W9-CFK-224

More Advance Comments on HOPE IN HARD TIMES:

"In a time of despair and anxiety we need this news, often hidden from us, of these courageous, active, everyday Americans working effectively for the continuation of the human and natural world." —*Grace Paley*

"I was enormously impressed with the chapter on children and the bomb." —*Robert Coles*

"Whether their metaphors are secular or religious, the ordinary individuals Paul Loeb portrays embody a new spirit of responsibility for the planet and those who inhabit it. We begin to sense what it might mean to treat the world as a sacred gift." —*Bishop Thomas Gumbleton*, Detroit, Michigan, National President of Pax Christi, USA

"*Hope in Hard Times* tells the stories of real people quietly changed by forces that would seem destined to overwhelm them, responding in extraordinary ways to the greatest peril of our times." —*Bishop Leroy T. Matthiesen*, Amarillo, Texas

" . . . Paul Loeb takes us on a frightening but somehow reassuring journey through the hearts and minds of myriad innocent citizens who are now stirring themselves to resist the unthinkable fate." —*John D. MacDonald*, author of the Travis McGee novels

"From these stories we can see emerging a new and healthier kind of patriotism—a love of country deep enough to include gratitude for the miracle of life and compassion for those yet to be born." —*Joanna Macy*, author of *Despair and Personal Power in the Nuclear Age*

"By reporting how individual citizen activists have made a major difference, Paul Loeb provides hope that by more of us exercising the courage of our convictions, we can arrest the growing threats to civilization. And in so doing, we can enrich our lives." —*Russell W. Peterson*, Former President, National Audubon Society

"This wonderful book is filled with interesting, inspirational messages from people who remain confident that we can and will avert a nuclear war. These dramatic experiences give us all 'hope.' " —*Gene R. La Rocque*, Rear Admiral, USN (Ret.), director of the Center for Defense Information

Comments on Paul Loeb's NUCLEAR CULTURE:

"An important book, wisely done . . . . A lot of smart people who have some influence on the course of history will read and admire you—and learn from you." —*Kurt Vonnegut*

"Disturbing, fact-laden and just plain interesting. . . . The questions raised . . . lie at the core of continued human survival." —*John Nichols, The Dallas Times-Herald*

"Loeb takes a gargantuan subject and brings it down to human terms." —*Schuyler Ingle, Los Angeles Herald-Examiner*

"Vivid, sympathetic and chilling to the bone." —*Clarence Petersen, The Chicago Tribune*

"A chilling portrait of this 'reservation,' where the makings of a global holocaust accumulate hour by hour." —*The Progressive*

"Most disturbing." —*Fred Shapiro, The Washington Post*

"A provocative account of the lives and thoughts of the men and women who make plutonium possible." —*Al Klausler, Christian Century*

"The book is fascinating reading." —*Seattle Times*

"Paced like a page-turning novel . . . essential reading for anyone seeking to understand the psychic numbing that permits a place like Hanford to exist. . . ." —*Sandy MacDonald, New Age*

"The spirit of this deep internal conflict we have inherited with the nuclear age, of doubt and despair at the periphery of what seems normal existence, of the struggle for life and belief in life while immersed in preparation for instant death, is exquisitely wrought in Paul Loeb's *Nuclear Culture*." —*Tom Gervasi, Penthouse*

"A disturbing lesson: those most directly involved in nuclear work are often those who think least about its implications." —*The Christian Science Monitor*

"Loeb has listened carefully to the Tri-City people he talked to." —*Roger Sale, New York Review of Books*

"One cannot give a higher recommendation." —*John Kenneth Galbraith*

# Hope
# in Hard Times
*America's Peace Movement
and the Reagan Era*

by

PAUL ROGAT LOEB

Lexington Books

*D.C. Heath and Company • Lexington, Massachusetts • Toronto*

*Library of Congress Cataloging-in-Publication Data*

Loeb, Paul Rogat, 1952–
Hope in hard times.

Bibliography: p.
Includes index.
1. Nuclear disarmament.   2. Antinuclear movement—
United States.   3. Peace.   I. Title.
JX1974.7.L63   1986        327.1'74        85–46044
ISBN 0–669–12929–1
ISBN 0–669–13022–2 (pbk. : alk. paper)

Copyright © 1987 by Paul Loeb

Illustrations © 1986 by Rupert Garcia

All rights reserved. No part of this publication
may be reproduced or transmitted in any form or
by any means, electronic or mechanical, including
photocopy, recording, or any information storage
or retrieval system, without permission in writing
from the publisher.

For information about quantity discounts, contact
Lexington Books, D.C. Heath and Company, 125 Spring St., Lexington, MA
02173.

Published simultaneously in Canada
Printed in the United States of America
Casebound International Standard Book Number: 0–669–12929–1
Paperbound International Standard Book Number: 0–669–13022–2
Library of Congress Catalog Card Number: 85–46044

The paper used in this publication meets
the minimum requirements of American National Standard
for Information Sciences—Permanence of Paper
for Printed Library Materials, ANSI Z39.48–1984.

ISBN 0-669-13022-2

87 88 89 90 8 7 6 5 4 3

# Contents

# Preface

I OFTEN speak in college classrooms, addressing those students who are presumably the most secure of their generation in affluence, access to power, and a sense that the world is theirs to inherit. Yet half of them consistently believe an atomic war to be likely. Few consider their actions remotely capable of helping to prevent this. They say they are afraid to act, they do not know how, that they fear even thinking about the bombs.

The students' fatalism is rooted in more than just concern about nuclear warheads; it taps into broader currents of apprehension and uncertainty running throughout our society. Yet because the atomic arsenals can annihilate all human creation, and because their existence requires at least our tacit support, they carry a uniquely personal and irrevocably universal threat.

Knowing this may leave us only further paralyzed: all the more impelled to grab our own small pieces of turf, cut the best deals we can within their bounds, and limit ourselves to the narrowest concerns. Yet signs of a profound national shift also exist. When I began this book in 1982, America's atomic arsenals had been building largely unchallenged for nearly twenty years—at least since the massive citizen effort that helped produce Kennedy's Above Ground Test Ban Treaty in the early 1960's. Questions of nuclear escalation were the property of distant experts. Discussion played on near-invisible stages. Yet a vision popularly embodied by the Nuclear Freeze campaigns soon sparked imagination throughout the remote corners of the nation. Individuals began taking on the most critical issues of our time.

A Los Angeles engineer described this process as learning to see beyond the boundaries of his own front door: beyond those private personal realms to which he'd always restricted his concern and compassion. A seventy-nine-year-old former National Mother Of The Year risked ten years in jail for joining a small boat blockade of America's first Trident submarine off the Washington coast, then said she acted because "the thought of going out and obliterating people" had simply become "very obnoxious." A Baptist preacher, who initiated an unprecedented peace march in his small South Carolina town, termed his involvement "a crowbar to my soul."

Whatever its metaphors, this engagement takes different forms in different contexts. No single person can represent the full chorus of voices; no one place the full reach of concern; no sole political or spiritual tradition the full range of dreams. Emerging from vastly disparate pasts, those who make up the resurgent peace movement forge a new and further-reaching vision out of this breadth and diversity. They embrace a common responsibility for a future which now must not merely be passively received, but actively earned. Their efforts succeed most when they rely not on instant solutions or magic cures, but on nurturing a connection both to human community and to that natural world of which we are inextricably a part. They seek a hope discerning and sturdy enough to endure.

As a writer in no way exempt from widespread strains of complacency and despair, I have found this hope demanding even as I have attempted to describe it. It is hard to break through the myths and rationalizations preventing us from coming to grips with our potentially terminal course; it is perhaps harder yet to nurture that courage and generosity capable of leading us down an alternative path. Like the Carolina preacher's crowbar, engagement with ultimate issues has a way of opening us up, unearthing corners of our hearts we might prefer to leave safely buried and hidden. Yet we may need these difficult efforts to rediscover who we are and what we must do.

This book rests on these stories of challenge and hope: on ways individuals have brought their respective traditions, gifts and strengths of character to bear on the fundamental questions we now face as a species. The narratives I recount stretch from Seattle to Boston, Minneapolis to Philadelphia, Los Angeles to South Carolina. Given that those presently engaged also confront difficult political contexts, and inevitably face frustration and doubt, I have also explored obstacles to reversing the arms race inherent in our culture—like the faith in technical salvation so profoundly called into question by events like Chernobyl—and have examined those visions capable of sustaining citizen efforts for as long as will be needed to steer a different course. Many concerned initially with the atomic arsenals alone have now taken on an array of interconnected challenges, like opposition to the mounting cataclysms in Central America. I have also examined that broader perspective beginning to emerge from these choices. Finally, the book returns to personal lives. For our future will ultimately be shaped—or relinquished—by the actions of ordinary humans, in all our fallibility and in all our strength.

# Ordinary Heroes

# 1.   Minneapolis: Respectable Resisters

A SKING Erica to make an angel, the volunteer gave her yarn, cotton, and instant plaster, and sat her down beside other inmates held for prostitution, forging checks, drunk driving, or stealing. She articulated each step as if leading five-year-olds: "Now take the cotton." "Now take the plaster."

Despite Erica's background as a skilled jeweler, she was having trouble, and the volunteer's guidance didn't help. She finally molded a crude plaster figure, slapped on a hunk of brown yarn for hair, and ended with something resembling a Raggedy Ann doll with wings.

Erica attributed the volunteer's silence on her creation to artistic disdain. So she was surprised when, four months later, the woman wrote her, explaining the prison guards had forbidden casual conversation, but saying she was so proud they had met that her church placed up for auction what Erica considered to be possibly the ugliest angel ever made.

The incident left Erica feeling odd, "like a piece of the true cross, a Christian relic." Yet implicitly it honored the common vision of nearly 600 individuals who she had joined in challenging the atomic arms race by blockading Honeywell Corporation's national headquarters. Erica had been singled out, she stressed constantly, solely because her husband, Tony Bouza, happened to be the Minneapolis police chief. And because extraordinary times led her to serve a ten-day sentence in jail.

Eight years before, Erica lived the life of "a middle-class Scarsdale matron": manicuring the house, raising two sons, learning ceramics, furniture renovation, and jewelry, and accompanying Tony to functions appropriate for the head police chief of the Bronx. Although she coordinated a Fresh Air Fund to give a summer escape to impoverished children, and agonized over Vietnam and civil rights, she only raised her concerns at an occasional dinner or cocktail party, and even that seemed rather impolite.

Then Tony received a letter from a couple named W.H. and Carol Ferry, complimenting him on a *Washington Post* article, "A Policeman in the Ghetto," where he said our society manufactured law-breaking and brutality, and concluded, "To the degree that I succeed in keeping the ghetto cool, to the degree that I can be effective—to that degree, fundamentally, am I deflecting America's attention from discovering this cancer?" The Ferrys turned out to be neighbors in the Bouza's affluent New York suburb, and the two couples soon became friends. Although Erica thought Carol's political activism was mostly tilting at windmills, and couldn't imagine herself similarly involved, she did wonder why she always found reasons to avoid troubling social questions, like those surrounding the escalating global arms race. When Carol mentioned attending a demonstration at New York's dangerously slipshod Indian Point nuclear reactor, Erica said, "Let me know next time and I'll come along."

But the opportunity never arose. A few months later Tony got the Minneapolis job offer, and in spring of 1980 the Bouzas moved. Wanting to nurture Erica's budding concern, Carol wrote Marianne Hamilton, a friend from the Vietnam era who had recently helped found a new Minneapolis peace group, Women Against Military Madness (WAMM).

Marianne deluged Erica with nuclear literature, filling her mailbox until she had to come and talk from sheer saturation. The two women struck a ready bond. Erica soon joined monthly leafletters at a major downtown mall.

Erica was already overloaded with cooking and entertaining for a new social circle; setting up her own shop to sell the jewelry she'd made during the past fifteen years; logging fifty hours a week crafting earrings, bracelets and rings; and painting and papering the Bouza's new house. She had no time for political planning sessions or other

WAMM projects like weekly leafletting at key freeway offramps; writing letters for outlets ranging from local papers to *The New York Times* and *Vogue*; and staffing peace tables at religious conventions and neighborhood meetings. But she willingly spent a few hours a month carrying signs, offering information to passing shoppers, and wishing herself invisible whenever a police officer passed by. Originally, the leafletting was just one more dutiful activity.

In late 1982, Erica had been working with WAMM a year and a half, standing vigil at the mall and producing gold pins for the organization to sell as fundraisers. Although she still preferred Victorian novels to treatises on nuclear strategy, she thought increasingly about what seemed an unprecedented global jeopardy, and wondered whether her modest involvement was enough. In November, when she read about thirty-six people who had been arrested blockading Honeywell, Erica began to further shed her cocoon.

The blockading group was part of the Honeywell Project, a renewed version of an effort begun in 1968 to oppose the corporation's production of cluster bombs, which sowed a hail of deadly pellets on Indochinese peasants. Because of delayed-release fuses, these bombs continued to take lives in Vietnam, Laos, and Cambodia. Fragmentation bombs of this type had helped helped devastate Lebanon, Angola, and El Salvador. Honeywell also manufactured fuses, mines, jet fighter components, and major systems for missiles like the Trident, Pershing, MX, and cruise. The corporation's annual report proudly called military programs a major growth sector, and management worked steadfastly to insure the continued flow of Pentagon generosity.

When the Honeywell Project announced a second blockade for April 1983, Erica's excuses no longer held. Planned participants included Marianne Hamilton and other friends she respected. Unlike Saturday rallies that took her away from her shop, it would be held on a Monday, at 6:00 A.M. Granted, she didn't view Honeywell as a particularly heinous institution—she and Tony had even dined at the home of the former company president, and she valued the support he and his 3-M heiress wife gave to local art and culture. But the blockade raised broad questions regarding the nuclear arms race, with far greater force than the monthly vigils at the mall. Erica marked the date and thought about participating.

Her involvement proceeded step by step—from a general concern to the initial vigils and leafletting, to a later decision to undergo arrest. She had no single leap of conversion, but rather an accretion of encounters, commitments, and flecks and shards of knowledge all exerted a common pull. Had she received WAMM's mailings three years earlier, she might well have done something then. Yet because others had broken the ground first, she would not have to "look like a crazy" and act alone.

For all that the initial blockade included respectable priests, nuns, doctors, teachers, and nurses, many old and trusted friends still told Erica not to get involved. It would reflect badly on Tony. There were other paths to change. America needed the weapons. But others believed it was her right and perhaps even her duty—a way of speaking not only through words, but through risk and sacrifice to insist this issue was so urgent, so critical, that ordinary business might have to be interrupted. They agreed that perhaps only acts like these would finally make the politicians listen.

Erica might have worried more about Tony's position had he not been a blunt and outspoken iconoclast, carrying few qualms about offending in the process of making police work the public trust he believed it must be. He grew up the son of poor Spanish immigrants, and was raised by his seamstress mother after his father died when Tony was fifteen. He became a beat cop in 1953, was made inspector after getting Bachelor's and Master's degrees through night classes at New York's Baruch College, and continued to rise in the force. Since blacks and Hispanics came in contact with the police most often, and were vastly underrepresented in the ranks, he said they should be hired over white applicants of supposedly greater objective merit. He testified to this end in connection with federal lawsuits. Despite patrolmen's fears of losing accustomed turf, he created extensive auxiliary policing programs to involve ordinary citizens in stopping crime. Considering himself "the ultimate square," he nonetheless accepted an invitation to address a Houston gay rights parade, and insisted that police should serve the law, not be its masters.

Tony also carried a quick-fire sense of humor, which would later lead him to tell reporters it was tough "living with such a notorious criminal" as Erica, but that he hoped rehabilitation would be possible if she would only "rethink her misdeeds and life of crime." Negotiating over the April blockade with Marv Davidov, the Honeywell Project's fifty-one-year-old founder, he teased Marv by asking, "Are you a Communist?" When Davidov answered that he was not, Tony continued, "Are you a subversive?" To which Marv replied with a grin, "Shit yes, chief."

"Well, you should talk to Erica," said Tony, laughing. "She likes that kind of thing. She's one of you."

When Erica said she was joining the action, Tony looked a bit startled, but then asked, "Is this really what you want to do?" Yet he felt no right to alter her decision, any more than she would have had to interfere with involvements about which he cared deeply.

Tony viewed laws as necessary "to keep society on an orderly basis." He believed in applying them to governments that, when they became criminal, as in the Nixon era, "totally poisoned the wells of justice." And to individuals, because otherwise there would be no check on greed or power, and nations would be run, without recourse, by the richest and strongest. But he also respected sincere acts of conscience, sacrifice accepted for ideals believed in.

It was 6 A.M. and barely light when Tony drove Erica to the April 18th demonstration. He had to be there anyway to command the police. Parking was scarce, and she could hardly leave her car in the Honeywell lot.

They rode in silence. Neither was talkative that early in the morning. Each kept their own preoccupations. Although Tony remained uncertain whether Erica would do more than simply stand in witness, he worried far more about the mechanisms of handling nearly 150 citizens simultaneously breaking the law. For Erica, apprehensions and uncertainties churned. Deciding once more to go ahead, she mustered her courage.

At Erica's request, Tony dropped her a few blocks from where the blockaders waited at an adjacent freeway bridge. They kissed goodbye and she walked to join the others, then passed through a line of several hundred supporters assembled at the roadside, as if preparing a Virginia reel. Halfway up Honeywell's five-story brick headquarters tower, a bas-relief thermometer recalled the building's original manufacturing purpose when the company was still Minneapolis Heating Control. The brick now formed a quaint backdrop to offices where managers punched out antiseptic paper trails beneath wall prints of sea birds and Mondrian cityscapes.

Outside, the blockaders carried flowers and wore different colored calico armbands for each group that took part. A few wove themselves in place with bright yarn, repairing their web as the police broke and tore it. A number celebrated an ecumenical Eucharist. A clown danced, while balloons with peace messages filled the air. The mood became almost that of a carnival. When Honeywell's security head announced that the corporation opposed all activity "destructive to anyone's personal health and safety," 500 people laughed.

Erica watched the initial arrests as if from afar, wondering why she was there and where this choice might lead. Some WAMM women began singing. Though Erica didn't know the words, she joined anyway, and sat still while the police said move or be arrested. She then waited in a paddy wagon circling the courthouse like an airliner on interminable hold over O'Hare.

A few hours later, when Erica was booked and released, the media descended. She'd seen her choice as an individual one, stemming from personal conviction that the threat merited a slight disruption to her life. She assumed she'd slip in quietly, pay her fine and return, as before, to private concerns. One hundred and thirty-four people were also arrested here for similar reasons, as over 5,000 others across the United States would be that year.

Yet Tony was not just any government official, but one vested with enforcing the very laws Erica had just finished breaking. Granted, she chose to plead guilty and to accept whatever penalties came, a suspended sentence, as it turned out. Others who pled innocent were later acquitted, leading the prosecution to appeal Minnesota's "claim of right" law, which allowed the principle of greater necessity. But the fact of the Bouzas' marriage highlighted Erica's role. Tony joked that he'd be sending her to Siberia and taking the bulk of the demonstrators downtown to be fed to dogs.

Erica would be asked to speak for herself and for the movement on every major network; in newspapers from *The New York Times* to *USA Today* and the *Peoria Journal-Star*; in magazines like *People*, *Family Circle*, and *The Ladies Home Journal*; and in media reaching as far as Tokyo, Mexico, and Rome.

Unlike those whose opinions on these issues were usually broadcast across the airwaves, Erica was no expert in politics and power, and possessed no privileged knowledge beyond her own convictions. Yet she received, for a brief moment, a level of coverage more commonly given to Henry Kissinger, Casper Weinberger, or rare dissident authorities like Daniel Ellsberg, Helen Caldicott, or Carl Sagan. People saw her as representing their concern in a manner even sympathetic celebrities could not, because she lived an ordinary life.

Letters soon arrived from Minnesota, New York, Oklahoma, Montana, Virginia, Indianapolis, San Diego, and Detroit. A few reactions were critical: "Keep your kids away from ours, you jailbird"; another, to Tony, "Please ask your wife to do her housework before she parades with the Communists"; a third signed the letter "Comrade Andropov" and said Erica was doing a terrific job for the Soviets. A few rattled off parades of obscenities.

But most saw Erica echoing their own fears, urgencies, and hopes. As one woman put it, many were "normal homemaker types" wanting to ensure a world for their children. A Boston friend asked, "If I come to Minnesota, do I have to visit you in the slammer?" An Illinois woman wrote, "I was with you in spirit. Someday soon, when my job allows, I will be there in body also." An activist from a small rural community described a local march she said was "a lot for one town, but not enough." A state senator acknowledged her courage. And a Moline, Illinois, police officer recounted his own suspension for protesting the arms race by wearing a purple ribbon.

Honored as she was by the letters, Erica considered the Joan of Arc media images a bit absurd. "It all began when I heard voices," she said later, teasing. "They told me to rescue the Dauphin . . ."

But because she was being made spokesperson for an issue she felt deeply about, and because she held high standards, she began to worry about not knowing each relevant number or statistic, about being unable to hold her own with the generals and diplomats. She went on national TV and almost expected her words to stop the bombs. When the world went on as before, she began saying, "I failed! I failed! I haven't made my point!"

For all Tony's faith in law and concern about individuals breaking society's codes for their particular causes, he believed Erica had harmed no one by her Honeywell arrest, had acted out of sincere motives, and accepted the consequences with dignity. If people weren't willing to risk, they might never know their true human choices. If we couldn't all be saints, we could at least honor that part of ourselves that seeks to act for a broader, common good. But, as he also told her bluntly, she was not the star of the universe. He said we were all "just slugs on the earth, going from rock to rock, doing the best we can." She had no right to act the anointed savior.

Erica resisted, briefly, then agreed. "Getting this much publicity," she said later, "you start to take yourself very seriously. Look into people's eyes for recognition. Start to think you are something special and unique. Which is of course absolute nonsense, because I'm no different now from what I was before."

Erica's enchantment with the limelight dissipated quickly. She returned to viewing her role as that of any individual acting from a common urgency, to asking herself and others, "Look here. Is this what you want to happen? Or do you want to do something?" To continuing on, the best she could.

"I'm sick of books like *Looking Out for Number One*," she said when we met in the Bouzas' modest green house in a comfortable neighborhood half a block from Minneapolis's Lake Calhoun. "If life's been good, it's my responsibility to respond in kind." Her living room walls held gilt-framed reproductions of rumbling Turner skies and aristocrats circling an outdoor ice pond. Mozart played on the turntable, and in the bookshelves were copies of Churchill's biography and Pynchon's *Gravity's Rainbow*, Philip Roth, and an analysis of Eichmann.

Erica sat thinking, then her broad features broke into a wry almost self-mocking smile, bemused at the role into which she'd been cast. It was as if she viewed herself in some exotic play, yet worked to redeem the part with everything she had. Disliking grim self-righteousness or wide-eyed sentimentality, she burst into laughter during one rain-sodden demonstration when a participant suggested beams of light were coming up from people's feet to surround and purify the Honeywell tower. But she also profoundly admired so many of those who now came together to act and hope for peace.

The phone rang, and a jewelry customer offered to open the shop during Erica's pending incarceration in a week and a half. It was one of a deluge of calls and interviews that had gone on all day and all month. She had become so beleaguered she wrote herself notes to keep each conversation straight, and they piled one on top of the other like stacks of dishes about to collapse.

Erica thanked the caller, fetched a pot of herbal tea from the stove, and returned to talk of growing up in London, where her father helped run the successful East End furniture factory owned by her mother's family. She hid, as a frightened nine-year-old, when bombs from the German air raids fell. Because her mother's multiple sclerosis made getting in and out of the shelters tremendously difficult, Erica's family evacuated to a city that was less of a target. Four years later, her mother died, and Erica was sent to a private school in

Switzerland, where she learned French and endured European history, sewed her own clothes to save money for sweets, and flirted with elderly businessmen at tea dances. When her father moved to the United States, Erica followed. She got a job as an assistant buyer for Macy's, and met Tony, then a young detective, at the party of a mutual friend.

"He was wearing some ghastly outfit," she recalled quite fondly. "He hadn't any idea of how to dress and still doesn't. But I looked at his face and decided this was a man I might marry." One night, after eight months of dating, Erica drank two martinis for courage and then proposed to Tony. He accepted, and then backed out. She let him go, keeping her tears to herself for three more months until he called at 4:00 A.M., drunk and lonesome, and they soon entered what by now was a twenty-six-year marriage.

The phone rang again, and Erica talked briefly, then hung up and continued. "A lot of people say, 'I'll do something when my child's out of the army. Or when my husband doesn't have this type of job.' And I want to say, there isn't a perfect time. There's never a perfect time. There's never something that you're not afraid of losing. I think the things you have and really value, you have to be willing to let them go and take the consequences."

Erica directly faced these consequences when the Honeywell Project announced they would hold another blockade on October 24, 1983. Because a second arrest would mean jail, she struggled at length with her decision. A respected friend, and survivor of the Holocaust, said violating the law invited social breakdown like that of Germany. Another person worried about Erica's personal well-being, and thought there were other ways to change the system, insisting, "You've made your point. What's the earthly reason to do it all over again?" But others encouraged her, particularly those who would also be joining the action. But they did not press, even though jail would undoubtedly bring major publicity—any more than the project prescribed individual choice on whether those who participated pled guilty or innocent.

So Erica debated, one day certain she would go, the next certain she would not. Tony intentionally shied away from the subject. Where before he would have discussed his responses to such a major demonstration—both the event's moral implications and his pragmatic reaction plans—instead he compartmentalized, kept silent. He made sure her involvement led him to neither unduly favor the resisters, nor bend over backwards to prove governmental loyalty.

In turn, she said little about discussions with fellow blockaders. And while she knew Tony would respect her decision no matter what, jail scared her immensely. Once behind bars, she wondered how she would respond. Most of all she asked, would it do any good? Given her initial avalanche of publicity, would people begin to view her as a kook craving center-stage? And what did it mean for her to be pushed into the role of spokesperson for others with longer commitments and a far greater understanding of the issues?

Erica ducked and turned, talked one way then the other, and after staying up half the night before the blockade, she finally decided. Much as she respected the friends who counseled caution, if she'd asked them in April they'd have told her not to go then as well. She had come this far, and would continue.

The arrests on October 24th echoed over 140 major actions nationwide, as well as a week of European marches involving over one-and-a-half million people. As before, the Honeywell Project called for production halts of atomic weapons components as well as cluster bombs and similar "conventional arms," and described ways the corporation could convert to nonmilitary contracting without loss of jobs. The company took out full-page ads in the St. Paul and Minneapolis papers, explaining that "Honeywell does not take a political position on the level of the defense budget or any specific defense programs," and erected an eight-foot-high fence around the building. Ironically, the fence prevented police paddy wagons from getting inside and forced officers to shuttle blockaders out using inefficient small vans. By the time they completed the largest arrest in Minnesota history, as well as the largest in a worldwide week of international protests, the complex was essentially shut down for the entire day.

As before, Tony and Erica drove to the 6:00 A.M. blockade in silence. In front of the dark gates, she joined 1,700 supporters and 576 other blockaders, including a group of thirty-six children and teenagers who called themselves "No Minor Cause," a number of Vietnam vets, a prominent black woman running for city council, poet Robert Bly, a twenty-nine-year-old engineer who'd recently quit his Honeywell job designing Pershing missile components, and a cross-section of ordinary Minnesota citizens. People linked hands to circle the building in clockwise and counterclockwise lines, each facing the other. Affinity groups held services and rituals, including the placing of flowers and photos honoring a dedicated activist who'd died since the April arrests. Again police asked if people would move. Again they said they wouldn't. A few employees clambered over the bodies.

Tony supervised the arrests from across the street, chatting and joking with Marv Davidov. The chief pointed out an infant as "a notorious midget" his department had been hunting for years. Tony spent eight years in the New York "Red Squad" and continued to take pride in running "an aggressive operation" in every aspect of law enforcement; Marv had fought for thirty years resisting government and corporate affronts to dignity and justice. That these two so respected each other stemmed in part from their similar tough humor, respect for human courage, and tenacity for ideals in which they believed.

Tony left early, at which point several police began getting rough with the demonstrators. The blockade lasted ten hours, until Honeywell closed for the day and the few participants who had not yet been arrested went home.

Despite Erica's uncertainty about a second arrest, she felt strangely calm once the demonstration began—far more so than the predominantly high-level Honeywell employees who stared as if the blockaders were alien predators. Arrested at 8:15 A.M., she had her hand marked number 140, and felt ridiculously middle class, carrying a handbag and small sitting cushion, while media cameras followed her to the paddy wagon. Because her plastic handcuffs were inexplicably loose, she wriggled out and, when someone said it would be great if they could all cut them off, began to offer a scissors from her handbag. Then she reconsidered, laughing and saying, "If I do that, I'll end up in Alcatraz." Seven hours later, she left Hennepin County Jail, ordered to return for a pending hearing.

Erica recounted the events of the blockade shortly before entering the workhouse to serve her sentence, saying she remained unsure where these efforts fit in with her life. She couldn't yet be "like Marv or Marianne, who give constantly."

Although it was late evening when we talked, the phone continued ringing with calls from a drunken woman who'd been in jail and told her how horrible it would be, and a drunken man who asked repeatedly for Tony until Erica politely excused herself. Similar calls occurred regularly; like Minneapolis mayor Don Fraser, the Bouzas felt a responsibility to be publicly available, and kept their home number listed.

When Erica got off the line, I asked whether the influences leading to her involvement included the fact that the feminist movement had given so many women a new permission to act and speak.

"Yes," she said, "I think that's true." And she explained that, like her generational peers, she was brought up "to believe I had to be married and reproduce by a certain age. Keep a house so clean that people could run their fingers down the furniture to see if there was dust on it. Otherwise I was a big failure."

Erica still prized being able to cook a perfect crown roast of lamb, but acknowledged other dreams had become more urgent than immaculate bedspreads. She no longer scrubbed their home top to bottom each week. While she loved her grown children, she had occupations other than waiting for their every call. She could argue and speak without the constant urge to hesitate and defer.

She showed me the pink sheet given to her by the court. "They say I won't be allowed in jail without it." The sheet said to bring a change of underwear, two paperback books or magazines, toothbrush, toothpaste, denture cleaner, comb and brush, and packages of cigarettes. Soap and towels would be available. She phoned a special number to discover that, yes, she could bring her herbal teas, although they would of course be inspected. "It sounds just like camp," she said, as I mentioned attending the earlier admission of three fellow blockaders. Then she paused and asked, nervously, "What did it look like?"

Shortly after the October 1983 action, the judge handling the Honeywell protests introduced a speech of Tony's to the Hennepin County Bar Association. Two days later, the same judge methodically asked Erica how to spell her last name, then handed out the expected ten-day sentences to her and six other repeat blockaders, including one of his suburban neighbors. Their daughters were friends and fellow high school drum majors.

Erica packed for jail under the lights of network TV. Reporters came at 7:30 A.M. to watch her fill a suitcase with blouses, jeans, a flannel nightgown, herbal teas, the complete works of Jane Austen, and over 300 letters she hoped to answer. They held her until she was almost late. Then she got a ride with the husband of Moira Moga, a deeply religious woman beginning her third resistance sentence, who in court had quoted Dante: "The hottest spots in hell are reserved for those who, in times of moral crisis, sit by and do nothing."

Before entering jail, Erica feared Tony's position might lead to some backlash. Although he told reporters he was preparing an escape route and ordering a cake with a file, and even though the authorities seized her dental floss lest she get desperate and hang herself in her cell, things quickly relaxed. There were card games with Moira and a fellow blockader who ran a sporting goods store with her husband, as well as with other inmates. She did her chores: cleaning the dining tables, washing out garbage cans, emptying and rinsing the coffee pots, and refilling the salt, pepper, and sugar. She heard stories of drunken families, foster homes, teen age pregnancies, and poverty. One pregnant girl had stolen $12,000, been abandoned by her boyfriend, and was hemorrhaging in solitary with a miscarriage—after being shuttled back from the hospital each time the bleeding eased. Erica felt only circumstance had set her on one path and these women on another.

Then, on the evening of Erica's first day, someone called in a death threat. The caller said it was because of Tony, that they had a friend "on the inside"; they would "take care of" Erica and she would pay. The jail superintendent chose to play it safe, and after a repeated threat to use poison, isolated her in solitary.

Before, things hadn't been particularly bad; she liked joking with the other women, and her cell even seemed slightly homey. But now she was locked in a six-by-ten-foot room, bare except for an iron bedstead, wash basin with push button faucets, an open toilet, and messages of "Fuck you bitch" scratched on the metal mirror and metal door jamb. Erica offered to release the administration from all liability for her safety if she could only return to general population.

Along with others, Tony protested outraged that the superintendent would let "any idiot with a dime" effectively run his institution. Although the administration admitted threats came in all the time, they said they had no other choice. Finally Erica was moved to a separate, minimum security facility for inmates on work-release;

then at last back to general lockup. With time off for "good behavior," she served eight days of the original ten in the sentence, all but three in isolation.

Between witnessing the hurts of the other women, and the frustration of solitary lockup, Erica thought of little beyond sleeping, eating, and passing the time each day. She felt jittery and restless. The peace issue seemed distant. She scarcely thought of Tony, whom she usually missed intensely during even brief separations. Her final night, she was almost drunk with relief at finally getting out.

Yet jail revealed to Erica a strength she hadn't known she possessed—allowed her to recognize that she could bear at least a brief stay without despair or collapse. After her release, on a bright morning with high clouds, she faced still further media: a solo interview on CBS morning news, several major women's magazines, and endless questions for the spread in *People* (whose editors, Tony said, wanted to get at "the real issues, like whether we had marital trouble, were we really happy, how often we had sex, and how kinky it was").

Afraid of becoming any kind of public spokesperson, Erica had refused public talks following her first arrest. She considered her participation as a one-time affair and was eager to return to her business and home. Then October came, the next step, and brought jail, the further avalanche of interviews, and a growing sense that by recounting her reasons for acting, she might stir others as well. So she changed her mind, figuring that at the very least WAMM could use the money she was paid, and went ahead, half-expecting to be greeted "with bad eggs and tomatoes."

Addressing churches, schools and community meetings, driving eighty miles to small rural towns, Erica spoke nearly a dozen times a month. She acknowledged her technical weakness, admitted she'd rather read Jane Austen than strategic theory, and focused instead on her particular experience. Without meaning for it to become so, she said her previous life had in a sense been "comfortable and lazy." Although she worked hard at myriad tasks, her routine preoccupations so immersed her that she left choices of the gravest ultimate consequence to distant experts. She talked of responsibility for generations to come, and how it rested first on those, like herself, old enough to have already lived. She decided she'd continue to give talks as long as there were invitations, "until they say 'enough, enough,' and get sick of me."

I visited her again four months after her jail sentence. Her eight-by-twenty foot shop was nestled on a commercial corner with a barber, insurance company, realtor, sleek computer store, and the orange ball of a Union Seventy-Six station. Inside, a desk's cubby-holes held pens, rubber bands, and credit card forms. Walls and cases displayed hammered silver necklaces, carved coral flowers, and translucent red and white hanging earrings.

I'd been dropped off by Marv Davidov, who Erica greeted with a warm enthusiastic hug. They discussed her quitting cigarettes and starting a diet on which she swore to lose ten pounds in the next ten days. "I can't smoke, can't eat, and can't drink," she told him, laughing. "The only thing left is sex, and Tony's away until Sunday."

They talked of ongoing projects: another blockade and the shopping mall leafletting, which Erica now coordinated by making phone calls, transporting signs, and shepherding those making their own cautious entrances into public dissent. Two years before, she'd been the curious outsider. Now the peace work had become part of her life.

Although Marv's history of activism stretched from integration fights in Albany, Georgia, to a decade of Vietnam resistance, to this sojourn at the Honeywell gates, he and Erica now shared a common purpose. When he told of a former Franciscan nun jailed earlier in the day, Erica said she found it unexpected, as an agnostic Jew, to observe such courage in so many deeply religious Christians. Marv agreed, guessed that half the Honeywell blockaders were from the churches, and talked briefly about the movement's rich blend of secular and sacred. Then he laughed and recalled his own recent offer to partake in a friend's communion ritual—if he could spread the host with a little bit of lox.

In a few days Erica would address the League of Women Voters, replacing Ruth Youngdahl Nelson, who died several weeks before. A former National Mother of the Year, and the sister of a Congressman and a two-term Minnesota governor, this seventy-nine-year-old woman had herself been a major force in American Lutheran circles. Now, in her last years, she had become a highly dedicated peace activist. Marv told Erica how Ruth joined her minister son and forty-five others in a 1982 small-boat blockade of America's first Trident submarine off the Washington coast, and how she participated in the October Honeywell demonstration, preparing for arrest by taking nonviolence training. Although she'd been released from the hospital for cancer surgery only three days before the blockade, Ruth came anyway, sitting as a supporter in her wheelchair and telling reporters she wished she could do more. For Marv, she exemplified the passion in the resurgent peace movement: a passion that prevented her from simply letting the species slip quietly into extinction through lack of vision or courage.

Marv finished the story, then said, "When this is over, I'm going to go to the St. Croix River and catch some real nice fish."

"You mean in a hundred years?" Erica asked.

"No," he answered, laughing. "When the next action is done."

"I think being involved is my duty, my obligation," Erica explained to me after Marv left to give a workshop. "I hate the idea of breaking the law. But if you think it's going to be the end of everything, it's not such a terrible thing to do. I don't know what the answer is, but I have to try, as I said, to somehow leave the world for the next generation."

Though she knew it sounded sentimental, she felt life had been good and that she owed something. Not justice but fortune allowed her to sleep at night with a full belly and inhabit a fine house in a world where so many starve and are homeless. She couldn't take and not give back.

Our talk continued as customers ducked in and out of the store. Erica glowed with delight when a woman raved over a necklace her husband had bought. Her son called from college, and she chatted briefly, then invited him home for dinner. On the barbershop radio next door, a country singer called out to his true love, Elvira.

Again, Erica stressed, she'd never planned her involvement beyond each step she had taken. It grew choice by choice, as she first turned one corner, then another, and as the movement she was part of grew as well. Commitment came less through revelation than through this slowly building change.

Participation in the movement had pushed Erica. "I don't suffer from claustrophobia any more," she laughed. "Just having to cope with jail and death threats made me stronger. I never expected to get anything out of it. Sometimes people ask if the publicity helped my business and I get furious and say, 'Yes, I only did it to sell more jewelry.' But the strength was an enormous return."

Carol Ferry once contrasted Erica and Tony by explaining that while he had always been "a public person"—flamboyant, articulate, often corrosive, and not the least bit shy about taking center stage if it served a worthy purpose—Erica was domestic and private. Her domain was the house, family, and her jewelry. She disliked attention and clamor, and had dreaded jail as much as anyone. But, Carol said, Erica couldn't duck her concern. So she went "against her deepest nature in becoming—a word Erica would laugh at—a public heroine."

I recounted Carol's judgment to Erica, as well as Marv's suspicion that because her talks were so powerful, they also gave her satisfaction.

"I think," Erica said, "that there's truth in both statements. I don't like being in the public eye. I've been turning down television since I've been back. I think the publicity makes me look, even to people who feel sympathetic, that I can't get out of the limelight."

At the same time, perhaps, she got "a certain psychic income" from "the feeling of doing good." And she certainly tried to do the job as well as possible. But she gave the speeches not because she enjoyed them, but because people asked her, and because they said her words and experience were of use, "because I feel I must."

That feeling was evoked in a letter Erica received from a retired Minnesota teacher. A brightly colored card depicted a European piazza with pastel row houses, families sitting on benches, and children sailing boats in a fountain. Inside the woman wrote of her experiences in the Holocaust: her father taken to Buchenwald, the rest of her family dying there as well, her memories of being "a very young woman when I had to witness how two- and three-year-old children were lined up, all dressed neatly in white and blue aprons, only to be loaded up and driven away to be gassed." She compared Erica's actions to her own work finding safe homes for nineteen young Jewish children before she herself got out in early 1939.

Erica had no ready answer to the woman's letter. She felt honored and humbled, frightened and moved. As she was already now active and as the letter was one of many speaking from intimate pain, fear, and hope, it created no dramatic turning, but added another voice to the call Erica felt.

That call, pushing beyond routine compromise and fatalism, stirred the respect of many for those in the Honeywell blockade. Marv often asked media people to imagine they themselves were participating and getting arrested: what it would be like "to go to your boss and say, 'as a reporter I have to do this'." To tell the person they lived with, "and ask that person, 'what will happen to us if I do this?' " To tell their family and friends. He said these questions sparked a light of recognition that broke normally distanced roles—that the reporters at times began to understand these extraordinary choices of ordinary humans, and understand them sufficiently to convey their complex import.

A columnist for the major St. Paul paper wrote about this process in terms of Erica, describing his initial impulse to write off the action as trendy glamor, one more opportunity for the Bouzas to have their say in front of TV lights. He even laughed with a friend about the image of Erica in jail.

"When I thought it over later," the columnist wrote, "I felt guilty about laughing. The fact is, I'm not sure I'd be willing to do ten days in the workhouse for almost anything that I seem likely to become involved in. The willingness to be arrested and jailed on a moral point takes guts, even if you are confident nothing terrible will happen to you while you're inside. . . . And at the bottom I admire it, and won't laugh about it anymore."

# 2. South Carolina: Baptists and the Hound Dogs

TWENTY-FIVE years after an atomic bomb fell just outside its city limits, Florence, South Carolina had a peace march. A B-47 lost the weapon in 1958 when a lock broke on its bay doors, and the bomb dropped 15,000 feet before landing outside a modest farmhouse. Fortunately, the plutonium and uranium did not go critical. Three years later, two more bombs fell 130 miles away in Goldsboro, North Carolina, and an atomic blast was prevented only when, after five safety devices failed, the final one held. Instead, the first bomb's TNT trigger, detonating on impact, dug a hole 100 feet across and thirty-five feet deep, sheared off surrounding trees, and caved in the adjacent house as if a giant had kicked in its side. The blast wounded three children playing in the yard. The family fought for years before getting the barest of settlements.

Although Florence could be said to have a particular relationship to the time we've fairly casually termed "the nuclear age," otherwise it differed little from its quiet rural neighbors. The bomb came, went, and was largely forgotten. Situated 110 miles up-country from Charleston and eighty east of the state capital in Columbia, this community of 30,000 went about its ordinary way, paying scant attention to grand and distant global issues. Its citizens paid the resulting costs, accepted the resulting consequences, and fell into line with the rest of the culture. Dissenters only appeared as exotic fodder for TV news.

Therefore, it was unexpected when sixty respectable local residents engaged in a "protest march"—a fundraising walk for the national Freeze campaign. In all, 200 people participated by marching or signing pledges, contacting the press, baking cookies, serving ice tea, or performing the myriad other tasks that made the walk successful.

Starting out on a clear October Saturday from Poyner, a former high school now used as an adult education center, they headed east out of town, past the black neighborhood's crumbling porches, rusting tin roofs, and glass-littered ground. They reached the pale stucco courts and dried-up swimming pools of motels left behind when a new interstate bypassed Florence; the Treasure City Bingo Jamboree, a parlor as large as a Safeway store, promising $400,000 jackpots beneath an Imperial Margarine crown; and then the Florence Air and Missile Museum, where Saber jets, Titan missiles and B-47s stood sentinel on cylindrical posts. Quaintly obsolete, no longer up to high-tech standards, they cast echoes of past military glories on walkers carrying signs reading: "No Winners Nuclear War," "End The Arms Race," and " 'Come Now, Let Us Reason Together' "—this last with chapter and verse citation from Isaiah. Another sign began "Blessed Are The Peace Wishers," with "Wishers" crossed out to "Thinkers," and finally changed to "Blessed Are The Peace Makers."

The six-mile march was to end at the atomic bomb site. But the property owners backed out after receiving threatening phone calls. The marchers walked as close as they could—to the campus of the 3,000-student Francis Marion College, a commuter school named after the Swamp Fox of the American Revolution.

For the marchers and for the town, such public dissent was a first. For almost everyone involved, this day marked entry into a country of new vulnerability and exposure. So they walked past oaks, pines, and poplars, slightly timid but proud, while neighbors watched from the Midas Muffler shop, Piggly Wiggly supermarket, from porches and storefronts. Cars rendered verdicts of thumbs up, thumbs down, honking horns, "fuck you," or smiles and waves. Four men in a black

Chevy said one woman had a nice ass. Most who passed just looked surprised.

Among those walking for the first time was Southern Baptist minister Bill Cusak. Bill proudly wore a square sign, reading 'Peace Now' on all four sides, above a straw hat on his bald head. It could be seen unmistakably from any direction.

The sign did make Bill look a little odd; his wife thought he resembled Carmen Miranda carrying pineapples. But he liked its visibility and stood fast on local roots, dating back to before the British shot his ancestor, Adam Cusak, for refusing to let them use his ferry to cross the nearby Pee Dee River.

Bill's concern began after the initial Hiroshima bomb, while he was still a young seminary student at Georgia Tech. The knowledge of what had occurred and might occur again frightened and pained him. But since no one seemed to share his apprehensions, he placed them on a back shelf until, in early 1982, he heard a group of British and American scientists—including several who had worked on the original bomb—express fear that an atomic war was entirely likely by the year 2,000. Bill's first grand-daughter was two at the time. He couldn't think of her and remain silent. It was his phone call to a Francis Marion biologist that led, nearly two years later, to this march.

The day almost had the air of a Sunday school picnic—men and women in jeans and walking shorts, clean-cut teenagers in Black Sabbath t-shirts. Although the surrounding culture ceded these teachers and nurses, ministers, counselors, and other respectable professionals far greater right to question than it did the men and women who worked in the surrounding farms and mills, they wondered where challenging government leaders might lead. Their actions suggested that the world was gravely threatened, not only by external barbarians, but by our own society's actions and choices. Some were jittery, like the young Methodist minister who nearly cracked up his blue Dodge pickup while driving over from a small town forty miles away. Others took heart because everyone seemed so wholesome and ordinary. A pastoral assistant who was here at the request of a daughter dying of Hodgkin's disease, said "I guess blacks started this marching—I realize they went through a lot worse." A young social worker marched with a Sony Walkman and a sign, made jointly with a mildly retarded client, depicting a soccer-ball planet, colored in oblong continents of orange, yellow, blue and green, and the words "Save The Earth, Stop The Bombs" in strong black letters. Most nursed tired feet, chatted with neighbors and friends, and hoped they would be heard. As Episcopal minister Ingram Parmelly said, "now they know there are others who care as well."

At the end-point rally, a rabbi led an ecumenical prayer and a local historian recalled the day the bomb fell. Ingram, who also taught sociology at Francis Marion, filled in for a hoped-for congressman—salving possible disappointment by saying this was a movement determined not by star speakers but by ordinary citizens "insisting that we don't wish our children incinerated." He ended by quoting Isaiah, promising a day "when nation shall not lift up sword against nation."

They all knew the quotation. They'd learned it in fourth-grade Bible school, then consigned it to the domain of ideals or distant futures. But given that the marchers feared being tarred as pawns of evil empires, it rooted them in familiar traditions.

How is a movement born in a place where none existed before? How does a community of conscience oppose a once-accepted culture? A year and a half before the October 1983 march, Florence had no peace movement. Fears of the atomic arms race remained mute. Then a Francis Marion biologist named Jack Boyce got a Common Cause mailing detailing the consequences of a nuclear war, the developing weapons buildup, and suggestions for citizen action. Boyce began researching the issue in books, government reports, and publications like *The Bulletin of the Atomic Scientists*. He wrote letters to the editor of the local paper on the MX vote, the chances of surviving an atomic blast, and the escalating global crisis.

Around this time, Bill Cusak saw the scientists speaking on nuclear war. It was an hour-long public TV discussion filmed by the British, and it stirred him to consider the almost incomprehensible possibilities they discussed. Remembering a few of Boyce's letters in the paper, he decided to call Jack to talk.

Although the two had not spoken previously, they began meeting Thursday mornings from 7:30 to 9:00 at the office where Bill did religious-based counseling. Bill also invited the educational minister of a rural Baptist church, and Jack brought his Methodist minister and a Francis Marion drama teacher.

Bill got thirty people at his church to view a Physicians for Social Responsibility film, *The Last Epidemic*, which counterposed Hiroshima footage with testimony on the consequences of a nuclear war presented by doctors, scientists, statesmen, and even a former admiral. Bill joined with the others to buy a $350 print and book it, free of charge, to churches schools, Rotary Clubs, nurses' associations, community centers, and whoever would let them show it.

As the group's initial participants began to speak before different organizations and to invite others to help, they drew on the morning meetings for emotional sustenance. Support also came from other activists in nearby communities. In Charleston, the Freeze campaign joined with a small, largely black local of the United Electrical Workers to hold a 150-person peace march—despite freezing rain. In Columbia, the Carolina Peace Resource Center provided the Florence and other groups with information, films, slide shows, and a calendar of statewide activities. And in June 1983, the state's Methodist ministers endorsed the Freeze. But until the walk, Florence citizens had no public vehicle for expressing their sense of community.

Just as different local groups inspired each other, so efforts like that of Florence made it possible for the national Freeze campaign to coordinate coast-to-coast "walk-a-thons" that October. A California office provided posters, advice, and general know-how, and the marches passed on part of the money they received. The actions built each organization as well as a broader movement.

The Florence group now called itself the Pee Dee Nuclear Freeze Campaign, named for the nearby river. Participants joined by twos and threes as the mailing list grew from thirty to eighty to 150. Jack Boyce, however, had now retired to North Carolina. The Methodist minister rotated 180 miles west to Greenville. But new people filled the gap. Drama teacher Denny Sanderson became the organizational hub: carrying the campaign office in his briefcase, sandwiching march logistics between endless rehearsals of the student play, and using his broadcasting experience to prime advantage on the Florence TV show, "Pee Dee People." A local printer ran off mailings and fliers at cost. Others gathered pledges, called various media, and helped in whatever ways they could.

Of course the walk encountered resistance. Letters to the paper talked of the "darkness of Communist hell" and said ministers should not "promote moral causes," but rather "preach salvation only by Jesus's love for sinners and hatred for sin." Police were urged to revoke the march permit. A prominent Presbyterian berated his pastor for participating.

I caught an echo of this backlash when I went, along with Bill Cusak and Ingram Parmelly, to view the site where the Air Force bomb had fallen in 1958. We walked past a low barricade of branches and broken TV antennas that Bill Gregg—the man whose home was destroyed—had erected to keep out the marchers. Ingram said he understood why—given the draining fight the Greggs went through— they shied away from inviting further controversy by offering their land.

The house was gone, marked only by wooden posts, a broken flower pot, sheets of crumpled tin, and thin young pines struggling to reclaim the site as forest. The hole held stagnant water, surrounded by red and blue shotgun casings and the perforated Budweiser cans of their owners. A stove, an old sink, and sheets of rusted metal rose jaggedly from the water, folding back like crumpled insect wings.

Six months earlier, the local radio station played their twenty-five-year-old tape of the accident report with great fanfare. But when Denny asked to use the tape at the rally, the station manager (whose anticommunist rhetoric would have warmed the heart of J. Edgar Hoover) said it was lost and unavailable. Bill and Ingram discussed buying the bomb site and a narrow access corridor, so citizens could gather without triggering the Greggs' harassment.

We sat quietly, thinking of how apocalypse had so discreetly grazed this modest community. Ingram—not a lace-curtain Episcopal but a husky coal miner's son—recalled growing up in Tracy City, East Tennessee. His father died in the mines, and Ingram said he might be alive today had the company cared as much about safety as it did about profits, or had the union stood up to them as they should have. He thought the real betrayal of the South had come "when they convinced the poor whites that blacks were their natural ene- mies, that everyone in the Confederate Army was an aristocratic officer, and that when your grandaddy fought with Robert E. Lee he rode side by side instead of following with the shovel for manure."

As a butterfly skimmed the water to alight on a twig, shouts came from the road, kids yelling "Eat shit . . . goddamn Communists . . . Eat shit." We saw a flash of them running through the woods.

"I wish they'd hang around to let us talk to them," said Bill, then he decided to check the cars. After Bill left and walked slowly down the pine needle path, Ingram told me, "One of the things that happens with people shouting at us as they drive by, and kids yelling 'goddamn Communists,' is that there's a recognition that things aren't quite right, but a real uncertainty about what to do about it. The verities of land and property, home and hearth have been so clear here for so long. And we still remember losing a war."

He said the march would bring out support and make people listen, but that the group would also "catch a little hell before this is over." He remembered when Vietnam was at its height, and he was dean of men at a small college near Fort Bragg, North Carolina. Visiting generals paraded through explaining "how God and Lyndon Johnson wanted America to kick ass in Vietnam." Finally a student asked Ingram to sponsor a speaker for the other side. The speaker came, and the letters columns filled with talk of Ingram's communism.

Most marchers, Ingram thought, had little "real perception of what could be awaiting them—that they could suffer some ostracism, coolness, or be tagged crazy. Or worse yet be the victims of some violence, however minor." But individuals had to find their own understandings of the risk, and realize that "if people survived marching on Selma and on the Pentagon, they ought to survive a march from Poyner to Francis Marion College."

Then Ingram smiled behind his salt and pepper beard. "Do you know what it means for a bunch of Baptists to sit respectfully silent in the presence of a rabbi leading them in prayer in Florence, South Carolina, the by-God buckle of the Bible Belt?" He said having the rabbi was a deliberate statement, "because this thing not only transcends our faith and our particular sectarianism, it transcends our very humanity."

If this was a time when the efforts of ordinary humans might well determine whether or not the species continued, these efforts were not without their cost. One hundred and thirty miles from Florence, the South's oldest newspaper, the *Augusta Chronicle*, described protestors at a planned rally and civil disobedience action at the Savannah

River Plant, South Carolina's plutonium production facility, as "shiftless failures as human beings," who were either "knowingly helping America's enemies," or "venting their spleen on an orderly society with which they cannot cope." Here, however, the *Florence Morning News* supported the walk with an editorial explaining that because of the "insanity of the expanding nuclear arsenals," it was appropriate for "upstanding citizens and loyal Americans" to "have decided for the first time in their lives that the cause compels them to be activists."

Yet, even with an unusually sympathetic local paper, involvement in the issue raised fears. In part this was related to the ultimate stakes. But citizens were also attempting to reclaim a sovereignty over choices they'd been conditioned to believe were not theirs to address. As political scientist Richard Falk explains, we have been living since Hiroshima under what is in a sense a "permanent emergency," where an implicit state of war concentrates power in the executive branch, and critical national decisions are kept secret in the name of national security. Although the Constitution mandates Congress with clear responsibility for the declaration of war, the legislative branch now attempts vainly to reign in military actions unilaterally initiated by the president. Following our 1983 Lebanese intervention, Ronald Reagan denounced even congressional discussion as having increased American casualties.

For the Florence marchers to take on the nuclear issue was thus to challenge significant aspects of this political order—and the vested interests of all who feed off the weapons economy or perceive it as a necessity. They faced as well, a national heritage of tarring dissenting movements as beyond the pale; a heritage extending from the 1798 Alien and Sedition Acts and the jailing of those who spoke against World War I, to McCarthy-era blacklisting and Nixon's Cointelpro burglaries, IRS investigations and use of violent provocateurs. Even as the marchers were given legitimacy by respectable scientists, clergy, and breakaway policymakers (like former Ambassador to the Soviet Union George Kennan), and even as most sought a very modest utopia—of merely preserving home and hearth—it is understandable that many feared being branded and shunned.

For some, these fears centered around the same intimate community that could also give nurturing sustenance. A Florence counselor who coordinated peace walk pledges remembered how, when she was a high school student in Montgomery, Alabama, her parents received threats for discussing racial relations with black activists. The paper of the local White Citizen's Council published their names and the license number of their car. The midnight phone calls rang endlessly. She retreated, frightened of judgment by peers, and of becoming marked for the crimes of those who did not know their place. And she watched in silence until Bill Cusak drew her in, twenty years later, saying, "There's going to be a nuclear film shown at the Baptist church. Sure think y'all would enjoy seeing it."

The counselor ended up meeting a young nurse who was part of the Ebenezer Baptist congregation, who had done nothing more controversial than wear a POW/MIA bracelet her freshman year at Clemson. Together they formed a chapter of Peace Links (the women's disarmament organization founded by the wife of Arkansas Senator Dale Bumpers), brought in a dozen other members, and began to show their own film—on nuclear weapons and children—to groups culled from a Chamber of Commerce list.

But activists' apprehensions extended beyond the potential reactions of friends and peers, employers, agencies of state, and others wielding institutional power. They touched as well on the paths they might be led to follow. Participation in even the Freeze walk, or any other mild initial step, marked a point of departure from a stance in which critical decisions were automatically left to sanctified experts: politicians in Washington, D.C., or the Carolina State House, executives running the local textile mills, heads of distant oil companies and banks. Finding an alternative to compliance began with the insistence that ordinary citizens should judge these matters that so affect their future. And it meant perhaps following their judgments into whatever harsh and winding night they might lead.

United Methodist minister Levon Hucks grew up in a 600-person town in the shadow of the Myrtle Beach Air Force base—a town where supporting the military was a sacrament. He now lives forty miles from Florence, in an even smaller community called New Zion. During the 1968 presidential campaign Levon followed his father's lead and voted with his eighth-grade classmates to give George Wallace victory in a high school straw poll. Levon liked Wallace's populist toughness, and almost joined his older brother in Vietnam. Instead, the war ended and he enrolled in a seminary, still believing we had no choice but to follow our leaders, and that morality meant peace in one's own household. He backed Ronald Reagan in 1980 because, like Wallace, he seemed strong and sincere.

His change began with theology, which he took as a personal struggle between truth and falsehood, God and Satan. After preaching in late 1982 on how Christ said his kingdom could not be defended with the sword, Levon started wondering what it meant for Christians to use military violence, much less to prepare global annihilation. Yet he questioned whether we could defend what we prized without military arms, and initially balked at ideas that might profoundly alter his sense of who he was and what he must do. As a matter of faith, he had always been comfortably resigned to easing private hurts and leaving a less than pure world to the Caesars who ran it. Yet his questions erupted again, a few months later, at a Benedictine monastery in Conyers, Georgia.

Levon took the three-day retreat mostly from curiosity, and began by rereading *Genesis*. Feeling alone, small, and yet connected to something far greater, he prayed aloud, as the monks suggested, to sense the world as fragile gift. Primed for new meanings and purposes, Levon was more than receptive when he picked up a book entitled *Waging Peace*. Put out by the radical evangelicals of *Sojourners* magazine, it explained the escalating arms race in detailed specifics, and explored how "nuclear idolatry" betrayed true religious vision. Levon read again of how Christ refused the sword, and was appalled that the Nagasaki bomb was aimed, for greatest precision on an overcast day, at the town's most prominent Catholic church, the Urakami Cathedral. The book echoed, with fear and fascination, through supper, evening vespers, and a silent walk the following morning.

His new understanding spun and turned Levon, shaking previous certainties. Back from the retreat, in between playing with his three children and ministering to his parishioners, he wrote to *Sojourners* for a magazine subscription and local contacts. He also began reading Thoreau on civil disobedience and accounts of Pacific island bomb tests. With his wife, Darlene, he saw the movie *Gandhi* and, further shaken, wrote in his journal: "All of this frightens me. Darlene said it last night—we have thought and changed more in the last six months than in all of our lives. . . . I don't know where it's leading me and how it's going to affect what has been a very comfortable lifestyle. Or how it's going to affect a ministry that had been pretty peaceful—but is now shaken with contention among and between my people and myself."

But much of this contention was inherent in the situation of which he was part. The chairman of his church board also ran an all-white private school for the 200-person community. An anonymous caller accused Levon of "trying to stir up trouble" by attending a local black funeral. After Levon preached a sermon comparing the vendettas between Americans and Soviets to those between Jews and Samaritans, a World War II vet dropped by to talk.

"You don't see," said the vet, "that the Communists are devils, and that loving your country is next to loving God. Yes, I was glad to see the first and second bombs dropped. And I'd probably be glad to see the next one as well. Do you really want America left defenseless?"

Levon found it hard to answer. Were there alternatives to military force or the continued nuclear arms race? Would he become like those he still regarded as "professional protestors," going from demonstration to demonstration looking for a cause? Driving to the Florence march, and wondering what his participation might lead to, Levon raced his blue Dodge pickup, passing car after car during the hour long trip from New Zion. Suddenly a green Pontiac turned hard in front of him, and Levon spun 180 degrees, skidded past a signpost, barely missing other cars, and ended on a gravel siding, unhurt, but half uncertain his bones still connected. Was this the Lord warning him away, or the devil dragging him back; reasonable caution, or the fear that cows and rots? He decided it was the devil and continued on.

At the march, Bill greeted Levon, wearing what looked like a box on his head, covered with slogans. Levon again saw images of TV crazies and almost turned tail once more. But he was reassured by all the respectable professionals, and joined in, walking slowly, hands thrust in his jeans. Talking of the Peace Pentecost, where people had marched from Washington, D.C.'s National Cathedral to sit in at the Capitol, he said, "I was fascinated that they were willing to do something which caused a definite reprimand." He thought being jailed in that way might be "freeing and effective."

For all that Levon sought universal truths, they needed to be reflected in a human world, in what Martin Luther King called "the beloved community." Solitary witness could leave one isolated and embittered. New Zion was far even from the nascent Florence group, and Levon lacked other local support. Later he would join the Pee Dee Campaign's executive committee, attend further rallies, and connect with other Carolina Methodists. But at the time of the march he asked only for the long term strength not to break and falter, hoping this strength would come from his faith. Given all his uncertainty, he felt right in what he was doing. He walked on, forearms bent, already knowing too much to turn back.

The town of Florence had long been isolated and innocent. A Francis Marion administrator recalled the student body president's polite reaction to her shock at Kent State; he could have been consoling her at the death of some distant aunt. But with the development of the college and with new industry the community changed. It helped that the newspaper was sympathetic and the economy rested on tobacco, soybeans, a Pepsi-Cola plant, General Electric, and Union Carbide, and not on the military. Yet the peace effort grew primarily from chains of individuals overcoming their own hesitancy and uncertainty to stake integrity and reputation on the simple belief that the atomic arms issue must be addressed. Again, small town visibility could personalize resistance as well as support. Yet those who marched in Florence addressed a community more intimate and perhaps less jaded than an urban metropolis, and risked far less the pride and factionalism that often accompanies beliefs that one's actions matter more when located in a center of wealth and power. And like their compatriots in New York, Los Angeles, and Chicago, they began with the risk of discussing what had been unmentionable.

If our present crisis is propelled not only by blind trust, but also by cynical acquiescence, it is appropriate that those who choose to grapple with these issues do it in part for the hope they consequently find. Though this gain need not be sanctimonious, it does involve a sense of linkage to some larger context. In the words of another marcher, a big bear of a college-educated Navy vet, and a sometime truck driver: "I like being serious about the walk or a Sierra Club meeting, but when it's over I like being able to watch Carolina football, drink a half dozen beers and cuss out Southern Cal or whoever they're playing. If there is a God, I'd like to be able to say, 'Yeah I drank a lot of Coors, but I cared'."

Put differently, individuals like Erica, Marv Davidov, and the Florence peace walkers root their commitment in more than just awareness of the atomic threat. As psychologist Robert Lifton explains, humans innately seek what he terms "symbolic immortality": connection with those forces transcending our particular lives. These connections can be manifested through identification with one's community, nation or with the planet as a whole; pride in the future legacy of one's work; religious faith, with its sense of ultimate purpose; or respect for a natural world in all its power and mystery. Desire to be part of a broader whole may produce barbarism as well as humanity, oppression as well as liberty. Yet the global arsenals not only threaten our immediate lives but also these fundamental links and bonds. And those citizens who act and offer a different vision, draw on a final mode of connection, one Lifton terms "experiential transcendence," that stems from "participation in the larger human process."

I thought of these sustaining frameworks during a conversation Bill had with a young waitress at the local Sizzler steakhouse. She'd known him for twelve of her twenty-eight years, believed the radio preachers who warned of Communists and humanists round every bend, and was surprised he'd be involved in a peace march. So he juggled technical specifics and Biblical citations. He described satellite verification, NORAD computer errors, and the risk of first strike systems like the MX, Pershing, and Trident missiles; then he switched to the growth of Soviet churches and the question, "If Jesus had a gun and a Russian had a gun, would he shoot the Russian to save his life?"

"But what about the Bible prophecy?" asked the waitress. Didn't it say "that the invaders would come out of the north, like the Russians? And doesn't it talk about a great shaking, mountains torn down, and God sending fire on the coast lands? And aren't we blocking God's will by trying to stop that?"

Tugging at the hem of her white ruffled apron, she agreed it might be good for Jesus to not shoot back, "but it isn't realistic." If both sides really could blow each other up eight times over, "then why do they keep increasing?"

"It's like growing tobacco," said Bill. "People have jobs and money invested whether it does or doesn't make sense." He suggested she call the sympathetic local congressman for specific facts and figures, and then explained, "The problem is that we follow the culture instead of following the Scriptures, just like the pastors did during slavery. You have to ask yourself, 'Would Jesus want the world destroyed?' "

Bill and the waitress shared a particular language, like the urban secular humor that helped join Erica Bouza and Marv Davidov. The movement inevitably proceeded along diverse paths. Yet for all his conversance with apocalyptic traditions, Bill was not a thunder-and-lightning preacher. Instead he invited, speaking softly and slowly, both from temperament and his counsellor's role. A phone call here, a push there, a Biblical image, a rack of weapons statistics—whatever it might take to suggest, 'Well, if y'all could do this, it might help.'

Bill lived in a cluster of low ranch houses adjacent to a former swamp that had become a pristeen boating lake. We watched Denny on the 6:00 P.M. news, and Bill gave a five-minute take to an Associated Press reporter who called. "Media can prepare the groundwork," he said when he got off the phone. "But it still needs to be done one by one."

Two hundred and forty other walks had been held around the country that day. But the network reporters made no mention of this, and instead cut to a half-million person peace march in Moscow. This one, the reporter said, "moved like clockwork. It should have," he stressed a half-dozen times, because it "was carefully orchestrated" to do so. Coverage moved on to Midwest tornados, the death of a swing era bandleader, and the final baseball games of Johnny Bench and Carl Yazstremski. When Bench left with his 389th home run, Bill said "That's a good way to go."

I met Bill the following day at the Sweetbriar Shopping Center, where his office was squeezed between an Italian restaurant and Nationwide Insurance. The office was spare but homey, the walls adorned with maxims like "Jesus is greater than any problem I have," a picture of people fishing off a bridge, the Rotary creed, and a Georgia Tech plaque.

In 1948, as a student at Georgia Tech, Bill found what would become a model for his later involvement. He hit rough times following a break-up with a young woman who he'd considered marrying. It seemed only his religious rebirth pulled him out. When some Texans put together a series of student-sponsored youth revivals, Bill "came back to the Baptist Student Union and said 'If they can do it in Texas why can't we in Atlanta?' " In the process of putting on similar programs, he chose to become a minister instead of joining his father's Buick-Pontiac dealership.

"The revivals weren't the usual thing seniors in college do," Bill said, looking very much the respectable Rotarian auto dealer with his plaid jacket, grey slacks, and balding Scotch-Irish features. "But I experienced something personally that was very saving. I wanted other people to experience the same. I saw a pattern in that youth revival, and I thought when we started this whole nuclear thing, that maybe all that happened back there might have been preparation.

"The parallel is that I've had to face my just hopeless sense about the possibility of life being wiped out in the next seven to seventeen years. I finally gained peace of mind about that by feeling that I'm doing all I can. Plus not trying to do it all myself but getting other people involved. And I'd just like for others to have that peace if this damn thing's going to happen. If somebody says, 'You got fifteen minutes before they land,' I want to be able to tell my grandchildren I did everything I could."

When I asked why it had taken so long to recognize these stakes, Bill said he had realized them, briefly, when the bombs first fell on Hiroshima and Nagasaki. "I got involved back then and worried and prayed, but didn't know anyone else was concerned. If there had been other written materials or other groups, if I'd been exposed to an anti-nuclear culture, I'd probably have been in the campaign since 'forty-five."

He did break from certain cultural traditions, and lost a campus job in Berea, Kentucky for supporting a young Nigerian who wanted to join the local church. And just as Bill's father "ran his own business—literally and figuratively," Bill always liked the independent path. But his feelings about the atomic crisis didn't fully emerge until he heard the scientists' discussion. Then, in a guest sermon entitled "How to Build a Spiritual Bomb Shelter," he recalled how he prepared his basement during the Cuban missile crisis, but realized he'd have to shoot his neighbors to keep it secure. Maybe, he suggested, we all grabbed at similar false security. Shortly afterwards Bill linked up with Denny, Jack, and the others.

"If you don't meet and share and make plans," he continued, "you go backwards. The key that made us fly was meeting here every Thursday morning. So one ingredient it really takes, whether you come from a Christian, Jewish, or some other perspective, is you need culture. You need people who've got some facts. And you just can't do it alone. You need nuts and bolts to support the individual pilgrimage."

Bill asked about these nuts and bolts when the coordinator of Carolina Peace Resource Center, Bebe Verdery, drove up from Columbia for the Florence march. She spoke briefly at the rally, and then rode back on the green and white bus from Ebenezer Baptist Church. On the way, she explained to Bill how best to computerize the Pee Dee mailing list.

Bebe acted as courier, translator, and weaver—helping disparate activists connect their work to a greater whole. Twelve hundred people received her four-page newsletter, which included resource listings and a calendar, plus stories on the arms race and relevant developments like the Florence walk, a Rock Hill peace conference keynoted by a retired rear admiral, and how Charleston generated a major chunk of their Freeze group membership through leafletting the film *War Games*. She drove from town to town and meeting to meeting, offering suggestions here, proposals there, news of others' efforts, and the concrete assistance of her slide shows, films, and resource files. Where groups faced isolation or despair from working against the grain of their entrenched communities, she affirmed that each modest effort mattered.

Bebe was hardly born to activism. Raised in the 5,000-person town of Hartwell, just across the Georgia border, she had listened attentively as her father, a respected wood pulp dealer, explained we fought in Vietnam for freedom and that segregation had averted trouble and conflict. When a friend ran into her Baptist Sunday School class, announcing, "Some students were shot at Kent State, Ohio," Bebe said, "Well they must have been doing something wrong."

Then came the push for a teen club, a place where Bebe and her clean-cut Baptist friends could hang out without being pressured to drink. They might have succeeded, had an open club not meant the possibility of racial mixing.

Schools had been integrated for several years by then, though no one had black students to their houses. But when the parents explained, "we might work it out in someone's home, but it would have to be only for whites," Bebe decided "it just wasn't right."

"Maybe it was church ideals about God loving everybody equally," she remembered, sipping a beer as we talked at her house in the mill town district of Columbia. "Or maybe some vague sense of justice." So while the parents kept procrastinating, she wrote an editorial for the high school paper and later sent it to the town's regular weekly, accompanied by signatures of a third of the school. A public meeting called her a troublemaker, while her own parents silently retreated in embarrassment. Only her young minister and a few loyal friends stood fast.

"People were threatened," Bebe explained, "because it hit a nerve. But it was like when they told us differences in class and power were because blacks were lazy, shiftless, drank too much and cut up their wives. It made me say 'That can't be true. That's not the full story. You're just not giving me the full story.' And made me ask the kinds of questions that would lead me to challenge the Vietnam War, or whatever—even in a beginning kind of stage."

Hartwell never did get its teen club, and Bebe went on to Furman, a nearby Baptist college, where she read Clarence Jordan and dreamed of true Christian communes. After training in psychology, she got "the very vague idea that because a lot of what was characterized as mental illness were problems of injustice or poverty, that I could work helping people change the system."

So Bebe visited the Arkansas headquarters of the grass roots organization, ACORN, and landed a job in Charlotte, North Carolina, where she worked at subsistence wages to organize poor neighborhoods around basic issues like streetlights and allocations of federal block grants. Though ACORN shied away from articulating visions of broad social transformation, success in gaining incremental change gave people a sense of shared power, and brought together poor whites and blacks who traditionally fought each other over the scraps. Later Bebe was arrested in civil disobedience actions at a nearby commercial reactor and at the massive Savannah River nuclear complex. She also organized a biracial organization, Fairfield United Action, in a largely black county where South Carolina Electric and Gas was building a new atomic power plant.

I drove with her to the Peace Center office, past the shining midway of a state fair, where the arcade freak show now included Skeleton Woman—direct from Three Mile Island, a svelte young figure jogging in the shadows of two reactors, her face a human skull. The

Peace Center occupied a blue-lettered storefront across from Charlie's
Cue and Cushion Arcade, with its side wall mural of an arm shooting
an eight ball towards the pocket, and just down from the vegetarian
restaurant that gave Bebe her first stipend for nuclear organizing.
Bebe folded newsletters and recounted how she'd left the Fairfield
project a year and a half before, after lining up support to establish
this center. Unlike many newer activists, her opposition to atomic
weapons was no grand, all-inclusive revelation, but an ongoing concern linked with others. For ten years, she'd driven dirt roads and
canvassed country stores, helping those wounded by the caprices of
power to voice previously unspoken pain and dreams. Resisting the
weapons meant working not only to pull the species back from its
apocalyptic edge; it meant changing political and economic structures
of which the bombs were only a part.

In the judgment of the Honeywell Project founder Marv Davidov,
a striving for justice springs from a combination of believing change
is possible and "feeling the hurt"—as he did when a black army
friend was refused at the Kansas City hotel where the two tried to
register, or when as a nine-year-old child Marv was called a "dirty
Jew". Bebe believed justice could be achieved through a community
of conscience, of the vulnerable and powerless, in particular.

Justice also means a climate where citizens feel they have a stake
in their future. While possessing only dry crusts in the present, it
is hard to address global threats. As University of Wisconsin agriculturalist, William C. Thiesenhusen, said, "What agricultural laborer with a year-to-year lease on a farm will go to great lengths to
save hillside soil if he knows that his back-breaking efforts at terracing
will merely save the resource for the landowner, who may dispossess
him as soon as his laborious work is complete?" At the same time
that one can see citizen involvement in these critical issues as por-
tending our society's generally increased democratization, this very
popular enfranchisement may be essential for the peace movement's
ultimate success.

There's a t-shirt worn by Columbia nuclear activists showing a
picture of an eighty-four-year-old black woman with the words, "I
am a statement." The woman's name is Modjesca Simkins. The photo
and phrase date from the time a Methodist bishop convinced her to
testify before the legislature on how gerrymandered districts ensured
a complete absence of blacks from the state Senate. "I got up before

this old hound who's head of the judiciary committee," she explained, "and told him 'I don't need a statement. I am the statement.' Just told him of all the shows I could have seen, books I could have read if I hadn't been fighting, fighting, fighting all the time. And they were just sitting up there like made of something other than meat."

Modjesca looked at quick glance like anyone's old and poor black grandmother. She wore ratty pink cardigans, faded dresses, and mumbled while she thought. Then she'd speak, in a backwoods preacher's style. And the meeting or rally would turn.

I visited her white house on the edge of downtown Columbia. She sat on a green and pink stuffed armchair whose cotton batting spilled out in cloud-like puffs, resting her legs on an equally old matching ottoman, and pointed out the dining room table where a young NAACP lawyer named Thurgood Marshall had composed his early briefs. Modjesca cofounded the state NAACP in 1939, and she handed me clippings from the newspapers blanketing her living room floor. "Main Street In Columbia Is Off Limits To Seekers After Freedom," explained a faded handbill from the late 1950's, as it advised black participants in an Easter boycott to trade with friendly merchants or "wear old clothes in real dignity," rather than patronize Woolworths, McCrory's, or the other stores "where you are most welcome to stand on your 'dogs' and gnaw on a Hot Dog while a simple request for a 'SITTING DOWN' lunch will mean insults and arrest."

They won the fight, just as they'd broken the all-white Democratic primary in 1948. They even desegregated the public schools and a state university system that squeezed blacks into a single, drastically underfunded state college at Orangeburg, which received less than a tenth of educational expenditures to serve over a third of the state's population.

Modjesca didn't blame ordinary whites hesitant at the potential price of ostracism: "loss of their job, their daughters not getting husbands of the proper class, kids having rocks thrown at them." The fight ultimately had to be "by those suffering."

South Carolina's racial progress came from local efforts, and from national pressure, as Modjesca and others spoke in Washington, New York, and other northern cities. "The power structure doesn't care what it does to blacks and the poor pitiful disadvantaged whites," she said, "as long as it doesn't get outside. But they don't like it getting outside."

Change piggybacked on hard-won victories in Mississippi, Alabama, and Georgia, as well. "We didn't have as much killing and beating up, which was good. But that meant the Negroes didn't go through as much." Nevertheless, gunmen shot at Modjesca's property. School districts fired activist teachers. NAACP organizers were threatened with lynching. And in 1968, when Orangeburg students tried to desegregate a bowling alley, state troopers injured twenty-seven and killed three.

The phone rang, and a woman asked Modjesca's help in tracking down her son in Chicago. "What the hell you calling him on the telephone so much?" she yelled back into the receiver. "You got that kind of money? Twenty cents will get you a letter. Tell him if he was the son he ought to be he'd keep up with his mother."

The daughter of a prominent black dentist, Modjesca attended the local black college, Benedict, studied further at University of Michigan and Columbia University, and helped her husband in real estate and as manager of three state liquor stores. Later she canvassed for the South Carolina Tuberculosis Association, began her work with the NAACP and a kindred group called the Richland County Citizens Committee, and organized the state's first black-owned bank. Though the movement had won much, she said the poor were still poor, the powerful and wealthy still on top. "They open that Palmetto Center Hotel and 2,300 people go for 230 jobs. A woman froze to death here last year. I pick up friends working at fine restaurants and see people eating out of garbage cans."

Modjesca mentioned John Bunyan's *Pilgrim's Progress*, written during more than eleven years in jail, and how it talked of keeping one's eyes on the light. The light for her was "the betterment of mankind," and not letting "the chintzy things get in the way." She said faith came from "exposure to suffering." And that, as Christ said, if you had as much faith as you could put in a mustard seed, you could move the world.

"I'm ninety-five percent antichurch," she explained, "though I'm not a heretic or an atheist. Lots of them think I'm going to bust hell wide open. But I don't think I'm going to hell just because I won't go up, eat a little cracker, drink a little wine, warm a chair and bow my head for an hour and a half to have some cat tell me what the Bible means. Christ never put a million dollars in a building. The

Bible didn't say give a tenth of your money to the church. It said bring a tenth of your harvest for the poor."

For all Modjesca's anticlericalism, religion was still woven into her roots. Last week she'd heard Billy Graham "do a masterpiece sermon on the Good Samaritan, as good even as one Ralph Abernathy preached one time, showing how you should cross lines when there's suffering." She said Graham took a lot of heat for racially integrating his congregations from the start, deserved praise for his action back then, and that he'd changed still more between his support for Vietnam and his present opposition to the arms race.

Unlike most local black activists, Modjesca involved herself substantially in the nuclear issue. She thought most blacks felt, "White man got the world messed up. Let him straighten it out himself." The community was used to being denied, fatalistic even about getting holes in the streets fixed. Like most Americans, they had "a disease where they run along like a feather in the breeze till they come up against something they didn't see." But if the bomb dropped, they'd "be pinched up just like pork skins, along with everyone else."

Modjesca had spoken at every rally at Savannah River, the plutonium production facility commonly known as "the bomb plant," and was moved by a Hiroshima survivor she referred to as "a pitiful little thing in a rolling chair." A few weeks following our initial visit, she'd be the only person over forty-five at a meeting of a statewide group, Palmetto Alliance, that focused primarily on nuclear power. She said nothing for most of the meeting, sitting quietly, and thumbing through an article on military budgets. Then someone suggested linking the weapons and power issues more closely, and Modjesca jumped in, talking of what it meant to have eight- and nine-year-olds afraid of dying. "Everyone goes when the wagon comes," she quoted. "That means the bomb don't discriminate—old and young, black and white, rich and poor.

"You have to begin with small groups," she continued, explaining to the meeting. "But you reach the people who matter. They reach others. Like the *Bible* says, 'leaven in the lump, like yeast in the dough' . . . it rises somewhere else."

It was hard raising these questions, because most people cared only "about what song's on the radio or what they're going to buy, not about what kind of world they're going to leave for their children." Even by the Savannah River atomic complex, you had "whites and Negroes sitting up on the porch wiggling their toes and not caring if their lungs get eaten out and they die ten years earlier as long as they get the money." But Modjesca would keep on, getting up at 5:30 A.M. the following Saturday to drive 170 miles in her battered tan Chevy and address an antinuclear rally in Savannah. "I never turn down requests from young people," she explained. "So as the song say, I'm 'gonna put on my high heeled sneakers,' and go, take two of my friends who like things like that. I hope I can get some good fish down there on the wharf."

The Savannah River Plant (SRP) complex that raised Modjesca's concern was also the site of South Carolina's first nuclear challenge, which focused not on its weapons production, but on the atomic enterprise's immediate toll. Located just east of the Georgia border, the 312-square-mile facility was chosen for plutonium production in 1950, following lobbying by then-Governor Strom Thurmond. Surrounding residents called it simply "the bomb plant." It was the state's largest single employer, and it brought in over 10,000 workers to staff research labs, reprocessing plants, a twenty-seven-million-gallon radioactive waste dump, and five production reactors that had supplied the plutonium for half of America's nuclear warheads. More militarily dependent than any state but Virginia and Hawaii, South Carolina was once called by James Edwards—former governor and future energy secretary in the Reagan administration—"the nuclear capital of the world." It is home not only to SRP, but also to the Charleston naval complex (which includes a major nuclear sub facility, the home port of the Atlantic fleet, and shipyards handling an array of atomic-armed and -powered vessels) and to seven commercial reactors, with as many as a dozen others once proposed.

Among those who led the initial challenge to this nuclear dependency was a former Navy ROTC cadet named Michael Lowe. Michael worked building one of Carolina's reactors in the mid-1970s—the V.C. Summer plant, located twenty-two miles north of Columbia, and named after the chairman and Chief Executive Officer of South Carolina Electric and Gas, the plant around which Bebe would later focus Fairfield United Action. Michael began casting around for work just after college, and soon secured a job as a grunt laborer. Working his way up to a skilled crane operator, he took pride in his craft, savored hanging out with the good ol' boys on the crew, and spent his spare hours watching bands like the Allman Brothers play local roadhouses. But half the supervisors seemed to have been hired solely because their brother-in-law had cozied up to the right contact. Waste and sloppiness were causes for bragging and joking. When someone forgot to check a crane cable, and a falling cage barely missed a veteran ironworker, Michael stormed furiously into his supervisor's office. Then a batch of wooden supports broke and crashed, again because an untrained person had built them, and once more nearly killed the men below. Michael quit with a two-page letter of protest.

Although his worries were more about sleazy construction than the atomic technology itself, an article on South Carolina's Barnwell reprocessing plant soon spurred Michael's interest. He joined a nuclear study group drawn from the small counterculture community centered around Columbia's two vegetarian restaurants, local food co-op, and the group of carpenters he'd now joined. Curious as to exactly what he'd been building, he looked up Summer's Environmental Impact Statement in a local library. An accompanying chart detailed how cooling water would enter the Broad River, from which Columbia drew its drinking water, and estimated routine radiation dosages. Michael remained unsure about how these supposedly acceptable levels affected human life. But he knew it to be a hotly debated issue whose impact would rebound not only on himself and other adults, but also on Malachi, his two-year-old son. It outraged him that the utility could proceed so cavalierly.

Eventually Michael would be arrested at the Summer plant, along with with twenty-five others who sailed in a flotilla of rafts, canoes, and inner tubes across the artificial lake that gave the plant its cooling water. But the initial challenge was to Barnwell—a private facility adjacent to the Savannah River complex—whose construction began in December 1971 with the purpose of separating plutonium from commercial wastes.

Operated by Allied General Nuclear Services (a consortium of Allied Chemical, General Atomics, Royal Dutch Shell, and Gulf Oil), Barnwell was viewed by the atomic opponents as embodying a new and untried technology more frightening than even the most questionable reactor: a technology threatening radioactive releases, widespread proliferation of plutonium, and toxins that would persist in the environment beyond human imagining. Inspired in part by events like the massive civil disobedience at New Hampshire's Seabrook plant, several members of the small concerned community quit their jobs and began working full time on these issues, scraping together twenty-five dollars a week for what they optimistically termed subsistence salaries, eating free meals at the two health food restaurants, and living with sympathetic friends. In April 1977, they convened the Nuclear Skeptics Conference at the University of South Carolina, and began speaking, researching, and writing. The next year, on Sunday, April 30th, 1,200 citizens assembled to protest outside of Barnwell. They heard from an array of nuclear experts including Dr. John Gofman, who helped isolate the world's first milligram of plutonium, and a largely unknown Australian doctor named Helen Caldicott. Jackson Browne sang "Before the Deluge." Two hundred and eighty-four participants stayed until Monday, when they crossed onto Allied General property to be arrested. As Michael said, most thought they had little chance of stopping operations. "But we wanted at least to get our names on the record against it. We did it as much as anything just to preserve some dignity."

Michael has a lean grin, dark wavy hair, and an intellectual good ol' boy style that might have made him a successful New South politician. He sometimes toyed with the role of a hard-ass: responding to a rash of neighborhood break-ins by decorating his back door with a sticker showing a hand pointing a revolver and the message "Never mind the dog, Beware of owner"; slicing through the living room with a flurry of karate kicks and punches; savoring stories of how he'd smuggled in VO whisky when nuclear construction became halted and the men got bored and restless. He drove ninety miles each way to see the Talking Heads in Charlotte, North Carolina; wore his prize Modjesca Simkins t-shirt to the state fair. He loved taking the rare Sunday off, lazing around with Malachi and his wife Laura, reading a Vietnam novel, and reeling through the channels on cable TV.

A dozen years before, Michael had his own teen club confrontation in the South Carolina mill town of Anderson, where he'd grown up as the son of a pharmaceuticals supplier. This time, the teenagers asked their Baptist church to add a gym to the basement of a million-dollar sanctuary they were building. When the congregation said, no, it would cost too much, Michael and his friends renovated an old barn on donated property and spent hours installing sheetrock, flooring, and wiring. Then the Baptists tore the building down for a parking lot. Michael left organized religion, never to return.

He carried the same pride and desire for justice on the nuclear issue. He got arrested again after asking to talk with the head of a Westinghouse nuclear fuel fabrication plant, the largest in the world, which was preparing to deliver uranium rods to the Summer reactor. When the manager ignored his letter, he showed up anyway, together with a woman friend, and refused to leave without a meeting.

In other trials magistrates had rejected defenses based on higher justification: the main judge in the Savannah River cases, a former law partner of Strom Thurmond, dealt protestors the harshest sentences possible, and tried to prevent a 1983 "bomb plant" blockade with an injunction that was eventually overturned by a higher court. But at Michael's trial, he and his friend got an all-black jury, who listened attentively while they compared their action to "trying to prevent bullets from going to a gun that's going to kill our children." To Michael's amazement, they were acquitted.

Although most of the newly organized nuclear activists wrote off the weapons issue as simply unwinnable, Michael and his coworkers soon challenged both reactor safety and the transportation of atomic wastes, which seemed to roll through, in green cask trucks, from every corner of the country. Taking the name Palmetto Alliance from the short bushy palm on the state emblem, group members released balloons to mark the potential paths of radioactive clouds, held community meetings, brought law students to interview nuclear workers on the effects of radiation, and jammed state media with discussions and questions. When they put together the boat flotilla to "Sail on Summer," Michael received his first jail sentence.

At the subsequent trial, they again tried to talk about preventing dire consequences. But, as Michael later explained, this judge "took the position that we were on the property and that was that." It seemed contradictory to buy out by paying the twenty-five dollar fines. So he, one other man, and three women spent fifteen days in jail that Christmas. Though Michael hated being separated from his family, the group held nuclear seminars for guards and other prisoners, passed notes among their cells, and wrote letters to the press and to state officials—including a major statement that Michael sent to newly elected Governor Richard Riley, building off an ongoing correspondence the two had been pursuing.

A few months later, Three Mile Island hit, and Palmetto's crazy warnings suddenly sounded cogent. TV networks blasted the state with revelations of its crucial atomic role. Trucks brought waste from the damaged reactor, and Governor Riley cited questionably completed paperwork in order to turn them back at the border. Palmetto gathered thousands of signatures at the *China Syndrome* box office.

It would be convenient to draw a line of expanding concern from this initial opposition, focusing largely on the atomic enterprise's corollary hazards, to current weapons challenges. In other regions an equivalent process frequently occurred. Activists opposing California's earthquake-threatened Diablo Canyon reactor remained concerned about that issue, but also formed much of the core of the group that challenged the right of Lawrence Livermore Laboratory to research an endless array of weapons, confronted the lab in 1982 with a demonstration involving nearly 1,400 arrests, and helped convince Livermore's public relations head to speak against the arms race after initially leaving his job for personal reasons.

After the first Barnwell demonstration, yearly Savannah River actions did link the complex's weapons role with immediate biological threats. Coordinated by Columbia's Grass Roots Organizing Workshop (GROW), and complemented by intermittent leafletting and religious vigils, these actions sought to reach a broad constituency with rallies addressed by such diverse speakers as Modjesca Simkins, a farmer downwind from the plant, a Furman religion professor, Philip Berrigan, retired admiral-turned-arms race opponent Gene LaRocque, a Hiroshima survivor, a former NATO general, and a leader of the atomic veteran's movement.

Demonstration participants remained, however, largely young and countercultural—primarily the already converted. And breadth of speakers could not substitute for grass-roots outreach. Issues like nuclear transportation, waste disposal, and the earthquake threat surrounding the Summer reactor's cooling lake could speak, at least somewhat directly, to those who worked the land, wove in the mills, pumped the gas, and preached in the pulpits. Municipal governments, including the Charleston City Council, limited transportation of nuclear materials. Bumperstickers of even the hardest drinking good ol' boys proclaimed, "Don't Dump It In Dixie." And when activists discovered a March 1982 Reagan administration cable inviting Mexico to ship its high-level nuclear materials to Barnwell, they gathered over 50,000 names opposing waste importation from any source. But for most ordinary citizens, including those who would later form groups like the one in Florence, the weapons protestors seemed largely ragged hippies on TV.

Leaving aside exceptions like Bebe, Modjesca, and the GROW people, most citizens involved in South Carolina's new peace movement had done little to actively oppose the atom's commercial sector. And many who first challenged the reactors, wastes, and reprocessing continued to focus on this clear and present danger, believing the state to be far too militarily entrenched to even question the weapons. They thought most of its citizens, as Michael said, only half-jokingly, "would feel just fine if everyone kept an atom bomb in the glove compartment of their pickup."

Yet even where these issues were not explicitly linked, addressing the atomic enterprise's incidental consequences eroded the legitimacy of the same government experts, who also insisted we had no choice but to continue our weapons escalation. And it brought dissent to a state that had rarely known it.

If the environmentalist challenge fed a broader stream of nuclear skepticism, so did a movement of women seeking both to define their own words and determine their own actions in a culture that had traditionally prescribed their silence. According to learning theorist Carol Gilligan, women, at least in current Western culture, view morality in "a different voice" by defining it less in terms of abstract right than as choices that balance conflicting responsibilities in an interdependent world. And this voice might particularly speak out about a threatened obliteration of the complex human web.

This is not to say every woman involved in the peace movement defines herself as a feminist, nor that pacific tendencies are biologically sex linked. Notions of innate female aversion to violence become at least questionable when faced with female SS guards, Margaret Thatcher ordering the fleet full-steam for the Falklands, or even the ordinary moms helping to replicate the blind and callous strains of diverse cultures. But to be a woman in the past decade and a half is to have lived in relation—whether of embrace or disdain—to some fundamental questionings of one's role. At their best, both the feminist and disarmament movements prize diverse experience and judgment over the will of those possessing the greatest physical force. Both decline to dismiss whole populations as being childlike, lacking in judgment, or expendable. And when women act, they often share a sense they are no longer going to remain silent.

South Carolina is hardly a feminist Mecca. The state legislature enshrined opposition to the Equal Rights Amendment in the same hallowed tones with which they once defended segregation. Myths of Southern women as pure nurturers or silky flesh still hang strong, and shifts in hearth or home are seen as Yankee invasions. Although Columbia and Charleston are more urban and diverse, in smaller cities a mother can't even talk about a son or daughter who is gay.

But just as Erica Bouza no longer believed women fulfill themselves solely by immaculate linen and perfect children, change has occurred in the South as well—within the culture's codes and traditions. While women like Bebe and Modjesca made no apologies for their course, visions of autonomy have also inspired others for whom activism is perhaps a more difficult vocation. Feminist visions have merged with other compelling belief systems, as in the case of a religious group that stood vigil for half an hour every Friday noon in front of the South Carolina State House. They stood without speaking, eight or ten respectable women and a couple of men, holding signs saying, "Pray For Peace." Drivers and pedestrians paused, watched, wondered, and maybe even reflected. For the moment, light shone on what was ordinarily hidden.

A number of key South Carolina activists were imports. A Pennsylvania-born biochemist sparked the first, Charleston-based, statewide Freeze effort. A New York doctor started the local Physicians for Social Responsibility. A Milwaukee psychologist initiated a parallel group within his discipline. But the State House vigilers had longstanding local roots. The family of Pride Carson, who worked in a local government agency, went back to the Revolution, and Pride's kitchen displayed a framed muster sheet and list of battles for the Confederate unit in which her former husband's great grandfather was a captain. Mary Mills—at age thirty-nine, a decade younger than Pride—supported two teenage daughters by working as a branch librarian, and came from backyard farmers who'd lived near Columbia since 1770 and who'd arrived at Jamestown, Virginia, just a dozen years after the *Mayflower* reached Providence. Margaret Van Adams, wife of a wealthy contractor, followed generations of blue-blood lawyers and judges by practicing in the family firm; her mother lived next to "a bore and a boor" named Strom Thurmond; her father said the only reason Margaret never liked Strom was that he didn't pinch her bottom the way he did the bottoms of the other young women who he knew.

But the vigilers still feared being tarred as irrational apocalyptics, like the wild-eyed man who stood opposite with his own sign saying "Repent. The World Is Going To End." "I got called a Communist at work," said Pride, laughing as the group walked to the nearly 200-year-old church where they gathered at the end of the vigil to chat. "Tell them Margaret Van Adams is there and they know I'm no Communist," said Margaret, who described how Vance Packard interviewed her in the 1950s for his book, *The Status Seekers*. He wrote her up as an anonymous Junior Leaguer without black or Jewish friends. She laughed. "I've come a ways since then."

I met Margaret a few days later at her law office, across from a Baptist bookstore and down the street from the unemployment center, where a half-dozen black men stood looking down at the ground. Photos of family friends in judge's robes decorated her office walls. She greeted me in a plaid cotton dress, stout Topsider boat shoes, and grey hair in a grandmother's bun. The previous day she'd cautioned a vigiler who was also a Sierra Club member that she didn't wish the nuclear issue to be mixed with any other. She now explained, squinching up her eyes, "This is very risky. I need to learn how many missiles they have, how many we have. All these facts I don't know." Continuing as the cautious neophyte, she assured me that she was not "going to lie down in front of any tractor at the Savannah Plant," or protest when President Reagan came, as had two other vigilers. She thought maybe she should worry first "about peace in my own heart."

Yet she also knew more than she let on, having followed these issues at least abstractly for the past ten years. And she'd spent a good chunk of the past three attending out-of-state conferences with speakers like former Yale Chaplain William Sloane Coffin and *Saturday Review* editor Norman Cousins; poring through drafts of the Catholic Pastoral Letter (its committee was chaired by Joseph Bernardin, a Columbia native turned Chicago Archbishop); watching films, reading articles, and continuing to learn.

To a degree, she kept her commitments tentative, echoing the Florence Peace Links cofounder who explained, "I'd a lot prefer to know that someone's interested before proceeding further. So it's sort of a step by step thing of raising a question, seeing how the water feels, and what they take me up on."

Margaret took refuge in an insulated world where loose ends were taken care of by a full-time cook, a part-time maid, and a part-time gardener. "I told you, I'm rich," she said, laughing as she had earlier when calling herself "the conservative Mrs. Van Adams." But for all Margaret's joking, her divorced or widowed peers had an ironic freedom, which she had relinquished in marrying "a backwoods Mississippi boy who never had a nickel when he was growing up," then had made it rich doing contracting throughout the country. Her husband, Van, worked hard for his money, she said, and liked the boat-and-country-club circle which he'd finally made it into. He'd been at the Reagan dinner the previous week, when Margaret's two fellow-vigilers joined a 150-person soup-line to picket outside the $500 a plate Republican benefit. Van showed up as well a few days later, at an elite group donating $1,000 apiece to the Democrats. He got along fine with everyone.

For all that Margaret felt a corollary pressure not to jostle the pot, she prized her own choices, just as she had in attending law school during World War II, in a chopped-down class with four other women and twenty men. Margaret remembered choosing the career as "no big deal," just a natural path, and then having the first of her five children and not working for thirty years. "I just hate that Phylliss Schlafly," she said a little later, with a laugh. "She wants every woman to be like this," and made a huge pregnant belly with one hand, while the other clamped tight on an open mouth.

For now, Margaret alternated, embracing committed engagement, then shying away with the sudden turn of a Coney Island Wild Mouse. She wanted to act on this issue that she called "the most important of any that could be," and liked the way involvement challenged her strengths; yet she doubted she'd "do protesting" beyond this single effort, and feared being cast as disreputable. "Van and I belong to all the social things," she said, teasing again about her background. "Ladies and Men's Debutante's Clubs. The Dance Club with the other couples said to be the top 100 in South Carolina. The downtown Summit Club, where my son caused an upset by taking a black date when he graduated from high school, and they sent a letter saying members were responsible for their offspring's guests."

Mortified at the time, Margaret now recalled her son's actions with relish; then she paused, thought, and said that until the Civil Rights Movement she had never known blacks except as servants. She believed real change came from "a vision, which religion puts forth, that the most important thing in the world is human beings."

When I asked Mary Mills about Vietnam—as another time of choice and crisis, when government experts insisted things were going the only way they could, and when an American movement helped halt a more modest apocalypse—she said she had all she could handle in raising two young children. "I pretty much stuck my head in the sand," she said as we talked in the small, neat apartment she described as "early motel" and shared with her daughters, now teenagers. "I thought 'If I have to hand out another book on Watergate. . . .' It wasn't that I found Nixon wonderful. They were just hard issues to think about."

She married during the mid-1960's while still in college, divorced eight years later, and "was left with the joy of raising two kids on $7,700 a year after my ex-husband lost his job." Like so many in South Carolina, she came to her politics through the church, to which she returned following the divorce. "They had a singles group of eight to ten people, but the few men who came spent all their time telling us what they thought we wanted to hear. We were too mouthy for them. Instead we got together and turned it into a women's support group."

Being on her own was undeniably difficult. During the worst years, Mary scraped by on food stamps, trying to give the children sufficient support, with no one else to rely on. But independence brought blessings as well. Mary understood what Pride meant when she said her divorce had made her "more of what I was before." That meant, in Pride's words, that she had to think, and make her own judgments. Slim and dark-eyed, Mary wore a small cross and gold earrings. Copies of *Ms, Sojourners,* and *Carolina Living* rested on an end table near the green couch, and her father's drawings of country rivers adorned the wall. Mary got up, saying she'd "be a Southerner and make ice tea."

When she returned, she told me about Cursillo, a religious retreat she attended several years back, and in whose wake first met Margaret and Pride. "I wasn't sure why I entered," she said sipping her tea. "I just got pulled into it. But you'd go through draining talks on purpose and vision, then return to a table full of presents and letters from Cursillistas who'd gone on earlier retreats.

"It could be like the cults where they bombard you with love, or the praise and prayer churches like the one which meets Sunday mornings at the drive-in where my kids saw *Return of the Jedi*. But it's not trying to estrange you from community or family. The idea is to see what being a Christian could be like, gifting and being gifted."

Cursillo held a form of confession as well, which was new for Episcopalians, and termed reconciliation by the leaders. Mary visited her ex-husband the following week, told him, "I have hurt you. Let me ask for your forgiveness," and broke a bitterness they had clutched for nearly ten years.

Mary found it hard to apologize without an implicit contract that said, in effect, "OK, I'm sorry. Now what will you do?" But the ability to give up insisting on one's measured pound of flesh seemed to carry a particular urgency in the nuclear age, where past and pending crimes have piled on each other until, at least among the giants, no nations are blameless. And in an age in which ultimate vengeance might mean all people would perish. Prizing forgiveness didn't mandate naïve sentimentality, but merely an acknowledgement that, as Mary said, "We either quit and do something about where we're headed or destroy it all."

Cursillo let her "see everything turned around." When Margaret suggested their Tuesday night Cursillista group "do something besides study and meditation," Mary went to work one night a week for a local food bank. That, plus raising two daughters and spending forty hours a week at her job (where coworkers included the wives of two generals and the mother of an atomic submarine crewman) kept Mary more than busy. But she went to the initial peace group meeting both from concern about the issue and "from a spiritual sense that I had to leave myself open to it." She thought the vigil mattered, regardless of numbers of participants or amount of media attention, and that it would grow and have its impact.

"There's a lot of affection in the group," Mary said. "Strong personalities. Margaret is strong. Pride is strong."

When I met with Pride earlier, she told me she didn't know "whether we can stop it all from blowing up," but would try and keep on trying nonetheless. She'd finally stopped caring "whether my peers at work think I'm crazy." When one man began telling everyone, "Guess where I saw Pride at lunch?" Pride answered, "Yes. We'd just be more than glad to have you, any time you want to stand with us."

I said Pride had backbone, a directness of intention and purpose, and Mary answered "Yes, like this," holding her hands straight as a tough firm spine. In many ways their former husbands were similar, though Pride's had never let her work. A dozen years back, both might have taken Cursillo as merely a private lesson. Mary said Pride still had little financial security, and that the burden of supporting aging parents made things hard. She thought a moment, then said quietly, "Pride takes a lot of risks."

Mary leaned back on the couch, thought further, and said she considered herself "hardly the likeliest person to get involved in this sort of thing. I'm pushing," she continued, "towards a more radical point, in four or five years when the kids are out and I can work at something that won't make much money. I could get distracted. I know I'll wander off. But my inner peace is now determined by doing certain things. It just means I'll have to come out of the closet on all these issues of peace and justice and whether another person matters in the sight of God as much as I do, whether in jail or Central America. To do all the things I don't want to do, that make me uncomfortable, that are difficult."

That Mary and the other vigilers combined their feminism with religious vision was consistent with a major stream of South Carolina culture. Without reducing the theological complexity of the Christianity embraced by individuals like Mary or Bill Cusak, for most their religion meant not only a faith but also a rubric under which an ordinary social life of volleyball games, bake sales, and coffee hours played as great a role as explanations of the cosmos. Christian norms have conditioned the state to the extent that church-supported blue laws prohibit people from even buying a frying pan on Sunday. Jewish-owned Sears joins major food chains Piggly-Wiggly, Winn-Dixie, and three dozen other retailers in a weekly newspaper ad detailing appropriate New Testament readings. To quote Biblical argument is commonplace.

Before the resurgent disarmament debate, church liturgies might have touched on related issues. But the morality they prescribed remained a private one. The secular priests—government experts—took care of actions of state. Now, a national movement spurred the consciences of local activists like Mary, Pride, Margaret, and the Florence marchers. They in turn pressured their churches. Discussion entered previously excluded domains.

If churches are not only religious vehicles but also institutions of common life, for them to raise the nuclear issue not only tests root faith but also affects the congregations' mundane worlds. Expectedly, this debate is not universally welcomed, and many Christians prefer the cleaner sanctuary of private salvation. Silence raises fewer awkward questions.

For this reason, one of South Carolina's seven Presbyterian divisions found itself debating both the church's national statement on war in a nuclear age and the right of a local peacemaking committee to exist. The earliest drafts of the national document emerged shortly before the first versions of the Catholic Pastoral Letter, and developed through parallel ecumenical dialogue. The Presbyterian drafts were duly distributed and for the most part ignored—just more paper for the files. But the final document hit amidst unprecedented discussion of the issue, and after the Carolina churches had been torn and scarred the previous June by a reunion merger between the main body of Northern Presbyterians and the Southern congregations, separate since the Civil War. A number of congregations had bolted to small, conservative splinter groups or lost substantial minorities of their members. Tensions were already running high when nurse-practitioner Carol Doty began a Presbyterian peacemaking group.

Like most South Carolinians, Carol had never been politically active beyond benign civic ventures. But she had discussed the nuclear threat in her previous congregation in East Lansing, Michigan, where she lived before her husband, a professor, received a University of South Carolina appointment. The more she learned, the more she became concerned. After discovering that a grant was available to address the issue in Southern churches, Carol initiated an official committee that distributed educational materials, held a peace fair attended by 250 people, and pushed for subsidiary groups in each congregation.

It was in her Columbia church, the 1,500-member Eastminster congregation, where Carol raised the ire of certain individuals. Contending the national document was "inflammatory" and full of "accusatory guilt," and that church members had no business interfering with government leaders, the critics pushed to reject it and decertify Carol's committee. The Eastminster elders backed this challenge on a narrow vote, then brought its motions to Congaree Presbytery, a ruling body representing Eastminster and twenty-two other congregations totalling 13,000 members. In October 1983, Congaree elders and ministers considered the issue at their regular meeting in a red brick church a half-hour north of Columbia, in the small textile town of Winnsboro. A minister named Jim Watkins, in charge of peacemaking for the denomination's main Southern office in Atlanta, began by recalling when he got his ROTC commission at Georgia Tech, where he learned "to close, contain, kill and capture the enemy by fire and maneuver." He did it well enough, he said, to receive a medal as the outstanding military student, and then went to Korea, "where I closed, contained, killed and captured the enemy there as well," and brought home another medal. Later Jim trained men in these same tactics at Columbia's Fort Jackson, keeping on until he retired as a captain.

Light filtered green and pink through the stained glass windows as Jim explained that there might be a place for an organization with such purposes. "But that is not the purpose of the church." And he described a diorama of the battle of Atlanta, where cannons boomed in the background and the final scene portrayed a dying Confederate given water by a Union soldier. "It was his brother. The Martin boys from Tennessee." The earth's people, he said, were all brothers now, all "God's children" in the face of a common threat. Peace had to become something more than just "the time between wars." And the role of the church was to seek that vision.

Because this was an ordinary business meeting, and the resolutions on peacemaking were only two of many, routine proceedings kept interrupting the debate. One moment, people addressed the species' future; the next, committees reported on benevolence budgets, and ministers gave testimonials honoring their retiring peers. When someone tried to use a technicality to dump the Eastminster challenge, parliamentary motions whizzed past each other like tracer bullets and the fate of humanity seemed to hang on Roberts Rules.

The national document, explained the opposition's main leader, suggested the United States was responsible for the world's ills. "It even implies the reason the Russians are warlike and belligerent is because we're so bad." He questioned whether peacemaking should, indeed, as the document asserted, be "the central activity of all believers individually and corporately." And, to be frank, he felt the word had "negative connotations."

"Peacemaking in the self, family, and congregation is fine," he said, moving to limit any committee role to those areas, "though I don't know we need a special group to carry that out." But congregants shouldn't be telling the president what to do. And, as he told a friend, he thought the activists were "duped."

Peace effort supporters stressed that they loved "the red white and blue as much any anyone." "Sometimes," explained one minister, also a major general in the National Guard, "our country is wrong. We must learn that it is not without sin, just as we are not without sin." He cited an array of weapons opponents, from Billy Graham and the evangelicals of *Sojourners* to "the conservative doctors," and said even career military officers were now speaking out.

Because routine matters pressed, the debate could not spiral endlessly. Most had scarcely thought about the issue, were unsure of their appropriate role, and feared another major split. So they first postponed a decision on the letter, and then on the local peacemaking committee. Instead, the Presbytery delegated a group to study the challenges, prepare a report, and bring the matter back when, four months later, they met again. The man who suggested this belonged to none of the factions, admitted he knew far too little, and said it was more than time he and others began to learn. People wanted to heal the wounds of the denominational reunion and make peace within a church wracked by loss and factionalism. In a sense, they buried the most difficult questions; yet, they spurred a more extensive and further reaching debate. For now each congregation would have to discuss and decide.

That these discussions took place at all was as important as their religious context. Whatever their theology, churches paralleled other ordinary institutions in their ability to maintain or breach the prevailing silence in which the arms race continued. Debates like that in Congaree Presbytery embodied this choice. The question was how responsibility got played out among those who filled the pews.

Eastminster pastor Ernest Thompson stressed that resistance to the document and the peacemaking committee might well spur further learning. "People heard [opposition leader] Ron Brown," he said, "but they also heard people like Jerry Hammett, who's a general in the reserves and who people have respected for a long time without knowing where he stood on these issues." Now every congregation would be wrestling with the document's understanding "that God has given us the world to work with, and that it's our choice to blow it up or not."

Ernest's own church consisted largely of affluent professionals from white-colonnaded plantation houses lining the nearby streets of Columbia's Trenholm Road neighborhood, and included a substantial number of retired military officers. Some criticized Ernest for supporting Carol's committee, or for implying, in a Christmas talk on peace, "that our President might be lying on whether we really trailed the Russians in missiles." He worried about pastors who'd lost their jobs for speaking too loudly during Vietnam and the Civil Rights Movement, like a Methodist colleague who was moved, in Modjesca's words, "way up yonder to a country church so small he almost starved." Ernest felt he evaded such censure by compromising: "sitting here with my nice new running shoes and my nice car and a kid I'm trying to get through Princeton"; just as in the civil rights era he spoke from the pulpit, housed traveling organizers, but never quite made it to places like Selma.

"I have the image of a race," he explained, running his hand through his greying hair and leaning back beneath a medieval hanging of mounted knights. "Some," he said, "like William Sloane Coffin, are in front, taking the prophetic tradition. Others look back, not wanting to get too far ahead of the pack. I know Christianity isn't supposed to be sitting on comfort, but how do I oppose these things without giving something up? I'm here as a change agent, but the situation's working on me also, pushing me just to go to the Carolina football games and not worry."

Both ministers and lay people faced the choice of whether to spark difficult confrontations within their congregations, whether to break both formal and informal codes that would keep peace work huddled in small private domains. Success in doing this might create forms of common expression like denominational Freeze endorsements and peacemaking documents, or secular equivalents initiated by unions, neighborhood councils, and professional groups. Legitimacy conferred by these organizations could allay individual fears of involvement. Speaking out might draw in those reluctant to be the first.

In the case of Congaree Presbytery, most churches held at least some preparatory discussions for the February meeting. As official moderator, Ernest Thompson picked the five-person committee to evaluate this challenge which had been backed by his own East-minster elders, and he mixed respected figures sympathetic to the peace movement with others more supportive of the military. To Ernest's surprise, the committee suggested unanimously that Congaree keep their peacemaking group and accept their national document, and the churches overwhelmingly accepted this recommendation. The peace question was not to be banished.

If issues raised by the peace movement were now voiced in previously silent communities throughout the country, the movement also linked these communities in a mirror echo of the weapons culture's complex reach. The weekend before our last visit, Bebe had been run frantic, coordinating statewide actions around the white train: a string of guarded armored cars beginning at the Pantex plant, in Amarillo, Texas, where the final atomic warheads were assembled. The train then carried them to be loaded and deployed at the Trident submarine base in Bangor, Washington, the Charleston Naval Weapons Station, and assorted other deployment sites. It ran unnoticed for years, until its purpose was discovered by the people at Ground Zero, a largely religious nonviolent action center, located immediately adjacent to the Bangor base, which had spent the better part of a decade challenging the Tridents. Now they added another task: gathering voices along the steel rails joining these receptacles of global fire with the diverse humans who sought to dismantle them.

Called the Agape community, the railroad network relied on spotters in the peace movement to relay progress, schedules and route information. Compatriots further along lined the tracks to stand vigil, blocked the train with their bodies, and did what they could to make the passage one of learning and witness. They tried, in the words of a Dominican nun from Ground Zero, to allow the train to run through, touch, and change their hearts, yet also to affirm their own choices about how they would act and live. In Portland, Oregon, people stopped one Bangor train for two-and-a-half hours by blocking the tracks. In Orchard, Idaho, a deputy who arrested a grandmother said he would like to join her in the vigil line, and the state's major paper praised the activists' moral vision. In South Carolina, the train headed east towards Charleston; it was originally due to follow a northern route through Greenwood, Catawba, and a town of 6,000 just twenty-five miles from Florence. The Pee Dee group gathered everyone possible on a single day's notice and prepared to head out to the tracks. So did students at a small Presbyterian college without the slightest history of activism, and residents of numerous small towns with similarly silent pasts. But the train left its expected route—possibly because of the size of planned Atlanta protests— and instead hugged the southern coast, speeding into the Naval Weapons Station just ahead of some Charleston vigilers.

The quick crisis over, Bebe relaxed in her living room, drinking beer. A tawny kitten clawed at her sleeve. The stereo played a National Public Radio jazz show: first Erroll Garner's elegant leaps and ballroom glides; then Ornette Coleman, with a somersaulting ghost dance, laced with Texas blues.

Bebe recalled her work with Fairfield United Action, and the utility executives' assumption that teenage bus drivers would calmly pick up first- and second-graders if the Summer reactor had an accident. The Fairfield group challenged this, asked as well why the evacuation plan carved around the major black school in the area, and bridged racial divisions by stressing a variety of common plaints against the banks, insurance companies, and other presumably un- accountable institutions ruling the region.

A train shook the house from tracks forty yards behind, and re- called the gleaming guarded machine that passed two days before on rails more commonly evoking dreams of lonesome freights headed for Chicago or Abilene. Bebe's walls were thin, and during the winter she fed a cast-iron stove with wood scrounged from the mill town neighborhood, where the poor were forced to burn oil or electricity because landlords feared fire in the rotting chimneys.

Bebe told me of a church program in which participants asked not only about the weapons she came to speak on, but also about radio- active waste and other presumably separate atomic safety issues. "I'd never seen any of them at demonstrations," she said. "They'd never written letters to the editor or come to Palmetto Alliance meetings. But it was clear they'd been reading throughout those years. Maybe they even agreed with us all that time but never did anything."

At times Bebe felt powerless, "like with Nicaragua, where we don't have any twenty years to change the American people's minds. Where the vote comes down today—do we or don't we overthrow their government." But she thought that on the nuclear issue people were learning. "Even if all they've done is read their newspaper, they've seen concern about nuclear waste, transportation, and evacuation plans. They've heard the word connected to radiation leaks, the plants' economic cost, and spills on the highway. And so when they see their national church statement, it rings a bell. People say 'Yeah, it seems they've been fooling around with this for a long time and don't really know what they're doing. They're building weapons that supposedly are going to be used for our benefit, not detriment. But look how they made their decisions on the wastes.'

"So we're talking about Savannah River's environmental problems. But we've also asked why the L reactor's plutonium is needed. If we hadn't done that stuff before, SRP would still be an invulnerable kind of place the Freeze people would be afraid to even talk about. They'd say that's our local plant and we can't go against people's employment. It would just be too big a jump."

Four years ago, Bebe stressed, South Carolina residents didn't think they could directly question atomic weapons. Addressing any nuclear hazard was an awesome task. But half a year after our talk, in the spring of 1984, local activists convinced the state Democratic caucuses to pass resolutions supporting the Freeze and opposing U.S. intervention in Central America. If anything was to happen in South Carolina, she thought, "because of national media, Reagan and so on," now was the time "to glimpse that little hole, that pinpoint of light, and run like hell towards it." She wanted to bring as many others to see and act as she could.

On the road from Columbia to Florence a billboard pictures a hand held to a cross by a huge and vicious nail. Blood drips from the wound. The hand is clenched in pain. Words explain, "Jesus loves you so much it hurts." The blood is a warning to all who pass.

Shortly after her first involvement in the peace movement, Bill Cusak's daughter Pam had a dream. She was a computer programmer, married to a former West Point cadet who was now a Physicians for Social Responsibility doctor. "It didn't make a lot of sense," she explained when we talked the day after the Florence march, "just like a lot of dreams don't. But for some reason my husband Don and I were in Fayetteville, North Carolina, at a couples' retreat. Apparently the person leading the conference was someone I knew.

And he said that we had fifteen minutes, that the Russians had launched nuclear warheads and that they were aimed at Fayetteville and somewhere in California. And the reason was that we shuffled our weapons between the two places.

"I mean it was just a crazy dream," she continued, hugging her knees together and crossing her hands over her pregnant belly. "But we happened to be in the prime target area. And it was headed towards us. And I remember Don and I holding each other, waiting for it to happen, but we were OK. We were at peace because we knew we were going to be with the Lord. We were going to Heaven. But there was a close family member, Don's brother, who doesn't claim to be a Christian. He doesn't want to have anything to do with those things. And I was thinking in the dream, 'I wished he would have listened.' But there was no chance to talk to him any longer. It was over."

The next afternoon, I asked Bill about my conversation with Pam and Don, and their statement that her brother was destined for Hell. He said their belief was indeed sincere, as was their compassion in wishing no one to suffer that fate. They'd told him years ago that if war came and the shelters had no room, they would surrender their places so non-Christians would have a final chance to save their souls. "Their concern," Bill explained, "is not some idle thought, but something they're willing to give up their lives for."

When I asked Bill if he agreed, he said he used to, but didn't any more. "They probably quoted you a Biblical phrase where Jesus says 'No man comes to the Father but by me.' It's based on the idea that if we come to the Father we are spared the natural process of disintegration, which some people call Hell. By staying in contact with the source of life, then we are spared the nonlife. But in my interpretation I tie it to some other passages that go 'Why call you me Lord, Lord, and do not the things I say?' Which leaves me thinking Jesus was more concerned for the spirit of the person and the style of life of the person, and that they demonstrate their faith in ways other than saying the classical Christian words. So I do think that passage is true, but that it means no one comes to the Father but in the Jesus way.

"For instance, Mahatma Gandhi never formally accepted Christ, because he lived in a Hindu and Buddhist country and knew that would separate him from so many of his people. But I just can't imagine a guy like Gandhi, who's probably one of the most Christ-like people I know in our day and time, quote, 'burning in Hell.' So I see Gandhi as being true to the passage they quote from—he does come to the Father in the Jesus way."

In part because involvement with the peace issue had pushed him, Bill's current notion of Hell was more existential, "a place where God is not." If humans rejected God "to a point that they're fixed in that position, then they separate themselves from the source of life." This was not necessarily in the afterworld. It could be in the present, and the disintegration could be ethical and spiritual as well as physical. "But you separate yourself from the source of life in this world and guys as mean as I am disintegrate real quick."

Bill smiled when I doubted his meanness, answering "You ought to ask Pam. She's lived with me. She knows." He said he feared his own explosive fury: "We get as angry against the Reaganites as they do against the peaceniks.

"It's like the other day when they called us Communists. I've been reading a lot of astronomy lately, and have begun to see God not as a blazing sun, but as a black hole which absorbs everything. What I'd like to do is go there and be a black hole and absorb their anger. Because I think only if that's done in a kind of chain reaction will we really disarm evil. That's true of Jesus and Gandhi and Martin Luther King. King understood the whole nonviolent thrust of the Scriptures, and so did that fellow I gave you the *Baptist Peacemaker* on, Clarence Jordan. Those boys understood what Jesus was driving at and weren't afraid to go against cultural norms to follow it. I ain't even touched the hem of the garment of where they are. But it's fascinating to be on the trail."

I thought of Bill's notion of "the source of life," and how it par-alleled other images of strength to be gained by reaching beyond one's individual self. Dietrich Bonhoeffer, a Lutheran minister ex-ecuted for his role in the plot to kill Hitler, made a parallel argument in an essay entitled, "Who Stands Strong?" He said that, without connection to that transcendent power he also called God, individuals collapsed into desperate gestures, pragmatic accommodation, or de-spair. For Modjesca, a perhaps less theological sustenance comes partly from sheer cheek, the brazen humor out of which she called Carolina's esteemed legislators "a bunch of old hound dogs," and from the compassion that let her care even about those who would spend their entire lives wiggling their toes and doing nothing. Novelist Alice Walker draws on that force which creates the color purple in a field.

I told Bill I thought the movement needed to break beyond its current constituency and reach others besides the white, the middle class, and the educated. He responded, quietly, "I agree. And that's the sixty-four dollar question."

Bill and Ingram discussed this issue briefly at the bomb site. Ingram attended local NAACP meetings. Bill had tried, without luck, to enlist a contingent for the August 27th anniversary of the original march on Washington. They talked of a local forum on King and Gandhi.

"I'm looking forward to meeting," Bill continued, "with a black pastor and evangelist who seems very interested. I think it's going to be done by finding someone like him and supporting him just like Jack and the others supported me. And maybe he'll grow into the catalyst to spot other people in the black community, and go from there. That would be my hope and prayer."

He said the same was true with young people, that except for a few children of adult marchers, the group hadn't "made a real break with the teenagers. But the way I see it is if we can get one youth group where it becomes the group norm and the group loyalty, then they can look for other kids—just the same way we did in that youth revival in Atlanta. They can share their enthusiasm with other people. And it will catch on like a wildfire.

"Because basically it takes likes to reach likes: youth to reach youth; blacks to reach blacks; Catholics to reach Catholics. And," he said with a sly smile, "I even think it takes Baptists to reach Baptists."

# 3. Los Angeles: The High Tech Road

T HE TV screen shows a young jean-clad mother, holding her baby's hands. They sit on a patchwork picnic blanket, on the lawn of a white suburban house. The baby takes a slow tentative step, then another, slightly more sure.

"Proposition 12 won't end the nuclear arms race overnight," an authoritative voice explains. "But it does call for a freeze on the production and testing of nuclear weapons by both Russia and the United States." The announcer pauses; the mother claps her hands. The baby looks around, tottering and frowning, persevering towards its father, who waits, clapping and holding out his arms in encouragement. The announcer stresses "strict safeguards" on cheating.

At last the baby makes it, wobbling, reaching for balance, finishing with a perfect Gerber smile. The parents look, proud and tender, while the announcer asks us to "take the first step for a bilateral nuclear arms freeze. Vote yes on Proposition 12. And help make sure there's a time and a place for all the other first steps—that have yet to be taken."

The ad ran in Los Angeles and San Diego, Fresno, Sacramento, and Oakland, Sonoma, Palo Alto, and Azusa. It ran in nearly every media market in the nation's largest state, endorsing a November 1982 referendum viewed by many as a watershed mandate. It affirmed that the most intimate domains are now threatened by the weapons.

In its fundamental message, the ad might have spoken equally to Bill Cusak's Florence neighbors, a grandmother in Soviet Tashkent, or a horseman on the Argentine plains. But what, within these particular situations, would lead one person to risk political involvement and not another? What allows some individuals to act and continue acting without capitulating to the inevitable difficulties and costs? Commitment to challenge the arms race requires more than mere technical knowledge of our present jeopardy. It seems to require, once again, a moral context, a sense of oneself as part of a larger whole, as with Bill Cusak's religious faith or the desire for generational continuity that the Freeze "First Steps" ad hoped to evoke. Involvement may stem from strengths of personal character, like those that created a continuum between Bebe and Michael's teen club sagas and their later opposition to the bombs. Or from a human capacity for unexpected leaps of vision, like those evoked in a book by Lawrence Weschler on the Polish Solidarity movement, when a French observer described how the goal of an independent trade union spread, during a brief week and a half in 1980, from the remote thought of a few dozen individuals to become "the central expression of the will of the whole of the working class of the maritime region, and within a few more days, of the entire country."

Involvement requires both persistence and strategic judgment: Weschler points out how the newsletter of the workers' support group KOR mentioned repeatedly the 1978 and 1979 detentions, minor arrests, and other political harassments of a then-unknown shipyard electrician named Lech Walesa. Solidarity did not leap, like Athena, suddenly into being. Yet the shift of individuals or communities towards broader concerns, must remain, in some sense, a mystery that, in Walt Whitman's words, "the talkers talking their talk" can never fully explain; whose roots can only be glimpsed through what Whitman calls "faint clues and indirections."

Those who break from prescribed roles often explain their profound personal shifts by the deceptively simple statement that they act because they have no other choice. It was in this vein that a Los Angeles machine equipment distributor named Bob Willard recalled an incident during the World War II Battle of the Bulge. He was a

young second lieutenant, working in a heavy automotive mainte-
nance company, serving the Red Ball Express, which kept the supply
trucks running. The major in charge of materials procurement turned
down Bob's request for some equipment to rebuild the vehicles. The
supplies were badly needed for the fight. Bob broke discipline, and
went on his own to find a sympathetic general. Although he later
found himself reprimanded for "failing to follow normal channels of
command," he nonetheless got the trucks to the front.

With the battle soon won and the war ended, Bob returned to a
culture that rarely sanctioned risk-taking for anything larger than
one's self: that instead channeled individual energy, skill, and am-
bition into buttressing private gain. He worked hard to support his
family—first as an engineer and then in his small machine equipment
business—and to succeed as a respectable citizen; but he shied away
from any taint of dissent or dissaffection. Although Bob cared deeply
for those in his intimate world, and wrote his quota of checks to
charity, more direct involvements largely stopped at the door to his
home.

The nuclear issue ultimately broke Bob's insulation, as he began
to get "a sense of the universality of life from the universality of the
threat," a sense that we couldn't afford to remain "just insular people
who don't have to worry about anyone else." Bob came to this sense
after being invited in by a chain of other individuals who acted—a
pattern that occurred again and again in the peace movement's resurgent broadening.

One could begin the particular process of which Bob was part
with Harold Willens, a Los Angeles corporation head who, during
Vietnam, cofounded a national organization of antiwar businessmen.
Concerned as well about nuclear weapons, Willens contributed heavily to the initial presidential campaign of Jimmy Carter because of
Carter's bold campaign speeches on the atomic danger, and Carter
appointed him as a delegate to the first United Nations special disarmament session. But the session did nothing, blocked by superpower recalcitrance—including that of Carter's administration. And
Willens returned to tell his old friend, Rabbi Leonard Beerman of
Los Angeles's Leo Baeck Temple, that perhaps the only hope lay in
the religious community. The two joined a Pasadena Episcopal minister to pull together what they called the Interfaith Center to Reverse

the Arms Race. And when they held the founding conference in the
fall of 1979, Beerman asked Bob Willard's friends Suzy and Wally
Marks to come and attend.

Invited in turn by Suzy and Wally, and stirred by the evident
gravity of the crisis, Bob spent the next six months reflecting on
what he'd heard. He had never been much for political reading,
preferring baseball almanacs or novels by Kurt Vonnegut and Isaac
Bashevis Singer. But he plowed doggedly through magazines like
*Defense Monitor* and *Foreign Affairs*, trained to go out as an Interfaith
Center speaker, and began writing elected officials and the local
papers.

He also helped begin a small Leo Baeck peace group. Although
Bob knew only Rabbi Beerman and the Markses, the meetings
strengthened his confidence that this issue was not "just one where
the kooks hang out." Group members gathered a thousand names
and accompanying donations to run a full-page pro-Freeze ad in the
*Santa Monica Evening Outlook*. Bob joined a Friday noon vigil at the
major west Los Angeles intersection of Santa Monica and Wilshire.

"Imagine me standing on the corner with a sign," he said, with a
quick ironic laugh complementing his engineer's gruff pragmatism.
As we talked over early morning breakfast, he described how friends
drove by, shaking their heads and saying to themselves, "No, that's
not Bob." He spoke at the American Association of University
Women, and at a chapter of the Jewish Hillel Foundation "where I
got the hell beat out of me in an argument with a couple of Russian
immigrants, then went back and studied further." He gained "a sense
that individuals could do something beyond their personal lives. That
you don't have to have the money of a Harold Willens or be able to
devote full time to it. And that you can do something more than
just vote."

When Bob stood vigil opposite the Beverly Hilton Hotel, he faced
different obstacles than did Mary, Pride, and Margaret in their weekly
sojourn at the South Carolina State House. There, the dominant
sentiment overwhelmingly assumed our military policies were necessary to back down the Red hordes. In west Los Angeles, many
people were ambivalent about further weapons systems; their resistance to involvement stemmed mostly from distraction, complacency, the press of more high-rolling affairs, and fear of appearing
part of a radical fringe. Yet the resulting acquiescence was often the

same, and Bob's vigil was as great an apostasy to his surrounding culture of casual detachment as was that of the Carolina women praying for peace in the shadow of Columbia's Fort Jackson.

"I'm a lifelong Republican," Bob said laughing. "I worry whether my business associates are going to consider me a Communist dupe. I don't want to lose friends and I hope I don't." But he also didn't want fear "of being associated with radicalism" to back him away from critical issues, whether the arms race, or economic systems that left some "with tremendous material wealth" and others in poverty.

When I asked Bob if he'd stay involved, he said his twenty-six-year-old son had told him, "Dad, you're going to surprise us yet." He laughed and said, "I didn't sign a contract," then suggested that Europeans who spend their whole lives on this issue often see Americans "as crazy people, because we expect to solve it all in one weekend study group." He doubted, though, that he could return to being just a spectator, "because what I know won't go away, and when I was passive it left me uncomfortable—always saying 'look at so and so doing this. I'm as smart. I'm as capable. I have as many ideas.' Maybe I learned it in high school civics, but it seems wrong to eat the grain but never water it. It feels better to participate."

Without journeys like Bob's or Bill Cusak's, broader change is impossible. Yet their personal conversions affect institutional choice only when joined to mechanisms for voicing common concern: the nuts and bolts that Bill said were as important as inspiration and vision. That Bill Cusak, Bob Willard, and the various Leo Baeck and Florence activists ended up working on an initiative called "the Freeze" was a result not only of their caring and commitment, but of a cross-country chain of efforts and choices.

In the summer of 1978, the United Nations responded to worldwide pressure by holding the special disarmament session to which Willens became a delegate. During an accompanying surge of discussion, several national peace groups raised the idea of a halt in nuclear weapons production as an initial step towards further cuts. A year later, Oregon Republican Mark Hatfield introduced in the U.S. Senate an amendment to the SALT II Treaty, proposing precisely such a U.S.-Soviet freeze. But SALT II was indefinitely tabled, and Hatfield's proposal succumbed undiscussed.

The following February, representatives of a dozen organizations met to respond to the SALT II rejection. Led by Randall Forsberg of the Brookline, Massachusetts, Institute for Defense and Disarmament Studies, and including members of Fellowship of Reconciliation, Women's International League for Peace and Freedom, Clergy and Laity Concerned, and the American Friends Service Committee (AFSC), the representatives developed a document entitled "Call to Halt the Nuclear Arms Race," suggesting the United States and the Soviet Union adopt "a mutual freeze on the testing, production and deployment of all nuclear warheads, missiles and delivery systems." Because the Freeze required a blanket halt, it could stop further escalation without diffusing activist energy by forcing groups to oppose an endless succession of new individual weapons. And because it was essentially verifiable by satellites and other technical means, and still left the United States with 30,000 warheads, it retained the cherished assumptions of deterrence. The organizations distributed the call to chapters and members, and then began soliciting further endorsements.

Supporters came close to making the Freeze a part of the 1980 Democratic platform. And in the same election that first made Ronald Reagan president, an initiative supporting negotiation of a Freeze passed three state senatorial districts in western Massachusetts. Activists from Deerfield's Traprock Peace Center and the Northampton AFSC office had worked for nearly a year, gathering several thousand signatures to put this "non-binding public policy question" on the ballot, and then informing churches, schools, and community groups how their support might help check a global arms race. Daniel Ellsberg sparked hundreds of volunteers with talks at local colleges. Doctors, clergy, and businessmen bought full-page local ads. A billboard owner donated seven massive signs.

Although Reagan carried the district, the Freeze referendum won fifty-nine percent of the vote; it captured thirty of the thirty-three towns and cities that supported the Republican ticket, and all of the twenty-nine that went Democratic. The victory was repeated four months later in Vermont and New Hampshire town meetings.

A month following the November election, a Los Angeles couple named Jo and Nick Seidita read a *Nation* article about the Massachusetts referendum. Nick was head counselor at an adult high school in Watts; Jo had worked for years in reform Democratic politics. Though California was a far vaster challenge, they saw no reason why the Massachusetts experience couldn't be duplicated, and began by approaching their Unitarian church. This highly ecumenical congregation was nicknamed "the Onion" after its brown shingled sanctuary. Its minister had worked on war and peace issues since becoming inspired over twenty years ago, by the voyage of a small sailboat into America's Eniwetok H-bomb test site. The church had set aside $2,900 to repair some roof leaks, but members decided to donate the money to finance the Seidita's initial mailings, phone calls, and visits to key organizations. Together with a small group of colleagues, Jo and Nick next solicited support from organizations ranging from other congregations and the national Unitarian assembly to the Grey Panthers, Church Women United, and the Democratic Party's State Executive Board, as well as a host of other bodies that first contributed paper endorsements and, later, members and resources.

By the following August, eighty-four groups were involved, plus numerous informal gatherings like the Leo Baeck community. Committees in each congressional district began to show films, hold educational gatherings, and prepare for the "petition parties" the Seiditas hoped would generate most of the necessary signatures.

Jo came up with the party model in 1968, when in eight hours she and other members of the California Democratic Council generated 39,000 names to put Eugene McCarthy first on the primary ballot. Hosts invited eight friends, who helped with refreshments, and each brought eight additional guests, preferably from diverse backgrounds. Participants talked, gave modest donations, signed ballot petitions, and picked up additional copies of the petitions to circulate further.

Once the Seiditas had enough support to expect this tack would again succeed, the campaign officially became Californians for a Bilateral Nuclear Weapons Freeze. The electoral effort would undoubtedly be both massive and costly, and the grass-roots groups were long on energy but barely meeting shoestring budgets. So a man named Marvin Schachter contacted his old business friend Harold Willens, the corporation head who helped put together Interfaith Center, and who he knew had been following the campaign's progress. After lengthy conversations, Willens decided to participate.

He began his job as campaign coordinator by convincing ten wealthy colleagues to join him in helping to provide $250,000 as further seed money. On November 23rd, the state attorney general released copies of the petitions, giving the campaign five months to gather a half-million names. In a two-week push, people gathered in 1,500 locations to consume wine, cheese, coffee, and cookies; discuss buried hopes and fears; and raise 110,000 names.

In addition to lining up funds, Willens enlisted the support of respected luminaries like Berkeley Nobel Prize physicist Donald Glaser and San Francisco Archbishop John Quinn. The Freeze soon secured endorsement by four more of the state's resident Nobel laureates and an array of other respected scientists, including polio vaccine discoverer, Dr. Jonas Salk; Caltech president, Marvin Goldberger; and numerous Manhattan Project veterans. Religious leaders echoed Archbishop Quinn's call, joined by executives and Hollywood figures such as Norman Lear, Sally Field, and Reagan's daughter, actress Patti Davis.

Nationally, the Freeze was being endorsed by groups ranging from the Wilderness Society and the National Council of Churches to the American Association of University Women, the National Conference of black Mayors, and the YWCA. And in part because of California's progress, parallel efforts began that would lead to referendum victories in nine states, from Michigan to Montana, and over fifty cities, from Philadelphia and Chicago to Miami and Galveston.

The ballot drive provided a framework within which activists could take the arms race issue to churches, shopping malls, movie lines, schools, neighborhoods, union halls, and Kiwanis clubs. Beachfront volunteers sold "Freeze Bar" popsicles for a dollar apiece. Ventura County, home to a half-million residents between Los Angeles and Santa Barbara, showed *The Last Epidemic* at each of its high schools. When Sonoma County billboard companies refused to rent signs, a young artist painted 700 of them on broad wooden flats, then hung them outside supportive businesses and homes. Storekeepers displayed petitions on their counters. Football fans placed them next to the beer and chips when friends dropped by to watch the Sunday games. After a black minister collected 440 names at one Sunday service, he gave thanks in prayer "for the opportunity of saying 'No more war.' "

Once the initiative qualified for the ballot with over 750,000 names, its core organizers faced a choice. They could continue engaging people group by group, neighborhood by neighborhood, constituency by constituency; or they could hope the outreach would continue from present momentum and focus their prime organizational and financial resources on a media campaign aimed at winning a majority of California's nearly 25 million residents. Because this was the nation's largest state, Reagan's home, and known—for good or ill—as a bellwether of shifts in national sentiment, Freeze supporters believed the outcome would echo across the country. They also assumed they'd encounter strong opposition, and were later proven correct when the Reagan administration delegated batteries of top officials to tour the state condemning the measure as a threat to national security. So, led by Willens, who had by far the most access to people with wealth, the campaign chose the high-tech road, and attempted to blanket the state with ads.

The baby spot was the first, pulled together by Bill Zimmerman, a forty-one-year-old psychologist who'd worked in the Civil Rights Movement, had organized and directed Medical Aid to Indochina (a highly effective Vietnam-era organization that melded political impact and direct human concern), and participated in an array of further causes, including an airlift of food and medical supplies to the Native Americans at Wounded Knee. Zimmerman first glimpsed the possibilities of political ads during Tom Hayden's 1976 U.S. Senate race, when he built up Tom's effort a year in advance, hoping that because of Hayden and Jane Fonda's visibility, they could generate ample press coverage without paying. They did—most of it fair and sympathetic. But Hayden's support rose in that year just a single point, to an entirely marginal fourteen percent. Then Zimmerman tried TV ads, leaving the sectored-off ghettos of talk shows or news columns and entering the real world where Hayden could be marketed head to head with MacDonalds, Excedrin, and Pampers. In three weeks his standing nearly tripled.

The election cut off further progress, but Zimmerman saw how similar commercials might aid a variety of worthy causes. He didn't consider the electoral realm the sole domain within which to act for political change, "or even a particularly good way to launch social movements." But once activists took on its challenges, there were rules to be heeded. Votes came "from doing a lot of things that social movements aren't particularly good at, like raising money and doing advertising." If citizens entered the arena, he felt they should enter to win.

The Hayden campaign led to the creation of a consulting firm, which Zimmerman formed together with Sid Galanty—a veteran director with CBS, the United States Information Agency and various commercial ad shops—and Jack Fiman—a young media expert who targeted commercials to the schedules and venues best supporting their impact. The group gained further experience in small local elections, trying to convince citizen's groups that, in Galanty's words, "television was not automatically and necessarily the enemy, but simply a tool that had to be used if progressives were to have a chance in modern campaigns." They slowly built up to major efforts, including the successful defeat of a 1980 attempt to roll back California's rent control codes, a near miss with one initiative that sought to tax the excess profits of Exxon, Mobil, and other major oil companies, and a major role in Harold Washington's 1983 victory as Chicago mayor.

The Zimmerman firm coordinated Freeze media from the start: lining up services donated by actors, technicians, writers and set designers; producing the spots; and buying air-time for maximum demographic reach. Willens chose the major themes in consultation with Zimmerman and a major ad firm partner who volunteered his time. The baby spot ran from mid-September through election day, coupled with another in which a former assistant secretary of defense spoke of the "dreamers" who supported the Freeze, "you know the sort," then listed a parade of hardheaded backers including former Secretary of Defense Clark Clifford, former CIA director William Colby, and former four-star general James Gavin.

In early October, viewers expecting a break for Miller time were instead greeted with Jack Lemmon and Paul Newman playing poker. The two sat on battered milk crates, laying their cards on an old worn tire behind which a tank leaked gasoline onto the floor. "There is no way you really got kings over," said Lemmon, tough enough to chew glass, while Newman paused long and hard—Cool Hand Luke with a dirty jean jacket and steel glint in his eyes—and then stated calmly, "The pot's the limit."

They backed each other down, splitting off matches from stockpiles in their hands, holding them out to test and threaten, barely glancing at the gas on the floor. "I got forty-four," said Newman, "How many you got?"

"Thirty-six," answered Lemmon, and Newman responded, "Aha," then peeled off another match from his arsenal. The two struck simultaneously. Their flames merged, fanned by the gas, to fill the screen. A retired Marine Corps major general compared the poker game's madness to that of the arms race.

Like all the actors, writers, and designers, Lemmon and Newman donated their services, as did the retired major general. Equipment was free as well, furnished along with technical crews by Norman Lear. Freeze ads ran in all California's media markets, at all hours and on all stations—paid for with the hard cash of a $2,000,000 warchest. The ads appealed, not for demanding involvement, but for the simple act of a positive vote.

Without Harold Willens, this high-tech strategy might not have been considered. Born in Russia in 1914, Willens fled with his family in the chaos of the post-Revolution civil war and came to the United States in 1922. While his father barely supported the family working as a tailor, Willens hustled and scraped, selling drinks at the Los Angeles Coliseum and clerking at a grocery—in awe of those who made princely sums like fifty dollars a week. Finally, he saved enough to buy a truck, and struck out on his own, marketing pickles, mayonnaise, and other specialty foods to various restaurants and stores. When World War II began, he enlisted in the Marines, sold his now modestly prosperous business, and used the proceeds to buy his first property in what was to become Los Angeles's booming West Side corridor. By the time he returned, three and a half years later, the investment had more than tripled in value. He went on to purchase shopping centers and further real estate, to found a company supplying textile machinery, and parlay his salesman's skills—what he sardonically termed "a nice eye for property"—into an eventual net worth of millions.

Just after the close of the war, Willens spent a year in Japan working with U.S. military intelligence. The shock hit hard when he visited the ruined, dead cities of Hiroshima and Nagasaki, but he soon buried the lessons "in personal life, building my family, my economic base." They remained buried until twenty years later when he became involved with the Santa Barbara based Center for the Study of Democratic Institutions. He enlisted the donors who kept the center alive, and listened and learned as luminaries like U Thant, Arnold Toynbee, and Aldous Huxley discussed the nuclear threat and other global issues. In the meantime, Vietnam continued to escalate, and Willens found himself backing dissident candidates like Eugene McCarthy and George McGovern, as well as joining the former chairman of Baltimore Life Insurance to found Business Executives Move for Vietnam Peace. One by one, prominent executives joined as Willens asked, persuaded, and staked his credibility on the importance of speaking out. Their participation lent the growing resistance respectability and clout.

When the war ended at last, Willens returned to the broader issue of our march towards worldwide cataclysm. He now calls the United States and the Soviet Union "two Marie Antoinettes proceeding to mutual destruction," and compares national security to "a three-legged stool" based on military defense, a healthy economy, and a humane and just society—stressing that for one leg to become vastly imbalanced undermines our nation's most fundamental strengths.

Six weeks after the Freeze's November 1982 election victory, we talked at the Beverly Hills Tennis Club, where Willens had just finished playing a morning set and eating breakfast with a friend. His greying hair closely cropped, he was immaculately dressed in casual wool slacks and blue deck shoes. He spoke rapidly, hammering successive chains of logic to explain the path to his present concern. Then he described how he enlisted respected constituencies individual by individual, by going after each key person just as he had when selling mayonnaise, and by drawing in those who could "buck the image of an issue only the concern of people on the social margins." Although he kept no temple affiliation, and embraced Judaism as cultural heritage rather than theological creed, he began the Interfaith Center to push church people to recognize the arms race as "the quintessential moral issue of our time." He sought out doctors as well, because of their status as healers, and scientists who "could explain the differences between this and all previous weapons." Willens worked endlessly on Jonas Salk, "who'd never given his name to anything except the Salk Clinic," and at last secured his endorsement through "begging, pleading, and arguing" and staking all on his persistence and charm.

"Being a salesman," Willens laughed, "is how I learned to get rich from being poor. Not just taking down orders, but really selling, offering something else when they say no, using imagination, creativity, not giving up." He was doing the same thing with the nuclear issue, reeling in men like Salk, Archbishop Quinn, and varied Nobel laureates—individuals no one could tar as discontented outcasts or cow with red-baiting. Their achievements, vision, and credentials might begin to balance the pronouncements of "a government which claims to have the right to decide global life and death."

Willens was working now to bring in his business colleagues, hoping to draw in "at least a few thousand" to join him in speaking and acting. He recalled how, during Vietnam, Lyndon Johnson "almost had fits when the first *Wall Street Journal* article announced that major executives were beginning to dissent. Johnson was shaken," Willens stressed, "because this would take away the underpinning of what he, Rusk, and Rostow were saying—namely that anyone who opposed his holy war was either soft on the Soviets or, at best, soft-headed. It's pretty hard to say either of those things about business executives, who are seen as the embodiment of free enterprise and antithetical to communism."

I asked about the recent nuclear dissent of Vietnam architects like former CIA head William Colby. Willens acknowledged that he knew only too well of Colby's role in helping originate the Phoenix Program, a Vietnam effort said to have killed as many as 40,000 civilians; Willens had, in fact, helped expose the program to public outrage. But that war was over, and the nuclear issue was "so preeminent that nothing comes in second." And, "because business does rub the edges off your ideals and makes you much more pragmatic than you might otherwise want to be," he could "erase the blackboard in terms of a William Colby or a Robert MacNamara and say, 'Okay, if they're willing to lend their particular credentials to this issue, their hard-line anti-Soviet backgrounds, fine.' "

Willens approached the nuclear issue as he did his business enterprises: concerned with efficiency and getting the job done; comfortable using high-rolling connections and the power of wealth and command; preferring not to spend hours wrangling over moral distinctions. Yet his pleas converged with those of Ingram, Erica, and others who have recognized that we are all vulnerable before the technical and political systems we have created, and that this vulnerability overshadows differences in belief, culture, or political vision. "I have a sense," he told me, "that many Americans are going through a process similar to that which I went through twenty years back. Only their catalyst is Ronald Reagan instead of Aldous Huxley. It's a process of seeing our blind movement towards the guillotine, seeing Hiroshima as a warning and a model."

Once people grasped this knowledge, Willens believed they could not erase it, and that it would call for involvement and engagement from that point on. He recalled Jonathan Schell having a similar feeling after *The Fate of the Earth* was released and Schell had his second child: a sense that, as Willens suggested, we were not "insects on the flywheel of history, but creators of our common future," with obligations to act not only as residents but as citizens. Yet Willens hesitated to call the new peace effort a movement, saying it was "maybe a nascent movement, which could still be fully born or not." He wasn't sure it could reach far enough in time.

When Willens spoke of individuals needing to become engaged citizens, or Bob Willard judged his previous sensibility as a kind of selfishness, they did not condemn others who were uninvolved, but rather highlighted a vision perhaps now necessary for human survival. Our culture makes it easy to slide, almost without thinking, into what Bob termed "a fortress" of comfortable indifference, one that entirely blocks those difficult, painful, or unseemly questions that lie just outside our front door. But a universal threat can also bring corollary lessons regarding a broader human bond. And these lessons steadily emerge the more one begins to act and risk.

According to Harvard educational theorists Lawrence Kohlberg and Carol Gilligan, moral development occurs as individuals progressively widen their sense of connection and responsibility: at first acting solely for personal benefit; then embodying a conventional loyalty to family, friends, and nation—in Kohlberg's words, "doing one's duty, showing respect for authority, and maintaining the given social order for its own sake." Finally, moral development enters a "post-conventional" stage, in which individuals act from an inner voice; strive to treat humans as equally worthy, regardless of nation, race, religion, class, or ideological perspective; and, in Gilligan's formulation, also defend their own choices and values against the abstract claims of distant institutions and belief systems.

Much as individuals may enter into nuclear resistance purely to save their own hides, involvement fosters what might be called a meeting point of morality and self-interest: a recognition that, as Bob said, humans are at last tied together, if not by innate birthright then by threats that now join the fates of even the bitterest enemies. As was suggested by the Congaree Presbytery fight over whether the church should go beyond "peacemaking in the self, family, and congregation," the nuclear age demands more than just traditional good citizenship, more than private virtue or rhetorical concern. Not that how we conduct our "nonpolitical" lives is irrelevant. Wes Jackson, of the Salina, Kansas, Land Institute, says those of us seeking alternatives to our society's present course can succeed only by becoming individuals "of stronger moral character" than those furthering a course of militarism, greed, and environmental rapacity; that we have no choice but to be more honest, more committed, deeper thinking, and even to raise more exemplary children. Jackson isn't advocating unctuous piety, but rather making clear that citizen action needs to further—not attack—present sanctuaries of respite and community, and to foster not particular factions, but diverse voices and ways of living. And that vision requires our ability to feel seemingly distant wounds as affronts to our core human dignity.

I drove from the Beverly Hills Tennis Club to the Catholic Worker soup kitchen, located in a skid row neighborhood just east of downtown. Less than a mile away stood the three sleek towers of the new Westin Bonaventure, a fortress hotel aping Detroit's Renaissance Center as its dark glass and enclosed brick terraces rose untouched by the pulsing streets surrounding it. Outside the soup kitchen, nothing was sleek. City life felt crushed and bruised, and people slept in doorways.

When I asked Catholic Worker activist Jeff Dietrich what he thought about the Freeze spending $2,000,000 on media, he said, "some things can be done with money—and they're important." He was very pleased by the election victory, but also believed the effort remained largely "a media event, without developing the grass-roots network that could sustain its momentum. It was necessary," he repeated. "I've no criticism of how it was done or its impact. But we have to go further, translate sentiment into political power, build the kind of grass-roots networks that can generate 100 letters at a moment's notice, or generate twenty people to sit in at a congressman's office until he'll meet and talk with us."

Jeff is lean all-American Irish, with red hair, a thick moustache, and soft-spoken style. When we met, he showed me a newly released book he'd written on his jail experience following the 1979 Military Electronics Exposition, an international arms bazaar held in Anaheim. The Catholic Workers joined local Orange County activists in gathering nearly 8,000 signatures from Anaheim residents who opposed the exposition. Fifteen hundred people protested the arms bazaar's opening, while Jeff and thirty-five others blockaded the doors. At their trial, the same judge who had already placed Jeff on probation for a four-person civil disobedience at the weapons exposition of the previous year, now handed down a harsh six-month sentence.

But the arms trade issue remained alive, fanned by coverage in the *Los Angeles Times* and the Orange County papers. The judge received over 1,000 letters supporting clemency for Jeff, including one from Los Angeles Mayor Tom Bradley. After two months, he called the press into his court, brought Jeff in, and announced "You win. The stubborn judge is releasing you." When Jeff said he'd feel compelled to blockade the coming year, the judge said "I don't think so," and pulled out an announcement of the bazaar's move to Weisbaden, Germany.

"We contacted Weisbaden," Jeff told me as he mopped the soup kitchen floor, "and they put on a huge demonstration which forced it to move again to Panama. It was something out of a fairy tale or Gandhi, convincing you to keep hanging in with your approach and faithfulness."

The twenty-member Catholic Worker community inhabits two large adobe houses in a largely Latino neighborhood overlooking downtown. Jeff's house was donated by a former American Airlines pilot who now ran a cooperative bakery employing inner-city poor and selling its products through church networks. The soup kitchen serves up to a thousand free meals a day to those who might not otherwise eat. The Catholic Workers also have a law center, medical clinic, playground project, co-op food store, and temporary housing shelter. They balance this attempt "to seek out and serve the poorest of the poor" with religious worship and witness against the weapons that both starve immediate lives and threaten to annihilate all human futures.

The community began in Easter of 1969, following the model of an earlier Los Angeles Catholic Worker house in the 1930s, which had developed out of the national effort sparked by the work of Dorothy Day and Peter Maurin in New York. The community's visions were fed by this tradition of following Christ by placing oneself with society's outcasts, as well as by complementary church currents, like the "liberation theology" being developed by Latin American priests, the Vietnam resistance of individuals like the Berrigans, and doctrinal developments like *Pacem En Terris*, the 1963 encyclical in which Pope John XXIII stated, "it is hardly possible to imagine that in an atomic era war could be used as an instrument of justice." The community supports itself through *The Catholic Ag-*

*itator*, a newspaper whose 8,000 subscribers furnish core workers with basic needs plus five dollars a week for personal use. The group proudly announces that donations are not tax exempt; they do not want legitimation by "governmental approval, regulation or reward." Yet their last Christmas appeal netted $70,000.

Jeff pointed out a huge ham donated earlier in the day, and described the individuals who line up, shoeless and in rags, for their regular noontime meals. "Sometimes you go in without anything in the refrigerator; then Jake comes over with a bag of dirty onions, saying 'I can't sell 'em, ya want them?' and it builds like stone soup."

Jeff grew up in Orange County, the son of a weapons engineer who took him to meetings of ultra-right groups like Fred Schwartz's Christian Anti-Communist Crusade and the Catholic Cardinal Mindzenty Society. The parish priest wore Gucci loafers and bought a brand new Buick every year. Later, Jeff hit the hippie trail, and bummed his way through Europe and North Africa. Although he resisted the draft, inexplicably he was never prosecuted. Drawn in initially by the Catholic Workers' service to the poor, Jeff now cherished the balance in his life that came from editing the *Agitator* and feeding the hungry. His writing brought in enough extra money to afford occasional movies and books. He'd hardly say he felt deprived.

When I asked his view of Harold Willens, Jeff said he liked and respected him, would far rather work under Harold "than go through an endless consensus meeting every week." But he thought Willens's wealth and power separated him from the ordinary people who needed to become involved, and that the tensions of his role reflected larger dilemmas—as when the Freeze effort disassociated itself, for fear of losing respectability, from Catholic Worker vigils and civil disobedience. Or when lawyers and doctors suddenly became concerned with global responsibility, yet with their sports cars, high-paced lifestyles and cavalier optimism, impatience, and "let's get moving attitude," left a trail of resentment among veteran organizers.

"Given the length and scope of the effort," Jeff said, "maybe the only viable model is the farmworker one, where people get subsistence, live in communities or with sympathetic supporters, set up house meetings, and build towards events. Imagine fifteen people every day at vigils, getting others committed—they might have to be young or footloose, but they'd have that time. Otherwise for full-time workers you have to raise too much money for salaries. Or else people come in wanting to help and there's no one to teach them to do a decent leaflet, make money on concessions, any of that."

He'd been with the Catholic Worker a dozen years now, including eight married to a former nun who shared the soup-kitchen work and was the main community administrator. He mentioned unexpected results of the group's efforts, like the way the Anaheim actions spurred creation of the Orange County Alliance for Survival, which was still strong four years later, and had fostered a myriad of grassroots projects. He said he took heart from sacramental rituals like the Eucharist, and from working with those individuals society scorns and discards.

"I'm not saying people have to flagellate themselves," he explained, with a smile. "I like to think of ego as a pet dog. Take it out and walk it periodically. But to remain in the world—to compete in the power structures, lift oneself above—defeats the core of Christianity and servanthood.

"I don't think," he said, "that what happened with the judge was an exception. People respond to sacrifice and risk, simplicity and gentleness. Not stupidity or supineness, but a willingness to chance looking a fool, to hear those wounded and in pain."

The Catholic Workers share common labor, home, and faith; not all dissenting communities define themselves so clearly. Yet for opposition to persist and succeed in the face of proliferating jingoism and continued military escalation, it must do more than merely break through the assurances that all is well. It must anticipate the more humane world for which the activists fight.

One could call this anticipation village politics: the creation of human-scaled efforts within a nation so vast and seemingly out of control—efforts that now span from small towns like Florence to sprawling megacities like Los Angeles, New York, and Dallas. Although in many instances, individuals have acted initially in isolation, spurred only, like the Francis Marion biologist, by a general urgency, most often engagement has proceeded, as Bill Cusak said, person by person, through citizens staking their integrity and history, and inviting friends, neighbors, and coworkers to join in common effort. Village politics is Leonard Beerman asking Bob Willard and the Markses to come to the first Interfaith Center conference; Erica Bouza being drawn in by Carol Ferry; a bus load of senior citizens riding from California's Leisure World retirement center to a 500 person Orange County rally, all the while basking in community pride; Bill Cusak taking the issue not only to the town of Florence, but to every school, church, or group that would show *The Last Epidemic* film. It is the owner of a Boston industrial painting concern writing his largest customers to ask that they think about the arms race and ways they might help to reverse it. And it is a Long Beach nurse arrested after being inspired by a friend she respected—a fellow Catholic and devoted mother of six—who then sparked her husband, a Los Angeles fireman, to speak out and change the views of a coworker once so unflaggingly promilitary he'd been nicknamed "the Hawk."

Complementing grand efforts like nationwide demonstrations or statewide referendums, these more intimate actions provide building blocks for broader change. They assert that power lies not only with the kingmakers in their insulated suites in Washington, D.C., but with ordinary citizens in the domains they inhabit. Such intimate actions create a situation in which those hesitant to join may draw reassurance from shared traditions, definitions, and social bonds. Less easily tarred as carpetbagging servants of alien powers than those coming in from outside, local activists can suggest through example and action that the task of shaping the most fundamental human choices rests upon our own ordinary shoulders. They can confirm Jonathan Schell's notion that, "Because everything we do and everything we are is in jeopardy, and because the peril is immediate and unremitting, every person is the right person to act and every moment is the right moment to begin."

Like the classic community organizing that was developed by people like Saul Alinsky, village politics addresses turf that is manageably human-scaled. But Alinsky-style organizing focuses so exclusively on whatever needs are articulated by community residents that it can readily breed parochialism. Even Alinsky's noted early success story, Chicago's working class Back of the Yards neighborhood, later used its new-found unity to keep blacks from moving in and buying houses. As Bebe acknowledged, recalling her efforts with Carolina Action, issues like atomic weapons almost automatically took a second seat to more humble, though certainly important, fights about whether the city would fund parks or sewers for areas inhabited by residents other than the privileged elite; whether downtown development would benefit owners or renters; how communities whose prime economic resources helped fuel the arms race would most equitably divide the leavings. Certain Alinsky-successor groups, like COPS in San Antonio, Texas, have made major strides towards building a broader vision out of the fundamental values of their constituent communities. And they have developed forms of leadership development and democratic organization that the peace groups might do well to emulate. Yet they remain hesitant to address root issues like the weapons escalation. In contrast, village politics demands that we look beyond immediate surroundings. Taking as a maxim the Rene Dubos phrase, "think globally, act locally," it demands as well that we grapple with our furthest visions—like the religious kingdom envisioned by Florence's Bill Cusak, or the belief of Honeywell Project's Marv Davidov that wealth should be equitably owned and controlled—that we articulate our most complex understandings of how humans might better achieve both dignity and justice.

Again, appropriate scale can strengthen committed action. In Florence, a march of one hundred people made history; in New York City it would have been nothing exceptional. But what if a parallel efforts grew in the Brooklyn districts of Bay Ridge, Flatbush, or Bensonhurst? Might city blocks become units of common voice? Could workplaces address the ultimate threat? Granted, any opposition community meets numerous obstacles: gentrification and shifting job markets destroy traditional neighborhoods; corporations attack even remnants of the long-shelved democratic potential of unions; social and economic fear makes many afraid even to speak. Yet village politics offers at least modest hope for bringing dialogue into untouched niches of the society, using what culture exists at least partly outside the sway of the atomic state, and inviting in those not initially leaping to act.

By prefiguring a world not entirely cynical or carnivorous, these local efforts can also push existing sources of information to challenge the false balm drummed in by official experts on the nightly news—push sources humble as church newsletters or Saturday bridge clubs. And they can help break the despair that breeds when activists become disconnected from the broadest streams of life, by giving individuals reason to continue when immediate rewards seem elusive.

As in South Carolina, familiarity can lead to fear as well as to support. Anonymity brings fewer costs and sanctions. In the words of the minister of a Methodist church just outside the Savannah River Plant, "William Sloane Coffin can preach all he wants on national issues. He doesn't have to live in a community like this." The Long Beach nurse and fireman's wife sparked a major family fight when she refused to cancel a white train vigil to attend a last-minute graduation party for her nephews. A Lubbock, Texas bar band was booed and called "Commies" for playing an antinuclear song. Convinced by a nun to participate in the Wilshire Boulevard vigil, one Los Angeles woman edged up to the corner and covered her face with a placard—briefly ducking out, then darting back, terrified that some long-term friend would pass and see her standing. After a dozen rounds of the woman's surging and retreating, the nun began laughing and asked, "Having problems?" She admitted, yes, she guessed she was, then ducked out a little further from behind her sign.

Addressing familiar turf can of course breed comfortable parochialism. It is relatively easy to staff a table outside one's liberal suburban market, but walking precincts draws far fewer volunteers: the door-by-door vulnerability risks too much. Yet just as Erica, Levon, and Bill began gingerly, were supported by others along the way, and ultimately helped shape movements they'd once looked on from afar, so individuals, in general, need community to recognize that traditionally buried fears and hopes are shared with others as well. They need this sense to further confront a common threat. In the case of a couple named Marty and Bob Coleman, they felt enough emotional support to sell the $600,000 house Marty had lived in for twenty years, move into a bungalow less than a third the size, and use the resulting money to allow her to volunteer full time at the Interfaith Center.

The Colemans lived in La Canada, a wealthy suburb north of Pasadena, where Marty's first husband helped build the low stone and wood home that had been featured in *Sunset* magazine and the *Los Angeles Times*. She loved its Japanese garden where ponds and fountains nestled amid firs, eucalyptus, and Monterey redwoods; loved the pastel sitting room and hand-built wine cellar. But other things mattered as well.

Although Marty still dressed like an immaculate suburban Junior Leaguer, and Bob was a respectable financial consultant, she had had her fill of organizing Girl Scouts and church youth groups. In the spring of 1980, a year after her first husband died of an unexpected heart attack, Marty decided to take a church course with the benign title, "Crucial Social Issues." The six-week class studied the basics of atomic explosions, as well as related questions of proliferation, nuclear power, and waste disposal. The implications of what she'd learned disturbed Marty greatly. In the meantime, she'd begun going out with Bob, and a half year later—the day following their marriage—the *Los Angeles Times* began running a Robert Scheer series on nuclear war. In one article, Reagan's deputy undersecretary of defense suggested we would all survive if we only had enough shovels to dig instant home-made bomb shelters; in another, Pentagon strategists casually munched tuna sandwiches while describing the selection of Soviet cities for weapons targeting. When Marty and Bob flew to honeymoon in Scotland and France, they saw, headlined in every paper, Alexander Haig's talk about firing an atomic warning shot over Europe. It unsettled Marty "that this could be occurring at the same time as such great personal happiness."

Although Bob had voted for both Goldwater and Nixon, Vietnam had made him wonder. He'd shared Marty's belief that war and peace issues "were just remote political questions, didn't have anything to do with me." But the couple were given pause by the actions of dedicated Christians like the Berrigans, and by thousands of others who marched in the streets. Between knowledge gained by taking the social issues course and the contradiction between their marital bliss and a world in crisis, they wanted to do more than talk benign words "with ashes in our mouth."

Bob wasn't ready to give up everything—"I can't talk to Stanford lawyers with holes in my shoes"—but with their children in college or working, they had fewer family obligations. After taking a related University of California extension course, they began to feel that they could not continue delegating a common responsibility to others. Marty remembered a doctor friend's description of D-Day as his finest moment, one where he used all his faculties for something that mattered. She felt incongruous "with such a weight of possessions, speaking in Bible class about being true to Jesus, then spending

$150 on dinner or buying clothes at Bullocks." She thought selling the house was "an opportunity of freedom."

Peace movement participants inevitably varied in their styles: some almost maudlin in sentimentality, others citing statistics and strategic theory at every turn, some talking constantly of the need to heed God's commandments, others determinedly secular. Marty recalled divisions between the older religious activists and ones younger and more countercultural, when the churches and the Alliance for Survival put together, on June 13th, 1982, an event they called Peace Sunday. One hundred thousand people filled the Rose Bowl, mixing those Marty called her fellow "sleepy Presbyterians" with those who came out to hear Bob Dylan, Jackson Browne, Graham Nash, and Stevie Wonder. "I found it delightful," she said, "here I was looking preppy, suburban, and middle class, living in the center of WASP-ville, working with guys who were writing 'Fuck You' on the walls of Berkeley—and I loved every minute that I did it."

At their best, these different styles can complement each other, sparking learning and respect for other cultures, backgrounds and beliefs. Village politics can make our society's remotest corners potential venues for addressing an overarching threat. Yet intimate community can, again, breed parochial isolation, as occurred when Vietnam-era students not only made their campuses into successful centers of shared culture, ferment, and resistance, but also defined themselves in often arrogant distinction to those inhabiting less favored worlds. And even the most well-intentioned ecumenicism often falters before those divisions of class and race that act, like firebreaks, to segregate workplaces, neighborhoods, and social circles.

Minister Jim Lawson wondered at times whether many involved in the new disarmament movement understood the broader cultural, political, and economic strains that push our species towards annihilation, or whether they were simply running scared of the worst of Reagan administration rhetoric. We talked at Holman Methodist church, his large congregation in a racially and ethnically mixed neighborhood in central Los Angeles. Inside the white stucco building, a choir practiced and children played beneath photos of Jim's former colleague, Martin Luther King.

Jim talked slowly and patiently, saying he worried not only about the steady increase of the nuclear threat, but also about the dispossession of the poor and the need for activists to "apply their own idealism" in linking these issues. He asked what it meant for Reagan to talk of a time when we'd never had it better, while the nation saw "millions of people sleeping in the streets, in the parks, in their cars." Or to say that racism was no longer a problem, when American blacks suffered higher infant death rates than the citizens of thirty-two nations in the world, and where black wages, housing, and access to health care were now proportionately worse than in 1955.

Yet Jim doubted a Democratic administration would either bring real justice or significantly slow the arms race, unless massively pressured by a popular movement. He would "work like hell" to mobilize the black community for a massive anti-Reagan vote in the coming fall 1984 election, but that was for direct survival, "my own congregation, the people across the street." Even if peace activists halted the most brutal weapons escalation, it might not alter the arms race's fundamental momentum, "Just as the nation cannot go back to pre-1963 in terms of racial segregation, yet we still don't have an open access society.

"I am one of those," Jim explained, "who has written to congressmen, been on delegations, talked to them many times over the years. But I'm pessimistic, if we make that our sole approach, about our chances for success.

"I learned long ago," he continued, "that every congressman, every senator is assigned a Pentagon liaison person who has the sole job of wining and dining them. That doesn't even count Honeywell, TRW, and Rockwell. We can't match that without a lobbyist in every office, which we can't afford. But there are other options. Instead of diligently going through secretaries to fit their schedules, making them final arbiters of the issues' importance, having them determine how long they'll meet, the usual decorum, you can call upon them at their homes, picket their offices, lie down in front of their cars. There are other ways to educate both us and them, but on our own terms."

Jim was no stranger to these paths, having played a critical civil rights role by training the Birmingham volunteers who withstood the dogs and fire hoses of Sheriff Bull Connor, the threats of Alabama Governor George Wallace, and vigilantes like those who killed four young black girls by bombing a local church. The volunteers registered voters, marched despite injunctions and brutal beatings, and challenged a bondage the white powers called divinely ordained. Jim drafted the pledges in which they promised to "refrain from the violence of fists, tongue or heart" and to "sacrifice personal wishes in order that all men might be free." He wrote the words, helped plan the strategies, and was preparing to lead a major march and be jailed when the effort at last won its victory.

To a degree Jim was merely following his father, a Methodist minister who sometimes wore a .38-caliber pistol on his hip while speaking out in Southern communities, and later went North to organize new chapters of the NAACP and the Urban League. Lawson first took up the atomic issue in 1946, by discussing it in national student debate when he was a high school senior, and by consuming everything being written on the new peril and its meaning. The next year, at Ohio's predominantly white Baldwin-Wallace College, he heard a lecture in which Fellowship of Reconciliation executive secretary A.J. Muste questioned America's tendencies towards global domination and rooted World War II in an international order that bred German and Japanese militarism by trying to freeze those nations into perpetual junior-partner roles to Britain, France, and the United States. Muste believed nations might be defended through civilian-based resistance, following examples like the Norwegian teachers who successfully refused to pledge support to the Nazi regime. He said individuals could challenge U.S. Cold War policies and institutionalized injustice by similar direct nonviolent confrontation, and suggested audience members could choose to resist the draft. Jim respected Muste's integrity, congruence with Biblical traditions, and skill in compassionately handling even the most antagonistic questioners. He also respected Muste's demand that pacifists concern themselves not with seeking some abstract private purity, but with pursuing their often stumbling paths of truth and justice through challenging systems that masked profound dehumanization by maintaining a sense "that when things were quiet, all is well."

Jim followed Muste's talk by reading Gandhi, Tolstoy, and Andre Trocme, a French Presbyterian minister who organized his small village of Le Chambon to hide and save thousands of Jews in defiance of the Vichy regime. Jim had originally filed with the Selective Service as a Conscientious Objector, relinquishing what would have been an automatic ministerial deferment. He now decided peacetime conscription was fundamentally immoral, and in 1949 sent his board a note saying he could not in good conscience cooperate.

Korea broke out the next year, and a judge gave Jim three years in jail. Friends called him a traitor because, as he explained, "blacks always saw war as a chance to prove our loyalty and commitment, to become part of American life—and we've accepted dominant beliefs as a result." But he entered jail anyway, served thirteen months, and after three additional years at a Methodist college in India, joined Ralph Abernathy and a white Texas minister to open a Fellowship of Reconciliation office in Nashville. He also enrolled in Vanderbilt's theological program, while spending the bulk of his time holding workshops in black churches and colleges using material on Gandhi and on the previous year's Montgomery bus boycott. In November 1959, he led a half-dozen students who tried to be served at downtown Nashville's segregated lunch counters.

The Nashville sit-ins preceded by two months the far more famed ones in Greensboro, North Carolina. They grew until 500 students took their turn during the Saturday rush at Woolworth's, Kress's, and McClellan's. Eighty students went off in handcuffs. Management closed the store. Vanderbilt trustees responded to editorials in the Nashville *Banner* by having the university chancellor warn Lawson to cease immediately. When Jim refused to compromise, the chancellor joined the Board of Trustees in expelling him, and the divinity dean led fourteen of the department's sixteen professors to publicly resign in protest. Over 400 letters soon joined the stack, coming from professors in law, medicine, the physical sciences, and an array of other departments comprising the core of the school. The controversy sparked international publicity.

Twenty-five years later, Florence minister Ingram Parmelly would remember the talks Jim gave, "standing audiences on their heads" over the school's and city establishment's affronts to human dignity. The discussion only fueled the civil rights campaign, and business and civic leaders at last accepted a desegregation plan that became, a regional model. On May 10, 1960, five weeks following Jim's expulsion, blacks sat down to eat at the downtown counters for the first time in any major Southern city. A few months later, Vanderbilt offered Jim reinstatement, but the chancellor also accepted the supportive divinity dean's tendered resignation—in effect summarily firing him as a scapegoat. Jim finished his degree at Boston University.

He thought current peace workers needed to create forces of vision and conscience similar to those that ended legal segregation. To a degree, the Freeze had done this "by taking the existing structure of election ballots and using them to raise our questions." The emergence of the Freeze movement might even offer "hope for ending a mean-spirited period, the beginning of a resurgence of awareness. But if we got five million votes," he asked, "how do we translate that into the next step? We can't do five million letters."

The answer might be what Jim termed "redemptive community," described in his keynote speech that helped found the Student Nonviolent Coordinating Committee as a vehicle for sit-ins, freedom rides, and other direct human actions challenging "systems of gross social immorality." It was during one fight against these systems—a local garbage collectors' strike, for which Jim garnered the support of even the most conservative black pastors—that Martin Luther King made his final trip to Memphis.

We talked of King's legacy, and of the work the two had shared—work that allowed those who had been pushed to society's margins to now connect militarism with being frozen in demeaning jobs, and with hopes constantly barred to their children. Some black leaders still saw the army as an opportunity for blacks to get ahead, but the community's voice had begun to be a consistent force for peace.

Jim criticized activists who have hesitated to address difficult questions like converting the arms economy—"putting 25 billion, or 30 billion, or 40 billion out of the defense budget into education, health care, housing, infrastructure rebuilding, figuring how Rockwell or TRW could produce other goods than weapons." He felt the movement needed to go beyond just theoretically studying this issue to actively organizing.

He thought "the community of middle-class good will" was uncomfortable with "those issues of homelessness and joblessness and racial discrimination—the way that every dollar spent on war, as Eisenhower said, is a dollar taken from the hungry and the poor." And that in failing as well to offer alternative visions for blue-collar whites, activists helped allow the election of presidents like Nixon and Reagan. Jim wondered, for instance, why the movement didn't actively support the Congressional black Caucus's alternative budget, when for the past eight years the caucus had said, "Look, here are the kinds of subsidies that you don't have to have," and attempted to cut off wasteful expenditures like paying out money to tobacco farmers, and to shift resources from weapons like the B-1 bomber to purchasing services that go "for food, for housing, for civilian needs." Jim thought the Freeze effort was still "often-times more an antiwar movement than a propeace movement, and more propeace than projustice."

I asked whether blacks were likely to return to widespread non-violent action. Nine months following our talk, the first of nearly 10,000 individuals was arrested while protesting America's South African policy, but that effort had not yet visibly surfaced. Jim said the Southern Christian Leadership Conference was still involved in boycotts, marches, and civil disobedience, largely in small Southern towns. Key leaders, including the group's present head, had been recently arrested while stopping a North Carolina toxic waste dump. But creating major campaigns was tough and costly.

The closest the Los Angeles black community came to widespread protest was during a series of 1979 marches against police brutality, culminating with sit-ins at the city council. But even those actions mobilized only a fraction of the community and lacked consistent follow-up. Ample immediate issues existed, like the health care crisis or the state of black schools, which were still overcrowded and segregated. But change required more than "little itsy-bitsy sorts of negotiating, which really doesn't put on any pressure."

Jim laughed at the antinuclear movement's desire to be well-liked and offend no one, then talked of the Sermon on the Mount as a doctrine "of resistance. And of struggle and coercion and power." He said Gandhian nonviolence did not mean passivity, "but aggressiveness to overcome evil with good. Wrestling with power as the ability to accomplish goals and ends. To build a community of justice."

Focusing Freeze resources on direct outreach would still not have erased barriers of race and class; even the Seiditas' proposed grassroots march had a heritage of becoming mired on the affluent side of the fields, of bridging beyond the economically comfortable with little more than paper endorsements. Yet the world presented in the media campaign was without exception white.

Bill Zimmerman justified this in terms of limited resources. Blacks and Latinos already supported the initiative in overwhelming numbers. The campaign needed those on the fence, those who still tarred this as an issue of the fringes. The ads were tools to win the votes of middle-class whites.

The initial spots presented reasons for acting—reasons as universal as a baby's first tottering steps—and addressed the escalating threat we were now resolutely embracing. Yet with Reagan administration officials attacking the Freeze in national policy speeches, and parading up and down the state to stress the need for further weapons systems, Zimmerman feared voters might still not be convinced. Ads urging people to get involved might mobilize 10,000 activists and help an array of varied local efforts. But in a state of 25 million residents, the campaign needed a majority of voters. It needed the magic fifty percent.

So Zimmerman convinced Willens to invest his own money in focus groups: professionally run sampling sessions with paid participants. Like those used by sophisticated ad firms to discern consumers' hopes, fears, and desires so that commercials could best play to psychic needs, the participants in the sampling sessions were drawn from a particular demographic group: the representative swing constituency of San Fernando Valley Democrats aged forty-five to sixty-five.

Told only that they were participating in a marketing study, the participants met over coffee, discussing varied concerns while Willens, Zimmerman, and Norman Lear watched behind one-way glass. Over a three-hour period, the moderator slowly worked round to the Freeze, which group members had heard about from ads like "First Steps" and the Jack Lemmon-Paul Newman atomic poker game, as well as from general media coverage. Eleven out of twelve planned to vote against it.

They'd heard it was bad, they explained. The president said it would remove our defenses and weaken us against the Russians. When Norman Lear asked if he could meet with the participants, Willens agreed.

The group responded enthusiastically, "Oh my God, we know him." Lear asked how they'd vote if they understood that the initiative required no direct action, but would merely send a message to the president and Congress saying, "We really would like you to stop the nuclear arms race—only, of course, if the Soviets do it too." The participants said unanimously that, in that case, they would vote yes. Lear stayed up all night writing new spots.

This time the broad themes were left implicit. Yes, we were toying with a common future, but even the urge to preserve the most intimate domains of love and hope might succumb, in a campaign laced with fear, to specters of enemies who respect only palisades of missiles. Thus, the new commercials did not stress grand goals of ending war and terror, or challenges to existing government leadership, and didn't even use the sentimental pull of children's faces. Instead, the spots presented only the most cautious aspect of this step—the degree to which it offered the beginnings of a different path, while maintaining the full weight of armed might.

The revised spots began running ten days before the election. "Both sides have more than enough nuclear weapons," said a woman carrying groceries from her car. "But how can we trust them? Proposition 12," she explained, practical as a tenth-grade geometry teacher demonstrating the Pythagorean theorem, "says our leaders should sit down with the Russians and figure out a way to stop the arms race. With no cheating," she stressed, looking sternly at the camera. "Any cheating and the deal is off."

"A yes vote just says," she concluded, "we want them to find a way to stop building more nuclear bombs. Isn't that what a vote is for? To tell our leaders what we want."

Other ads featured a Marlboro truck driver, and a grandmother in an orange summer dress, as well as celebrities like Martin Sheen, Lee Remick, and Kristy McNichol. A final variant presented a chat between an amiable, thoughtful interviewer and a series of skeptical voters who included, in different takes, a young couple, a construction worker on his lunch break, and a woman in her mid-thirties who might have been a secretary.

"I'm sure not in favor of nuclear bombs. But I don't see voting for a law to stop building more," explained the construction worker cautiously. "But it isn't a law," responded the interviewer, just a message "to Washington and Moscow—to figure out a way to freeze nuclear weapons." The construction worker nodded and thought, gestured with his sandwich, explained that he didn't trust the Russians. "I don't either," answered the interviewer, with a laugh that said, what reasonable person would? "But if there's no way to prevent cheating there's no deal."

"Is that the nuclear Freeze?" the construction worker shook his head, shrugged and thought. "Well I can vote for that. I will vote for that."

Straightforward and simple, anticipating expected objections, the ads concentrated on the proposition's most modest reach, affirmed the fundamental moral soundess of America's previous choices, and distanced Proposition 12 from any utopian associations. One did not have to disarm to take this step, or even usurp presidential privilege; one only had to ask that the arms race be addressed, and pull a single lever to affirm this. If the ads muted the peace movement's furthest implications, they also stressed the unarguable logic of at least beginning to challenge endless weapons escalation.

In April 1981, Jo and Nick Seidita sent out a progress report to individuals and organizations now interested in the Freeze. They summarized nearly four months of endless mailings, phone calls, and organizing trips through which they'd enlisted support from every corner of the state, sparked an array of groups that were now centers of activity, and made the dream of a California initiative a likely reality. They also submitted a budget for all expenditures—including a trip to Washington, D.C. to discuss strategies with other organizers—a budget that came in just under the $2,900 allocated by the Onion's congregation.

The same $2,900 bought thirty seconds of almost prime time on a major Los Angeles TV station, sending a Freeze ad to flicker across the consciousnesses of approximately 700,000 people. The Seiditas and some others involved in the campaign's earliest stages suggested that the initiative would have been far wiser to have used its $2,000,000 media budget, and the million-and-a-half dollars spent on other aspects, to fuel the most massive grass-roots organizing effort in California history.

Compared with the cost of the weapons themselves, the campaign expenditures were pocket change: $2,000,000 would purchase all of two-thirds of a single M-1 battle tank, one two-hundredth of a B-1 bomber, one one-thousandth of a Trident submarine. Yet given the scarcity of peace movement resources, the high-tech choice may have made other options more difficult. Bebe Verdery's entire Carolina Peace Resource Center cost $30,000 a year, including rent, phones, mailings, travel, and two staff salaries. Could Proposition 12 have created similar matrix centers throughout California—further nurturing existing networks like the one growing out of Leo Baeck? Could it have sparked new efforts where none had existed, and forge bonds more durable than those of TV images? Or did the ads draw in resources that would have been denied to less flashy, more humble efforts; did they act—in Willens' terms—as "catalytic agents" that spurred direct activity through their sheer massive presence? Should the campaign have pushed towards more intimate outreach, even if this meant abandoning what perhaps was the most practical path to election-day victory?

As Willens stressed, media could not replace the Beermans, Willards, Colemans, or thousands of others who worked across the state in all manner of contexts. Just as the Florence effort flourished without any massive influx of cash, so the person-by-person, institution-by-institution process of engagement continued, with the initiative providing a ready framework within which to act.

The ads might have encouraged greater popular involvement by showing citizens working together in churches, neighborhood groups or other community forums. Instead, they depicted isolated individuals, isolated couples, and isolated voters, didn't even present the notion that more direct actions might be necessary. Zimmerman pointed out that people voted as individuals, and most were not part of activist groups. Trying to build community might have made sense, he admitted, "for a long-range organizing view. Were we more confident of victory we would have been more concerned about the postelection situation. But we didn't have that luxury, felt that if we lost it would do lasting damage to the Freeze movement. Everything had to be sacrificed to the goal of winning on election day."

By placing the Freeze in the domain of a consumer choice, the media campaign helped frame it as a tame and legitimate involvement. The ads fostered a sense of omnipresent concern, as they appeared interwoven with Dallas, Hill Street Blues, and the nightly news. The need to gather the money to air them sparked grass-roots efforts like a new round of "12 by 12 parties," in which people followed Jo Seidita's earlier model by inviting a dozen others to meet, talk, and contribute twelve dollars apiece; or like the cards one woman created to buy and pass on like a mail order chain letter—except that revenues supported the ballot effort, and the cards displayed arms race statistics and an Eisenhower quote on the need for citizen action.

Unlike the election of prodisarmament senators, neither this vote nor others scheduled concurrently throughout the country could directly halt the deployment of even a single warhead. Yet the voters' message would not be blurred by personality politics, and could serve as a mandate not only to California's representatives, but to all those who regarded sentiment in the nation's largest state as a political bellwether.

As Zimmerman stressed, dilemmas faced by the Freeze activists paralleled those of all social movements focusing on electoral mechanisms. Similar choices were echoed in the decision of South Carolina's nuclear waste petition initiators, Energy Resource Foundation, to invest in offices finely decorated enough to be respectable for visits of even the most steadfastly Old South politicians and reporters. Yet, in the process, the foundation burned up resources which might have supported, for instance, a full-time Freeze staffer in Charleston.

For Willens, the Freeze resembled any economic enterprise in which one gambled, risked, and staked one's capital; the effort would bear fruit if the choices were wise. He recalled an early decision to purchase a full-page *New York Times* ad, which generated a fair amount of "anger and condemnation" because Willens had spent the money without group consultation. Yet the ad sparked a *Time* cover story, a wealth of international media attention, and contributions equalling twice its original costs.

"I'm a fundraiser who's had 23 years of experience," he explained during one of our discussions. "And I find individuals provincial who feel people who give have only so many dollars in their pocket, and if somebody else takes those dollars, they're not going to get theirs. You teach people how to give, and then others benefit."

As numerous peace workers reiterated, issues and personalities readily blurred. Willens could be curt and elitist; he dismissed the Seiditas' alternative as a suggestion that the campaign stake its entire existence on "creating one or two little branches of something in Oxnard." He was, by his own admission, "obsessed with the issue," and perhaps also a bit overenchanted with his personal visions. He readily launched into soaring descriptions of this new project, this political button, this study which, if only properly marketed, might provide the magic spark. The urgencies of others could slip by unheeded.

The Seiditas, however, could be equally proprietary. For all their persistence, vision, and invaluable work, they saw the Freeze campaign as their issue, their child, or at least the child of the dedicated few who'd nursed it for years. Whereas Willens listened closely to others' ideas, and then did exactly what he thought best, Jo Seidita often appeared not to listen at all.

Beyond different character styles, the Seiditas considered it suspect and unsavory to market the Freeze like soap: the stuff of sellouts and passivity. It also seemed wrong to them that simply because Willens had the money—directly or through his varied contacts— he could call the ultimate shots. They said the campaign could have succeeded by continuing to reach out to new organizations and extending the direct personal networks until the entire state was reached. But what of those who had no community? Could one create instant education in half a year's time? And were there enough networks to break through the saturation of Weinberger's steel edged voice and Reagan's genial smile?

Conversely, persuasion by the quick-impulse pull of ads could be readily transient. Just as the initiative's initial two-to-one lead began to erode under the Reagan administration counterattack, so the Freeze could also be supported in the detached, abstract sense that allowed congressmen to vote it in and then turn around and back an MX or Pershing; that allowed two-thirds of 1984 Republican convention delegates to believe both in its proposed bilateral restraint and in the near-divinity of Reagan; and that allowed the goals of nuclear disarmament to become just fine ideals, like talk of peace at Christmas. To a degree, this was inherent in the initiative's limited scope, which was purely advisory, dependent on executive branch negotiation, and left untouched the 30,000 warheads now deployed. In order to resist the pounding repetition of those who insist we have no choice but our present path, individuals need intimate community as a framework to provide the historical memory and sense of context often blurred by the caprices of *Time*, *Newsweek*, and NBC. The degree to which the Freeze ads built these frameworks was open to question.

In virgin soil, like that of Florence, South Carolina, the moral and practical approaches might be the same. Merely raising one's voice both educated and challenged. But where there was a hope of directly affecting institutional decisions—as in the later stages of the South Carolina radioactive waste fight, or the chance of gaining a statewide endorsement of the Freeze—activists faced additional dilemmas.

When I asked Willens about these choices, he framed the Seiditas' perspective as a belief that "you activate certain people and groups, and those people and groups remain absolutely committed and active, seven days a week."

"That's just total nonsense," he concluded. "Maybe a few could do that, but in terms of moving a society—even moving activists to stay with an issue, there are inevitable tides that flow." Media allowed the alternative vision to crystallize in the public mind with enough visibility that citizens could grasp and endorse it; to reject this chance would only have doomed the effort.

Yet most participants in the movement could hardly run a *New York Times* ad unilaterally or call Norman Lear to plot media strategy. Few had Harold's wealth and contacts. The relationship between Willens' circles and those of the Seiditas resembled that of a developed metropolis to its impoverished periphery. Not that the Seiditas or their coworkers lived in tin-shack destitution—Jo and Nick owned a pleasant house on a tree-lined street, dressed like any other middle-class human service providers, and sent their children to respectable colleges. But their projects ran on a shoestring, barely scraping by on shards of support. Although Willens continually asked for the help of others, the Seiditas had no spheres in which they could simply commission and command.

Before the Freeze, Jo had begun "to consider myself obsolete, to think that only money counted in political campaigns and the door knockers and precinct walkers no longer mattered." Now, once again, she felt ordinary citizens were being relegated to the background, as spear-carriers for star fundraisers and media whizzes, and that her approaches were considered almost naïve.

Yet one could also magnify the differences, and gloss over the common visions that allowed vastly diverse constituencies to create the November victory; one could forget too easily the steadfast commitment that drove both Willens and the Seiditas to play their critical roles. With the stakes of choice being, conceivably, the human future, they were far from the only activists who could bring into play not only courage and compassion, but also stubborn egos itching for the fight. For all that Willens and the Seiditas flirted at times with messianic airs—seeking the lights, the stage, and the helm—they also shared a willingness to risk, a dogged tenacity, and the chutzpah to place no bars on who they addressed with the possibility that, in the words of a Chinese proverb Willens frequently quoted, "If we do not change our direction, we are likely to end up where we are headed."

Granted, different allocation of resources might have supported individuals' longings for voice and community in a manner that would have better sustained their ongoing involvement. The ad campaign did, in and of itself, leave the viewers passive spectators. But most of the people working for the Freeze took on their humble local turf as a matter of course. The ads appeared almost as supplemental gifts.

In the view of most California activists, the initiative's eventual 52.5 to 47.5 percent victory required both village politics and high-tech muscle. In any case, the effort gained tremendous exposure for the arms race issue. As emphasized by a high school teacher who quit his $25,000-a-year job to help coordinate the Alliance for Survival, a loss for Proposition 12 would have buttressed a sense that the endless escalation reflected popular will, that even the idea of a challenge was unthinkable. And the referendum's mandate could be cited from now on to press both elected officials and fellow citizens.

Even if in another situation they might not find it so, most of those involved in the movement judged this pragmatic choice to be worthwhile. Yet the referendum's true impact would come only if ongoing work could create the very bonds of opposition community that the Seiditas hoped could in themselves provide election victory.

When I first talked with Harold Willens, just after the successful 1982 Freeze vote, he said the movement would grow through groups of occupation and affiliation, like the nurses, lawyers, and architects already involved; he hoped "we'll soon have Plumbers against Nuclear War as well." When we met again, in July 1984, he'd followed his own advice: he had moved from the general politics of the referendum to organizing fellow executives, suggesting to his peers that they use their resources of wealth, skill, and standing to address this ultimate human threat.

Willens pulled up in a brown Mercedes to his low stone house in the affluent Brentwood neighborhood where Westinghouse security signs sprouted from every yard. "Have you seen this?" he asked, handing me a copy of his new book from a pile in the back seat. "It's been mentioned twice in the *Wall Street Journal*, twice in *The New York Times*, *Time Magazine*, on television and radio in twenty-six cities. And I didn't leave one city without meeting with some business group and usually leaving an organization behind. Not just a few maverick liberals like the ones during Vietnam, but conservative Republicans, much more highly placed in the corporate hierarchy."

Willens' book, *The Trimtab Factor*, is simple and straightforward. It is an arms race primer, salted with comments by leaders ranging from President Eisenhower and General Douglas MacArthur to the British Lord Mountbatten, and it provides one of the numerous conservative deescalation plans that would allow the United States to begin disarming on its own, then continue after the Soviets reciprocate. Willens frames this material in the language of business; he compares the United States to an enterprise squandering its capital on an Edsel of endless security systems. He explains that no sane corporate leader would "bet the whole company" in the manner we now risk the earth, and suggests that executives possess key leverage to head our society from its present course—by playing roles analogous to the tiny "trimtabs" that turn massive ships by aiding their main rudder systems.

Sitting in Willens's comfortable living room, I thumbed through the book while he answered the call of a long-time friend who had turned out 200 Silicon Valley entrepreneurs to hear Harold speak at the Palo Alto Holiday Inn. The two chatted briefly, discussing an upcoming forum. Willens hung up, spelled the man's name so I would get it correctly, and talked of executives' groups blossoming in Chicago, San Francisco, Philadelphia, Milwaukee, Boston, and even Salt Lake City.

"I don't ask them to do anything," he said of those who attended his talks, "just to open their minds, sense their own self interest, and factor the issue into their personal priorities. 'Once it becomes a part of your life,' I tell them, 'you're going to figure out all kinds of ways to deal with it. Whether it means calling the president, if you have that kind of access. Or people around him. Or your two senators—and I know you have that kind of access because I've always had it and any businessman does.' " He laughed at this power and at his own role, laughed with the charm of a salesman unafraid to knock fruitlessly fifteen times, knowing he'd get the account on the sixteenth round.

Then he paused, his face a bit more lined and tired than when I'd seen him last, yet still not even remotely flagging. He leaned back on the couch where we sat adjacent to a low Chinese table and a stone fireplace whose flanking shelves held studies of Picasso and Georgia O'Keefe, novels by Gabriel Garcia Marquez and Leon Uris, works on arms race alternatives, and a row of family photos. Willens thought another moment, then told me about the involvement of executives as diverse as the founders of Midas Mufflers and Aamco Transmissions, executives of Polaroid and Pepsi Cola, and the head of a major California electronics company who limited weapons contracts to under five percent of his total business. In Cleveland, the president of one of America's 300 largest companies had commissioned a *Trimtab Factor* audiovisual presentation to screen at his international managers' meeting. A Seattle executive distributed 1,000 copies of the book. Other supporters chipped in for a two-page *New York Times* ad, then helped send copies of the book to members of Congress, college presidents, Chamber of Commerce heads, and an array of religious leaders, media figures, and corporate officers who they deemed to be the nation's prime movers and shakers.

Some concerned business people thought it easiest to focus on military waste, "the $1.50 screwdrivers for which the Pentagon pays $875.00." Others stressed that the arms race could run lean and mean, cost far less, yet portend the same catastrophic results. Willens took the latter perspective, preferring "to say 'being dead is bad for business,' and to hit hard frontally on the arms issue and the need to redefine national security." He hoped diverse groups would foster "indigenous ideas and energy," while still exerting a common force for change.

With the corporate community's own lives on the line, Willens stressed ideals of "pragmatic flexibility and tendency to look at reality rather than mythology, which personify the best in business leadership." Companies that are too rigid end up "where they belong, in the Dun and Bradstreet graveyard." He believed that perhaps only flexible realism could lead us out of our present trap.

Among *Trimtab Factor*'s central metaphors is the notion of an honorable corporation, USA Inc., lowering itself by aping the sabotage, threats and sundry ignoble methods of its unscrupulous competitor, USSR Inc. The book suggests this path casts aside our most fundamental strengths. Yet for all that Soviet barbarism—Poland, Afghanistan, the echo of the gulags—helps Americans rationalize their reciprocation, our nation took on the imperial mantle well before Lenin ever reached the Winter Palace: in Cuba and the Philippines; Mexico and Nicaragua; in our crushing of nascent socialists and nascent unions. For Willens to root U.S. militarism solely in external threats seemed to gloss over both our own dark and brutal historical strains, and those institutions that still proclaim our leaders' right to play global straw boss wherever and whenever they feel so inclined. It was to blur unpleasant realities for the sake of more effective marketing.

When Willens spoke again of business strengths, I asked whether there weren't also dangers in this emphasis. For all of their get-the-job-done practicality, didn't our captains of industry end up frequently corrupt, manipulative, and callous in their pursuit of bottom-line success?

Willens explained his praise as "normative, not descriptive," and said he tried "to challenge them to behave in a way which of course I realize that most of them do not. There are two business Americas," he continued, "the Rockwells of the world, and those who manufacture shoes, clothing or housing, who pay the hundreds of billions of dollars that are sucked away by the military economy." Willens said he believed in humane progressive capitalism, "not the rearward-looking benighted capitalism under which I worked seventy-two hours a week because my ten dollar earnings were all the family had." He spoke of full employment, safeguards for the poor, the possibilities of shared power through co-ownership.

"But that gets too far afield," he said. "Like my friends who say, 'We'll never really resolve this problem until we have world government.'

"I tell them, 'God bless you. I'm thankful you are working on that. But that's not where I belong. I want to use the few years that

I have left, and the energy I have left, and every other resource, in trying to stop and reverse the nuclear arms race so that people like you will have time in which to make the other corrections that are needed.' "

I asked again whether a double bind might be created when people of affluence and position concern themselves with this universal issue, yet remain silent about the inequities from which they benefit. I described an incident a dozen years before, when I worked in a New York bar alongside a Greek immigrant in his early thirties. The man was bitterly right-wing, embraced the Nixon administration's every military escalation, and suggested protestors and dissenters should be shot. My final day on the job, I learned he'd been a member of the Greek Communist Party, had resisted the brutal regime of the Colonels, served time in prison, and then discovered that his party leaders were comfortable doctors inhabiting elegant coastal villas. In the wake of his sacrifice, something snapped.

Willens worried little about the peace effort being resented as a movement of the "haves." "I was raised in desperate poverty," he said. "I'm not black, so that helped. But I saw what happened to my father when he couldn't get work. I sure as hell lived in conditions that were degrading." He said such conditions could make those who encountered them "legitimate revolutionaries," but that wasn't where the most important changes necessarily came from. He cited Thomas Jefferson, the aristocratic slaveowner, creating something "far more healthy" than the French Revolution led by the underclasses. In any case, he believed the arms race threat transcended particular backgrounds and divisions.

Before the Freeze vote, Willens frequently doubted whether any course of opposition could succeed. But he saw 1982 as a year of "the political miracle," when the movement gained the support of Catholic archbishops, Nobel Laureates and Republican executives, as well as a vast array of ordinary citizens. "Instead of turning their backs, individuals turned round and faced the issue. And now that the first step has been taken, never again will the American people ignore it."

In his introduction to the anthology *Protest and Survive*, Daniel Ellsberg points out that the United States has used atomic weapons repeatedly since Hiroshima, at least in the sense that a gun is used when held to someone's head in conjunction with a demand. We have brandished our weapons in this fashion at least twenty-two times, including the following instances Ellsberg and others have described in annotated detail:

Truman's deployment of B-29s to British and German bases during the 1948 Berlin blockade.

Truman's 1950 press conference warning that an atomic strike was under consideration, after Marines were surrounded by Chinese troops at the Chosin Reservoir, Korea.

Secretary of State Dulles's 1954 secret offer to the French prime minister of three tactical nuclear weapons to relieve troops besieged by the Indochinese at Dienbienphu.

Eisenhower's secret directive to the Joint Chiefs of Staff, during the 1958 U.S. intervention in Lebanon, to prepare to use nuclear weapons, if necessary, to prevent an Iraqi move into Kuwait oilfields.

Eisenhower's secret 1958 directive to use nuclear weapons if the Chinese should attempt to take back the island of Quemoy, occupied by Chiang Kai-Shek.

Kennedy's naval blockade and nuclear threats during the 1962 Cuban Missile Crisis.

Discussions in 1968, in newspapers and the Senate, of Nixon's deliberations on using atomic weapons to defend the Marines surrounded at Khe Sanh, Vietnam.

The 1980 Carter Doctrine, promising to protect Middle East oil with whatever weapons necessary, that was reaffirmed the following year by President Reagan.

Among other occasions Ellsberg cites was one Richard Nixon later termed his "November Ultimatum." In 1969, Henry Kissinger conveyed to the North Vietnamese Nixon's threat that they could either capitulate and force the National Liberation Front to do the same, or face massive escalation including possible nuclear strikes. Targeting was planned, down to mission folders containing photographs of the sites for potential atomic attacks. But the deadline Nixon gave was bracketed by a massive Washington, D.C. march and the nationwide "moratorium." Nixon decided the peace movement had so "polarized" American opinion that he could not carry out his threat.

Nixon's retreat echoed an incident in 1966 when advisors urged Lyndon Johnson to launch non-nuclear bombing raids on Hanoi and Haiphong, and blockade the Haiphong harbor. They told Johnson, as David Halberstam describes in *The Best and the Brightest*, that they had programmed a computer to compare the number of American lives that would be saved by these actions with those saved in 1945 by the Hiroshima and Nagasaki bombings. Johnson called a meeting with the programmers, and asked, "I have one more problem for your computer—will you feed into it how long it will take five hundred thousand angry Americans to climb that White House wall out there and lynch their President if he does something like that?"

In the Johnson case, the peace movement delayed the terrible bombing by over five years. In Ellsberg's view, only massive demonstrations prevented the probable use of atomic weapons during the Nixon era. But those who resisted knew nothing of their impact until long afterwards. And as Jonathan Schell describes in *The Time of Illusion* (a study of atomic weapons and presidential power that he wrote immediately before *The Fate of the Earth*), Nixon undertook his final Vietnam air attacks as much to demonstrate domestic "will and credibility" as to achieve a by-then unwinnable victory. By the time the war at last ended on April 30, 1975, most who'd resisted treated the event as an almost-unrelated historical occurrence—forgetting both their role in bringing back the troops and in checking, at least partially, a relentless annihilation.

Like their counterparts throughout the country, the Los Angeles activists desired tangible impact: success not only in shifting public sentiment, generating endorsements, and moving dissent to the mainstream, but in at least beginning to curtail the actual arms race. When campaigns to halt the arms race won electoral victories in state after state and when the House of Representatives passed the Freeze, expectations rose that progress would be made. But when the same Congress in turn approved production and deployment of a cornucopia of new and even more dangerous warheads, frustration pushed activists to doubt their power, and wonder whether even their best efforts might well be fruitless.

As when Nixon doggedly watched football during the very Vietnam-era demonstrations that would make him change his course, dominant institutions will continue to assert their own immaculate legitimacy, and portray dissenting individuals as, at most, bothersome flies to be casually shooed aside. When citizens focus solely on the grand theater of national politics, they consequently risk slamming up against seemingly unmovable walls, or being seduced into what Todd Gitlin calls "organizing with mirrors"—staking everything on millenial projections and apocalyptic goals, breeding roller coasters of soaring hopes and crashing despair. As much as the momentum that E.P. Thompson terms "exterminism" needs more than parochial challenges, work on a more intimate scale can offer signs that the social fabric is shifting slightly. A conversation takes place at the local bar. A community college holds a new class. Block associations challenge nuclear waste transport or zoning for weapons contractors. Responses from workmates, neighbors, and others outside the committed core can help anchor activists tempted to paint the entire world with their assumptions and projections.

Yet, no matter how wise and rooted are the paths pursued, citizen engagement can readily devolve into frustrated bitterness. Acts of commitment seem unreciprocated. Coworkers nod indulgently, explaining, "Mary sure does get talking on those nukes." Acquaintances suggest, as did friends of the Orange County nurse arrested at Rockwell, "You have such an important profession. You shouldn't let this stuff disrupt your work." Many people simply insist all the more loudly that individual choices cannot matter.

In the peace movement's most recent flowering—the surge of concern sparked by Reagan's talk of winnable nuclear wars, the massive European demonstrations, books like *The Fate of the Earth*, and the legacy of patient work by myriad unheralded activists—new participants bloomed in rapid succession. In some circles, nearly everyone suddenly seemed concerned, as they talked and learned. Then the momentum slowed. Those most ready to jump, leap, and risk—at least through the forms of dissent developed so far and the institutional contexts presently touched by heat and discussion— were already involved. To draw in others took work.

"We're trying to reach people who are harder to convince," Bob Willard explained when we talked again in July of 1984. "We interested a great many when we started out," he said, "accomplished a lot. I'm willing for us to take a little credit for how Reagan is talking now." If the Freeze in some ways "failed, because it seemed to be a clear statement of the people's will with no action following," its passage was still a victory. And given that politicians were "the most conservative of anyone," the tail of the dog to an increasingly concerned general populace, the goal remained to create a movement so massive it could "wag that tail."

We visited at Bob's modest apartment, nestled in a two-story stucco court between Willens's wealthy Brentwood district and the sprawling grounds of the Veterans Administration. He drove up in a red Mazda with the bumpersticker, "One Nuclear Bomb Can Ruin Your Whole Day," retrieved a sheaf of peace group notices from the mailbox, and changed from his suit to jeans and a sweatshirt from classical radio station KUSC. We sat down opposite photographs of his children posing and grinning during backwoods hikes. Bob retrieved another slew of messages from his telephone tape, then relaxed and drank some wine from a Los Angeles Dodgers baseball glass.

Laughing at his own efforts to save the world, Bob described a nuclear play, "Alice in Blunderland," which he was pulling together with Leo Baeck amateurs. The play's Ohio creators had supplied both script and production kit. The project had drawn universal enthusiasm. But earlier in the week, Bob lost his lead, "a wonderful young woman who decided she needed more time for her studies and disappeared yesterday. Now we need another Alice."

For all of the play's difficulties, Bob found it "a different type of experience, a different approach," one perhaps able to reach people "tired of being scared by pictures of Hiroshima." Blunderland had spurred standing ovations throughout the country, and for three-quarters of the Leo Baeck actors it was their first political involvement. Bob contrasted its excitement to the slow, hard task of trying to draw in other Reform congregations, and to his other major project—serving as treasurer for a local Political Action Committee (PAC), Southern California Freeze Voter 84. He laughed at the endless minutia required when pushing peace people "to submit budgets, not get all their money from one place, follow rules and regulations so the community doesn't end up in jail." He called the PAC "necessary work," but admitted it took him far from his original passion.

He stopped and thought, greying hair slightly mussed, his face tired from a full day in eighty-five degree heat. "I'm not unhappy," he said, "that the good guys from our original group are out doing other projects. If we can encourage people to work politically it might matter." It frustrated him that the present Leo Baeck committee expended all their energy on fundraisers instead of reaching out to other congregations. And that Interfaith Center spent so much time studying conflict resolution and debating about which computer to buy. "That's nice stuff, but for now? They should be mobilizing people, doing the different work of bridging, plowing the field for the elections."

The phone rang and Bob briefly discussed a Freeze Voter project. Then he scrambled eggs and chopped scallions for an instant supper. When I mentioned my talk with Jim Lawson, he agreed that a multiracial movement was necessary, but said some of the burden was mutual—that it would help immensely "if someone like Jim, a terrific guy and wonderful leader," joined the board of the almost all-white Interfaith Center. Bob suspected white activists would—rather than approaching those who'd trust them the least—still go where they found "the best and quickest response, remaining in their communities, exercising muscle, at least until November."

"You need constituency building," he stressed, "so we aren't lone voices in the wilderness. Unless you're Isaiah," he laughed. "And we haven't seen him for a while."

After another phone call about the Alice crisis, I asked Bob if he ever considered cutting back at his factory machinery business. He said he'd dropped extra meetings and projects, but felt a responsibility to the firm's employees, and needed, in any case, to support himself and help his former wife. He didn't like being overcommitted, but had little choice.

"Lots of people voted for Proposition 12 or its equivalent," he continued, thinking. "Reagan ignores it. Congress votes the Freeze, then the MX. It's not a thing you can jump on as a bandwagon, not a feeling of victory. I was talking with the social action person at University Synagogue. She said when people supported her food bank, they saw hungry people eat. Here what do they get?

"I've heard people saying the only way to succeed is to have one of the bombs dropped—elsewhere, Libya or Pakistan. That's terrible."

Bob paused, briefly, recalling the bitterness. Two years before, immense numbers of people had suddenly tipped, turned, faced the issue, and committed significant parts of their lives. Although the process continued, at the moment the going was harder, resistance greater, rationalizations more calcified with fear.

He found it hard to be "confronted with a specific occasion that seems important, as this coming election does. You can take the long view that it's worth it no matter how long it takes. But that changes when you have specific goals. I want to produce that play by October. My star quit last night. What am I going to do? I wish it wasn't political. It's much more interesting trying to influence people when each individual is important. The Thursday Night Group's still doing that—they'll send a facilitator to any gathering of ten or more, and I like their direct education process. But in an election, ten people mean nothing. You need thousands."

He paused again, reflecting and pulling in. "I'd never say I wasn't glad I got involved, learned so much, met so many fine people." Even when frustrated, he got "enough support so I don't feel like quitting. It would get a lot harder if I didn't feel close to so many of the people who are working on it. The excitement of being involved in something important. Feeling that guys like me have had some impact." Before this effort, the subject was hard even to mention. "Now, debate is happening. We've made an issue out of it. Even those who disagree recognize its importance."

He laughed ironically about a t-shirt he saw with the flip slogan "When the Going Gets Tough, the Tough Go Shopping." "I don't want to be one of those guys," he said. "I don't want to be like that. As long as this thing doesn't happen we have a chance of arresting it."

# 4. Boston: Children and the Bomb

IT was story time at Charles River School. Ten first-graders, barely reined in by their teacher, alternated between charging wildly around their suburban Boston classroom and cuddling close together, as the girls played with each other's hair and tied it in braids. Their teacher Carlotta patiently gathered them together, "Ladies and gentlemen, please sit down," then began reading the story of an orphaned Chinese boy and a dragon who took the form of a pot-bellied old man. The city's Mandarins, merchants, and generals knew real dragons were rich, wise, fierce, huge, and warlike, so they scorned the old man as a liar when he offered to save them from a horde of descending barbarians. But because the orphan boy was kind and shared his bowl of rice, the dragon blew the invaders back to their native land.

Carlotta read while the children asked questions. One said the town shouldn't worry about the barbarians, "because someone's gonna come and kill the bad guys." Carlotta asked whether the town leaders thought the dragon was good or bad, and the children said they thought he was bad and didn't believe him. Were the leaders nice to the dragon, she asked; the children agreed that they were not. How did the leaders know dragons were supposed to be big and fierce and not pot-bellied old men? If they mistakenly thought the dragon was bad and a liar, then how does one tell a good person from a bad person?

A little blonde girl paused as she smeared on red lipstick to suggest "a good person to someone might be a bad person to another."

"A bad person," explained a stocky boy, "would do what you don't like even though he knew you didn't like it."

"They might steal your bike," said another. "My bike was stolen last year but I got it back. I called the police."

"*You* called the police?" the boy's friend asked skeptically.

"Well my mom did, but I know the emergency number. It's 911."

"When we're home we put on the alarm."

By the time another child began quoting the Crime Dog, the lesson had clearly reversed its original intent, of cautioning against blind stereotypes and instant judgments. Instead, the six-year-olds offered image after image of how they would defeat the lurking criminals. Carlotta shifted tack, asking how they would know if someone at school was a bad person.

"They wouldn't let him in if he was a bad kid," the class responded at first. "They'd say 'Special Delivery'," a girl suggested, "then come in with a gun."

"Take a gun out of a Bible," said a boy in shorts.

"What if he came up and didn't say anything?" Carlotta asked.

"He would be mean." "Mean or shy," one girl finally admitted, allowing that maybe, just maybe, a child could be a stranger but still not be bad.

The dragon story was long forgotten. When Carlotta said "Sometimes somebody has to feed their children, and they are so hungry they have to steal," the class didn't believe it. Was anyone "all good and all bad"? "No." "Except for Jesus," said one red haired boy, looking up, expecting to be praised.

"And maybe," Carlotta continued, "someone who seems bad turns out to be good."

"Like Wynette," agreed a girl in a blue jumper, pointing at her friend and giggling.

But the children kept returning to talk of dangerous villains. Their teacher finally conceded and suggested they draw dragons, horses, or whatever animals they'd most like to be.

Even at six, the students were creatures of their culture: inhabiting a world with horizons substantially defined by the Crime Dog, electronic alarm systems, and whatever heroes and demons occupied toy stores and TV screens at a given moment; replicating the fears of an affluent society vigilant against those who might seize its worldly goods; preparing themselves to readily annihilate those cast as present-day barbarians—inhabitants of the evil nations who threaten us. It was hard enough to secure the children's acceptance of benign dragons who were not regular characters on the morning cartoons. How could one even begin to prepare them for ultimate global threats?

The difficulties faced by Carlotta echo dilemmas to be encountered by anyone who would bring critically important issues into the domains in which we shape our society's prevailing values. And those faced by all who would bring their ideals into the workplaces where they create perhaps their greatest impact on the world. To challenge the atomic arms race in our communities is to confront not only a general denial, but also fear, atomization, and isolation—the varied ways we live side by side, unable to talk about what matters most. And work in our communities alone is to squeeze our efforts into the often-beleaguered private time remaining after we have gone in to log the hours to earn our necessary living.

In attempting to make our jobs venues for alternative visions, we face different hurdles: the difficulty of meshing personal urgencies with our designated tasks; the arbitrary power that prevails as we labor in contexts we neither own nor control; assumptions that political controversy belongs in remote distant realms. Yet in asking how our work can best honor our dreams, we can both draw on existing traditions of skill and craft, and directly affect the everyday culture of our society.

Carlotta's classroom embodied more humble lessons as well. On some days, as she said with a laugh when the period was finished, the children will simply go their own way no matter what. One can only let them try what they want and start again tomorrow. The situation also illustrates the profound challenge in presenting difficult issues of tremendous consequence to individuals who have widely differing perceptual frameworks—in this case differences produced by a more than thirty-year difference in ages. Yet just as the Florence movement would not exist if Bill Cusak and his Thursday morning group had not begun their early discussions, and just as the actions of Harold Willens set off unforeseen chains of concern from Leo Baeck to the business community, so a nationwide push to teach questions of war and peace in the atomic age has blossomed out of the efforts of ordinary individuals.

Previously, these issues were addressed only in obscure alternative classrooms. But students across the country now discuss, depending on their age and vulnerability, not only soft-voiced dragon tales, but deterrence theory and nuclear language, MIRVS, the Soviet Gulag, U.S. interventions, Cold War history, and a Hiroshima legacy of collapsing buildings, burning hands, and corpses soaked with radioactive rain. The dialogue has even reached America's largest teacher's union, the 1.7-million member National Education Association, which—together with the Union of Concerned Scientists—drew up a draft nuclear curriculum they tested in thirty-seven states in the spring of 1983.

One of the many streams feeding these developments began in 1977, when the assistant principal of Maine's Bangor High School began a new disciplinary program. Every period of every day over the P.A. system he barked the names of ten or fifteen students he called to his office and probable Saturday detention for crimes like smoking, cutting classes, or being late. This was not what a twenty-nine-year-old teacher named Shelley Berman had entered the profession to embrace. Although a few individuals had been running slightly wild, Bangor was not Stalag 17, and Shelley did not want to play guard. The broadcasts disrupted the very learning process the discipline purportedly served. Shelley watched as the school successively closed off a once-open campus; exchanged community-sponsored cultural programs for strict-silence study halls; and squeezed education into a back-to-basics mold teaching everything but how students might critically consider the world they were about to enter as adult citizens. He tried protesting to the administration, objecting in faculty meetings, and refusing to banish students for trivial offenses. Then, following the exit of his supportive department head, he picked up stakes and moved to Boston.

Eleven years earlier, Shelley had entered the University Of Wisconsin believing that vested authorities invariably spoke the truth. Neither of his parents had attended college; his mother worked as a bookkeeper and his father was a sewing machine operator and later a foreman in a factory that manufactured suitcases and purses ten miles from their home in the largely Jewish Chicago suburb of Skokie, Illinois. Shelley's enthusiasm and innocence began to erode when he saw fellow students beaten for protesting recruitment by Dow Chemical, the napalm manufacturer. Although loyal to his country, he was also loyal to his now-resisting friends. While protests escalated and tear gas burned, he began attending Vietnam teach-ins and taking related courses. He felt shocked at America's global interventions.

Soon, Shelley was putting together antiwar education himself, and he moved to Washington, D.C. to lobby and organize for the National Student Association. But in the face of a seemingly endless war, the peace movement began to factionalize. Particularly in Washington, everyone had their own manifesto for the revolution; their own dream that would lift them to the level of the Chicago Seven or the Black Panthers. Most activists barely even stopped to listen.

Shelley didn't reject the root visions, the need to democratize America at home and abroad. But he was tired of constantly aiming for the network news, and wanted to speak to ordinary individuals whose choices would ultimately matter. He left Washington to read philosophy for a year in a beat-up shack on a friend's Maine farm, then got a Master's degree in counselling and began his Bangor teaching. He explored face-to-face politics as vice president of a statewide consumer's rights organization, for which he wrote a curriculum to be used in Maine schools. After leaving Bangor, he took another year of transition working for the United States Fencing Association (he'd practiced the sport since high school), and then secured a job in the Boston area at Brookline High.

As was becoming true with schools in all but the most elite environs, slashed budgets and adolescent frustration had left Brookline with battered halls, peeling paint and broken light fixtures. Yet the school's high-tech pacesetters learned on new computers, and it served a diverse community unusually willing to break from traditional forms. In 1969, Brookline began a small alternative program, "School within a School," in which 100 students joined their teachers in a weekly town meeting to determine courses, set rules, and hire new faculty. Shelley joined this program in 1979, and then helped create a more limited democratic governance system for the entire 2,100-student school. This system gave a voice not only to administrators, but to students, teachers, janitors, secretaries, and cooks as well.

Shelley thought responsibility conveyed to students the value of community and their right to make a difference in the world. He kept his own views almost translucent as he taught, offering an occasional question or word of encouragement, but mostly just giving sanction to discuss what was important but ordinarily banished. He pushed students to question the bases of their judgments, as he would later by showing first a film portraying the Freeze as Soviet-inspired, and then one on how children want peace. Afterward he asked his class to examine potentially manipulative approaches in each. In the fall of 1980, following a discussion on atomic energy, two of his students came up to talk. "You say a lot about the pros and cons of nuclear power," said one. "But you haven't even mentioned nuclear weapons, and they can destroy the world."

When Shelley raised the issue to the rest of the class, most echoed similar fears. Searching for relevant teaching materials, he found few until a colleague steered him to another Brookline teacher named Bobbi Snow, who recently had begun working on a curriculum she called "Facing History and Ourselves: Decision Making in a Nuclear Age."

Bobbi and Shelley shared Vietnam-era roots. She had gone South for the Freedom Rides and joined SDS to oppose the war, but then stayed within mainstream institutions, like public schools, while dedicated coworkers explored alternative education and mass civil disobedience, or—in response to the war's constant pounding—embraced revolutionary millenarianism like that of the Weathermen. When Bobbi pioneered a unit on the World War II Holocaust, discussing how a nation turned a blind eye to mass annihilation, some students asked if nuclear bombs portended a similar future. The nuclear issue seemed a chance to raise important questions. Along with two other teachers, Bobbi and Shelley began meeting to exchange ideas, then posted notices and involved additional colleagues.

Debate over the arms race also grew in the surrounding community. Vietnam opposition left the Boston area with a strong dissenting presence, and the mix of intellectual luminaries and activist organizations had already spawned concerned professional groups like the Union of Concerned Scientists and Physicians for Social Responsibility—the latter revitalized after a post-Vietnam limbo by a mix of young doctors and esteemed Brahmins like Howard Hiatt, the dean of the Harvard School of Public Health.

Seeking to strengthen these varied currents, and spark the creation of further organizations, a Harvard campus minister pulled together a conference entitled Waging Peace. During a weekend in May 1981, 1,000 people gathered at Harvard's Kennedy Institute of Politics to hear John Kenneth Galbraith, Robert Jay Lifton, Harvard theologian

Harvey Cox, Machinist Union head William Wimpisinger, former Yale Chaplain William Sloane Coffin, and Nicaraguan Cultural Minister Ernesto Cardenal. Accompanying workshops spawned what would become ongoing bodies of concerned clergy, media workers, high school students, and businessmen, and helped strengthen nascent groups of lawyers, nurses, social workers, and hi-tech professionals. Forty-eight teachers attended a workshop on nuclear education and ended up forming Educators for Social Responsibility (ESR).

Over the following months, ESR developed and tested additional nuclear curriculums, established a bimonthly newsletter, and worked with local teachers, parents, and administrators. They had not thought of going national, but after *Parents Magazine* ran an article on Bobbi Snow in January 1982, an Ohio woman wrote, "How do I start a local chapter?" A deluge of other letters followed. The coordinators pulled together an ad hoc packet describing the group's genesis, and mailed it to everyone who wrote in.

Reagan's Cold War escalation had already spurred Los Angeles and Seattle teachers to form similar organizations on their own, and chapters in New York, San Francisco, and Vermont grew from Boston's inspiration. To continue serving as a national force, ESR needed to move beyond an organization of solely spare-time volunteers. By spring 1983, Shelley had left his teaching job to work as one of two full-time staff members; Bobbi developed teacher workshops for a parallel project. ESR had groups in over half the states in the country.

I drove with Shelley to Charles River School, which had just joined 500 others in a fall 1982 ESR-sponsored national Day of Dialogue. When we met with the principal, she hesitated regarding further nuclear education, explaining, "We have a peace committee." Then paused, looking uncertain, and continued, "One voice says we should stand up and support it absolutely, raising its questions in every way. The other asks, where does our funding come from? Will our trustees think it's too political?" I asked what she'd do without such constraints, and she said she wasn't sure, but assumed some controlling outside pressure would "always be there."

Shelley and I watched Carlotta's children, then switched to another classroom where sixth-graders discussed similarities and differences between the United States, Canada, England, the Soviet Union, Japan, and China. Hovering just before the edge of teenage cool, some looked barely out of their mothers' arms, while others sported slouch hats, Doors t-shirts, and stylishly flipped hair. Shelley listened and asked periodic questions while they decided that China had "no nukes, no TVs, no cars, and shorter people," and that, compared to the United States, the Soviets had different money, alphabet, government, food, were unemployed, always had to stand in line, and "if they demonstrate there, they come up with a bunch of machine-guns and just blast them away." No one thought the two nations were the least bit similar, until a boy suggested "we both have a good military, even though theirs is better." A couple of children raised the nuclear issue spontaneously, saying, "If America and Russia got in a war, it wouldn't be fair, because all the other people in the other continents would blow up too."

Afterwards, Shelley met with a half dozen teachers, who told him about a film called *The Toy*, in which GI Joe dolls fight a battle and one burns up at the end. Three quarters of their third- and fourth-graders said they never realized this was what they were doing in their play; the others couldn't wait to rush home and light their own on fire. The teachers talked about the elegant paper cranes being folded by even the youngest children to decorate the walls of this and nearly every other school concerned with the nuclear issue. The cranes were inspired by Sadako, a Japanese girl who came down with leukemia at age twelve, ten years after surviving the atomic blast at Hiroshima. Legend said that whoever folded 1,000 origami cranes would get their wish, and Sadako wanted world peace. Although she died before finishing, friends completed the rest and, by placing them in her grave and on the Hiroshima memorial, made them a worldwide symbol.

Shelley liked the Sadako story because it allowed the children to do something direct and optimistic, and offered an alternative to an all-too-prevailing despair. He mentioned a scattering of useful books and curriculum guides, saying with a laugh, "At least we Americans are always good at getting out materials," then passed out ESR brochures and invited the teachers to join.

As elsewhere, peace work in the schools grew through chains of inspiration, learning, and engagement. One Brookline ninth-grader's reaction to the nuclear issue—"Knowing is terrifying. Not knowing is terrifying. But not knowing is hopeless. And knowing may save us"—traveled, via the cover of an ESR brochure, to students at a

Madison, Wisconsin, high school who were about to spark international attention by declaring their school a Nuclear Free Zone, and then to Japan, as a radio station interviewed the students after they journeyed to Washington, D.C. to present their petitions.

The Madison students began their concern in a nuclear education class at Malcolm Shabazz High, a public alternative school founded in 1971 to mix counterculture dancers and artists with students who'd bucked up once too often against more conventional environments. When I met Shabazz students Kathy Bryant and Sheila Strobel, they were sitting in an art deco restaurant with polished railings and beveled glass sidings, tasting each other's cake and chocolate mousse. "Should have dressed up for this," Kathy said, delighted to be out on the town on a spring afternoon. Wearing jeans, a t-shirt, and pastel leg warmers, she was tall and athletic, with blonde hair hanging off her shoulders; Sheila was darker, more mercurial, like the gold in her bright metallic scarf. Kathy talked carefully, deliberately, and for the most part seriously; Sheila's speech was more flip and quick-fire.

Their class, "Four Minutes to Midnight," began in the fall of 1982, half a year before we talked. When their teacher, Michael Brockmayer, showed films of Hiroshima and Nagasaki, Kathy nearly cried after seeing them, thinking, "I would never do in another person like that."

Five days a week they studied Cold War history, theories of deterrence and counterforce, arms race economics, nuclear language, and various alternatives. At one point Kathy told Michael "I can't take any more," and the group backed off from the most apocalyptic images to discuss the process of overload and fear. One student in the class read how a Nuclear Free Zone in Garrett Park, Maryland, had both declared the community off limits to the atomic arms race, and asked to be removed from all target lists. Though action by a school like Shabazz would be even more purely symbolic, it would echo legislation enacted in several U.S. towns, and by the governments of Norway, Sweden, and Denmark, as well as treaties preventing an atomic arms race in South America and Antarctica. The example might spread to other entitites with potential legal power. After Michael's class discussed the idea, a group took petitions to be signed by 117 of the school's 130 students and most of its staff. Shabazz's principal accepted this expression of sentiment, and the students notified peace groups and the president, Pentagon and Soviet embassy.

Because an eight-student Washington D.C. field trip had long been scheduled, the group saw a chance to deliver the school petitions by hand. When they arrived, Soviet Cultural Attache Anatoli Dushov gave them forty-five minutes and said his nation had already agreed to a freeze. A Pentagon major, who Sheila said was "the kind of guy who takes his kids for a drive every Saturday and to the park every Sunday," lectured them first, as if they were eight years old, "just some dumb students," then admitted after a few tough questions, "You kids sure bent my ego down." A young guard, who Sheila and Kathy promptly named "the robot," showed them a film on how much glass the Pentagon used and how many stairs and bricks it had, then led them through a hall of paintings—including one of a shell-shocked man with a 200-mile stare.

"The guide was just nineteen," said Sheila, "not much older than we were. He'd joined to program computers to shoot submarines. He'll be in the Navy his whole life."

"Unless something happens," said Kathy, more hopeful. "I came out from the Pentagon," she continued, "feeling my brain was really weird, all tangled up—that the defense budget hadn't really increased and everything was fine." Then the White House passed them from department to department, until the mailroom at last assured them the president would of course get their material. "He could at least have sent someone down like the Soviets did," said Kathy, still hurt. She felt her government didn't care.

The group returned via a detour to the Great Smoky Mountains and the fifty-year-old labor and civil rights education center, the Highlander School, where they met Pete Seeger and Montgomery bus boycott initiator Rosa Parks and watched bandy-legged eighty-year-olds dance on Highlander's main stage platform. When the students got back, the media hit. It began when Madison's afternoon paper ran a cartoon of a mail clerk mouthing comforting words while feeding bags of mail marked Pro-Nuclear Freeze and Pro-Arms Control into a massive incinerator. It continued with Madison and Milwaukee TV, Associated Press, National Public Radio, *The New York Times*, even the radio station from Japan. "I started feeling, 'Oh boy, more publicity,' " said Kathy, "then began thinking about why I'm doing this and got lots more serious. We tried bringing in other schools and a few students said 'God, yeah, no kidding.' But mostly they just didn't want to be bothered."

A red-haired woman entered the restaurant, dressed sleekly as a panther, and Kathy and Sheila stopped talking to watch her pass. Kathy toyed with strands of her hair as she listed churches and neighborhoods that had followed Shabazz's lead to become Nuclear Free Zones. A Nuclear Free Madison campaign had begun with the goal of converting the entire city; by the next fall it would gather over 7,000 signatures and pass the Madison City Council. For now, the two young women served on the campaign's board, fondly calling it NUFFUM, and took heart that their actions had helped spark this response. Sheila said she felt tougher and harder "understanding that people have a capacity for evil greater than anything on earth. Not like a wolf killing a rabbit, because that's trivial. I used to be more idealistic." She left to meet her boyfriend, summing up preemptorily, as if to a newsman's microphone, "some people care about it all the time, do everything. Some don't even want to know. I'm kind of both."

With Sheila gone, Kathy grew more reflective. The two had known each other for five years, first in the larger public schools, from which Sheila switched in tenth grade, reeling from her parents' divorce. Kathy followed a year later; because she felt shy and unable to ask for attention, she was drawn to Shabazz's "small classes, couches not rows, not always watching the back of people's heads." The two entered political activism together, competing, supporting, stepping tentatively out, like the Los Angeles woman hiding behind her sign at the Wilshire Boulevard vigil. They held each other up and nursed each other when down.

Kathy described how her mother had begun to canvass their local neighborhood. "It was like the hundredth monkey. Parents learning from children. My mom getting involved because of me. When we came home from D.C., Mom had just gotten back from the neighbors, and she said 'Kathy, Kathy, we got an idea to have Greentree a Nuclear Free Zone.' She just jumped up and down and hugged me."

But the January following the trip, Kathy was depressed. She'd written a letter to President Reagan, saying he was seventy, she was seventeen, and she wanted the chance to experience life. She wondered often whether she'd die in a flash or survive in a wasteland, whether the bombs would fall no matter what anyone did. Why should she have to fight for her life at an age when she wanted to do so many other things? Why should she have to do this?

She and Sheila had been canvassing what Sheila referred to as "the rich neighborhoods with yappy dogs and fear of abortion and blacks." It seemed no one cared but themselves, their teacher Michael, and a handful of others. Kathy wondered what she was doing, giving talks at other schools and trying to give them support when she was so low and had lost her hope.

She ended up talking with Erwin Knoll, who edited *The Progressive* from the magazine's Madison office. She also talked with her teacher, Michael Brockmayer, and with Sam Day, who'd been fighting for thirty years putting out small Idaho papers, contributing regularly to *The Progressive*, and being in charge of the *Bulletin of the Atomic Scientists*. "Look at what you've done, what people have said," Sam told her, stressing that fear was simply part of the situation. "It still took a while," Kathy explained, "a month to get to the point where I was saying, 'yes, look at what I've done.' I realized that even if I was just doing a little bit to help reverse the arms race, not even knowing what exactly would come out of it, then it was worth doing that effort with all my emotions and all I had. It was like slapping myself in the face, saying 'it's ok to be afraid, but don't stop living.' "

Kathy credited these talks with pulling her up out of the trough, letting her continue, "keeping reality in my sight." Then she canvassed the liberal Jennifer Street area, and met an old man who started crying "God damn, I'm just so proud of you young children fighting for this world."

To the old man, Kathy was inspirational because of her youth. Others almost automatically consigned her and the other concerned students to the tricycle brigade: like the father of another young Boston woman who lectured his daughter on World War I, World War II, and the dastardly Russians. Then, when she cried because they didn't understand, he told his friends, "Oh, she's just sixteen," and tried to be kind.

The same consignment to a half-real world was felt by another high school senior, Vanessa Kirsch, who served as one of four students on the twenty-member official city peace commission. At the first meeting, an older woman poured her a glass of wine. "I looked at her, surprised—it was in City Hall and Mayor Velucci was there.

Then she took it back, saying 'Oh no, I can't give this to you, you're a teenager.' I felt really stupid drinking apple juice, eating cheese, getting bored, and wondering what I was doing."

Although Vanessa and the other student commission members had full voting rights, they were uniquely ghettoized into associate status. She thought most of the adults "shut off as soon as we said three words" and regarded them as cute decorations. Then during one meeting Vanessa spoke up, with her freckled smile and intent steady gaze, interrupting a nearly endless discussion on how to extend peace education through the presumably nine foot high bastions of the school committee bureaucracy. She explained how she'd done just about the same thing in pushing through a Day of Dialogue week at her school.

From that point on, the peace commission members largely dropped their condescension. "Also," Vanessa smiled and admitted, "it was the first time I'd really talked, so it was partly my fault as well."

Even most ninth graders already know more about the nuclear threat than they would wish to—much as they may also need further facts, contexts through which to understand the evident danger, and visions of how their actions might somehow matter. But what of far younger children: those who, in the words of one ESR teacher, "still believe in the tooth fairy"; those, like Carlotta's, who, when you say dinosaurs lived long ago, wonder if that means when their parents were small. At what age should they be asked or told about what they may not yet know, or only know in images hovering like ghosts at the edge of their vision?

It is almost a truism to say the bomb is woven into the fabric of our time. Yet even five- and six-year-olds often raise not only the inevitably difficult questions of why people die, where they then go, and what it means, but also historically specific images of universal destruction. By accentuating the images that, as Robert Lifton says, reside "at a border of life and nonlife," the weapons threat feeds both disconnection and powerlessness. It also breeds—as psychologist Milton Schwebel has found in twenty years of studying junior and senior high school students—a more cynical sense that adult culture, the world of "the old men," represents only betrayal and lies.

In studies done in the mid-1960s and early 1970s, psychologist Sibylle Escalona discovered that seventy percent of a diverse group of children and teenagers spontaneously mentioned nuclear weapons and destructive war as likely possibilities, and many expressed profound pessimism about the future. Such apprehensions were confirmed by a major Boston-area survey done in 1978 by Harvard's John Mack and William Beardslee for the American Psychiatric Association. Again, children from diverse social contexts similarly described nightmares of bombs slowly floating towards them or vast clouds enveloping the earth; doubted whether they'd ever have children of their own; and feared being left alone in the face of danger, death, and cataclysm.

This is not to say that awareness of nuclear peril lurks round every corner taken by those growing up in the past forty years, erases every vestige of ordinary childhood or adolescence, prevents any connection with fundamental human continuities, or even that it hits every eight- or ten-year-old with equal strength. While those who came of age in the 1960s were often called "children of the bomb," most regarded it largely as a strange unseen presence, something to joke about in the grammar school air raid drills. Or, as they grew older, many viewed the nuclear threat as an absurdist coda to the litany of sins spearheaded by the quite-immediate holocaust burning steadily brighter in Vietnam. The presence of the weapons may have bred a generation particularly loosened from traditional roots and, therefore, particularly disposed at first to reject and risk, create and challenge, and then to flip back all the more to ordinary dreams of home and hearth, or to take greater refuge in the cynical or mournful detachment of those Hannah Arendt termed "inner immigrants"— private dissenters publicly silent. But when the bomb slipped off the TV screens following the 1963 Above Ground Test Ban Treaty, it largely receded from the active concern of those who grew up beneath its sway.

In Gregory Bateson's double bind theory, schizophrenia results from conflicting messages and commands, which leave their object no place to be, no manner to act, no way to win. These messages may be as direct as two parents demanding contradictory responses, as muted as instructions to "eat your cherry jello because mommy loves you," spoken with an overlay of bitter resentment, or as diffuse as the impact of bans by missionaries on rituals integral to the life of New Guinea tribes. Whatever their genesis, such conflicting messages blur internal and external perceptions, literal and metaphorical understandings, and abilities to inhabit a coherent world.

If today's children encounter unexplained images of mass annihilation, a similar process may occur, wherein denial of the threat by adults undercuts the stability, security, and comprehensible order children need to partake in. If they are not made participants in the discussion, if their concerns and questionings are not heeded, their fears will still exist, festering and unassuaged by the intimacies that heal more ordinary wounds.

Family relationships matter in part because they can confirm a still whole and caring world. ESR has worked, in the words of moral development theorist Carol Gilligan, to ensure that children are not being "left by adults in our society, to stand alone." And the organization has cautioned "against separating children ideologically/emotionally from their parents, their most important source of security." Yet even the most supportive environments cannot, by mere affection, erase legitimate fears about the future.

Like adults, children intersperse their apprehensions with concerns far more mundane and parochial. In the explanation of a Seattle nine-year-old, Amanda Domingo, "We kind of talk about it, but not all the time. Because we'll be playing stuff like jump rope and everything, and we won't get to talk."

I met Amanda after seeing her in "Peace Child," a musical adapted from a British writer's fable of how the world's children ended the global arms race, produced in over 100 American communities. The play focuses on a Soviet girl and American boy, children of diplomats, who meet outside an embassy in Washington, and decide to work together to stop the bombs. They get on TV, meet with their respective leaders, then overcome the standard accusations of reciprocal perfidy by marshaling "700 million letters" from kids of all nations and sparking a worldwide strike where the children stay silent. The play ends with a mass exchange of visiting children, so intertwining the two societies as to make future wars unnecessary.

Wearing rags and living on the street, Amanda played one of the poor children who surrounded the American twelve-year-old, tried to take his money, then recognized him from TV and offered him a song about Martin Luther King. Amanda spoke in her family's native language of Tagalog, "*Ako ay galing sa Pilipinas. Ang nais ko ay katahimikan*—I'm from the Philippines and I want peace," mirroring children talking in Hebrew, Chinese, Basque, Ukranian, Cambodian, Swahili, and over twenty other tongues.

Amanda had studied ballet since age four, and could flirt, charm, and mimic with the best. While taking part in a local production of "The King And I," she saw a bulletin board notice for "Peace Child," and joined other children recruited from churches, schools, and community groups.

Hiroshima was terrible, Amanda said, wrinkling her nose and shaking her head. She had heard about the bomb before, but didn't know America had dropped it. She was "sad that people do that kind of stuff with nuclear weapons," hoped the play would "get to the people, get to the president and tell them not to make nuclear weapons 'cause it will just destroy the world."

Amanda worried about the bombs, sometimes even discussed them with her friends when they weren't jumping rope, playing with Cabbage Patch dolls, or riding their bikes. She didn't talk much with teachers, because that would take time from recess and she hated to stay inside. She told me of an eight-year-old friend she rode to school with, "She had a mouth that would just be running to me with all these questions," and how the girl had suggested kids could take buses directly from the play to Washington, D.C.

"Expensive idea," said Amanda's mother, Nilda, laughing, as three younger sisters ran in and out of the Navy post duplex where they lived while her father, Ramon, served as a medical corpsman on a supply ship.

"She said we could ask our parents," Amanda continued, "to give us twenty dollars to rent the buses."

Nilda laughed again, saying she had seen a one-way airline special for $109—maybe the kids could walk back. She brought cupcakes for Amanda, her sisters, and a parade of visiting friends the girls had made during the family's two years in Seattle. This was their latest stop in a chain of Navy assignments that wound for sixteen years through Charleston, South Carolina; Barstow, California, Norfolk; Las Vegas; and America's Subic Bay Philippine base—ninety miles from Ramon and Nilda's original Manila home. Nonetheless, the family had made this place their own, with dried wildflowers on the walls, twin dolls of Flamenco dancers on the bureau, and a portrait of the Last Supper in inlaid wood. Nilda wrapped a Cinderella game for an afternoon birthday party. Amanda fooled around on an upright piano, then said with high-spirited enthusiasm that if the president got enough protests he'd finally have to listen.

Some "Peace Child" kids, she continued, already knew a lot: mostly older ones who "were always talking, using words we didn't understand, about, what do you call it? Radiation. They said that was a poison in a nuclear weapon." The younger ones just asked, "What are you talking about?" (Amanda imitated the exaggerated voice of an impatient five year old.) One fellow fourth-grader just responded "I see," told her "Bye, I've got to go," and skipped right out.

But most of Amanda's peers admitted their concern, like the children on her bus six months ago, who wanted Reagan to win and were going "Boo, Mondale," because they thought Reagan would get rid of nuclear weapons. The Mondale kids answered back, "saying, 'You guys are stupid. He's going to make more.' I wasn't really sure," she admitted, "so I go, 'I don't know anything about it'."

The children alternated, she explained, between getting through rehearsals and "talking about the thing for peace." They spent three months singing, dancing, and hamming. On Sundays they ate cookies. When the director wasn't looking, they flipped on the rehearsal studio's ballet bars and hid the loud drumsticks. "Peace Child" adult volunteers talked about the bombs, but also about models of hope like King, Gandhi, and some American children who traveled to meet their Soviet peers. Yet, as when students discussed nuclear issues in schools, Amanda found some of the knowledge disturbing. "It just gets you scared sometimes just to think about it," she said, pausing and deliberating. "And I hate it, I just hate to think about it when they're talking on the TV. Then I change the channel to another channel because I'm scared." She paused again, pressed her hands together, then continued, as if watching her own reactions. "The minute you think about it, you think it's going to happen."

Yet when I asked if she would rather not have been in the play, she said, no, she was glad. Because it was scary as well "to think about it just by yourself. You think that nobody will understand how you feel about it. But there is people who will understand. Like teachers and parents. Because I thought they would never understand, think I was strange."

Even as we talked, concern with the weapons both pressed and subsided. One moment, Amanda explained how "Peace Child" adults worried about the weapons as well, and wanted the play to "be a message to all of the people to try to get the presidents to talk to each other and make peace." The next moment, she called her sisters "yucky brats," announced her delight in poking them and bossing them around, then picked up a newspaper photo of a one-and-a-quarter-pound baby. "You could just squish it," she exclaimed with a fascinated grin. "Just go like that [she pushed her hands together], say 'Hi Baby,' and squish it easily."

Amanda's four-year-old sister came over to cuddle, and she teased her perfunctorily, then began braiding her dark waist-length hair. She said she'd like to talk with the president, but advisors always told him what to do, "and advisors never talk to little kids, they just say 'Get away kid, you're not very important.'

"But kids are people too," she continued, concerned and thoughtful. "They think that just because you're a kid you're stupid. Sometimes grown-ups make mistakes."

When Ramon came home, he greeted the children, holding one on his lap and rough-housing with another, then went in the back to play further. Amanda described her hopes of growing up to be an actress, a doctor, a model, maybe even a ballerina or a Navy Admiral.

When I asked if the play caused problems for Ramon's job, Nilda laughed, saying, "I'm a neutral party. I don't take sides."

"Be against Daddy," said Amanda, laughing about the idea of being bad. She wondered if she was "kind of embarrassing" him, and then paused, worried, when asked if the play was really against what he did.

"No," she said, after a bit more deliberation. "Just telling people. Just asking people," she laughed, "to get out for peace."

Ramon later told me she once had asked him, in a worried voice, "Does your ship have nuclear bombs?" And she didn't seem wholly reassured when he explained that it was too small. Sometimes she'd sit with him to watch the news, and he'd note her worry not only about nuclear weapons, but about the Middle East wars and African famines. It wasn't there before, he stressed, but he could see it in her face. It wasn't just a fear, but a caring, a "concern with all the people," which was the same as the love "for your neighbor, your fellow man" that their parish priest said might be the world's only hope. Ramon thanked the play for helping teach this.

However Amanda acted in the future, her new awareness did not destroy her childhood world. She was glad she'd tried something to make the adults listen. If she couldn't single-handedly make whole a world others were shattering, she wanted to continue doing more. We talked about the play's silent vigil and she said, giggling, that she had her own idea: "We won't go to school." When I asked if she was afraid, she paused and thought, with great seriousness. "I'm not really sure if it will happen or not. But I'm kind of worried about it." She said this knowing something must be done.

For all that students like Amanda accept the difficult burden of the knowledge they gain, and for all that concerned teachers stress respect for their students' youthful vulnerability, educational activists are still accused of violating virgin innocence, manipulating, seducing, and misleading. After the National Education Association (NEA) developed its initial nuclear curriculum entitled *Choices*, President Reagan attacked it in a July 1983 speech to the NEA's rival union, the American Federation Of Teachers (AFT). Reagan said *Choices* was "aimed more at frightening and brainwashing American schoolchildren than at fostering learning." He echoed the charges of AFT president, Albert Shanker, who asked if the NEA would approve of the Moral Majority or the Ku Klux Klan shaping courses according to their beliefs, and called the unit "lopsided propaganda" that contains "almost no discussion of the near-universally accepted concept of deterrence," is loaded with "moving accounts by survivors of Hiroshima and Nagasaki," and geared towards transforming innocent students into hardened disarmament cadre.

Much of the AFT attack was rooted in long-term interunion rivalry, although AFT members did endorse the Freeze over Shanker's opposition, and some outside the sway of the New York office even used material from *Choices* to address the issues in their classes. Like the mailing from Phylliss Schlafly warning parents of this and other pending evils in the schools, Reagan's reaction seemed to have less to do with specifics taught than the fact that, merely by presenting the arms race as subject for discussion, the nearly two-million-member NEA was at least implicitly questioning government policy. Yet the teachers themselves wanted the children to do more than parrot dissenting beliefs.

Aside from now-defunct civil defense drills and warnings about our "bitter fight for freedom," schools have dealt with nuclear issues essentially by ignoring them. As of a 1982 study, America's single best-selling high school history text, Lewis Todd and Merle Curti's *The Rise of the American Nation*, gives atomic weapons one sixty-four-word paragraph, recounting the number of dead at Hiroshima and only explaining that, "A new force had been added to warfare, a force that would enormously complicate the post-war world." Perhaps because publishers feared offending the school officials who order the major texts, neither this book nor its major competitors made more than perfunctory reference to the weapons' steady development since the original devices were exploded. Two of the top four books failed to even mention the H-bomb.

As a result, America's classrooms have contributed to a prevailing silence about nuclear war. The issue has remained invisible, like blacks or Hispanics in pre-civil rights era textbooks. As an eighth-grader wrote in a letter to Bobbi Snow, "My teacher says we cannot study about nuclear weapons or what to do, because it is not part of American history or biology, math or English. . . . I asked the principal and he said that I should ask my parents or learn about it in church. . . . my father thinks teachers should not be interested in politics and I should learn more enjoyable subjects."

The new nuclear curriculums—whether the NEA's *Choices* or others developed since that are still more complex and far-reaching, like ESR's *Perspectives*—discuss what an atomic war might be like, how the weapons build-up has come about, paths for pulling back from the brink, and the questions of individual responsibility essential to shaping a just and peaceful world. Games and role-playing involve kids in imagining possible consequences of various courses and in working through the diverse perspectives of those who both support and challenge our present course of weapons build-up. Where other classes assume an inevitable progression of graduations, grades, and exams, future work, and future life, nuclear lessons make all futures contingent—preserved not by letting well enough alone and doing as we're told, but by acting with enough wisdom, imagination, and heart.

Admittedly, some of the initial curriculums focused far too much on the weapons' overwhelming horror, and too little on alternative paths of hope. Or they primarily stressed the need to roll back our burgeoning arsenals, without letting students work through the rationalizations that keep the arms race escalating. But the nuclear units, even in their experimental, germinal stages, are not taught in a vacuum. They confront assumptions already created by *Time* and ABC, and by the textbooks explaining how Truman had no choice but to drop the bomb and justify further atomic escalation as inevitable technical momentum. The arms race is buttressed as well by what Frances Fitzgerald calls "the natural-disaster theory of history," in which the ills of our time are "created by no one," but spring up of themselves, as acts of God. Unless schools acknowledge the possibilities of a different course, they end up helping to delegate the future to those very experts who have built careers on magnifying fear.

Children's private worlds reflect a similar tendency to detach actions from consequences. For instance, they play with toys that, as Canadian educator Norma Law suggests, go far beyond primal needs for assertion, aggression and contestation, beyond "the war games, which children have played in all times and in most cultures." Instead we have, as Law explains, "toys that explode, dolls that bleed, death-rays that topple, tanks or ambulances that roar to the kill. . . . [not] materials that children invent for ferocious outpourings [but] the commercial war equipment that adults present to them. . . . without rules or imaginative variations or socializing resolutions."

Granted, no inevitable continuum winds from the TV set or video parlor to the automated battlefield. The generation whose corporate and political leaders have spearheaded the atomic arms race grew up with no such high-tech devices. And fascination with military icons does not mean children either embrace their violent contexts or would casually relish destruction of the earth. That Michael Lowe's son Malachi beelined for a tank at the Carolina State Fair, and could hardly be torn away from its machine gun, does not place him on an eternally militarist course. G.I. Joe can become a cherished friend and confidant, He-Man a flexible trickster replacing the old-time Gumby dolls, and fighting Transformer robots, intricate puzzles. For all that Star Wars Storm Troopers are just expendable enemies replacing the Apaches of an earlier era, such movies can inspire courage as well as "evil empire" jingoism.

It is also a mistake to assign toys and TV images more weight in shaping children's psyches and characters than we give their direct relationships with parents and siblings, teachers and friends. Yet it hardly bodes well that U.S. sales of war toys have increased almost four-fold from 1982 to 1985, reaching a record $845 million. Unless at some point we break the web of culture that makes death appear casual and bloodless, and again defines exterminating the barbarians as the only resolution in a rough and difficult world, children will be offered few visions beyond their everyday routines or clouds of annihilation over the horizon.

Activists do not take the issue of children's vulnerability lightly. In *Thinking about the Next War*, writer Thomas Powers speaks of a need to pierce our culture's thick carapace of denial and thrust into common awareness the possible future that might end all human futures. But his daughters are four, nine, and eleven. "Can fear possibly do them any good? How can children live with a knowledge of the world as it really is when adults find it so difficult? Wouldn't it be better to brush by the question [when one of his children asked about his book] with some short, neutral answer—'it's about the Air Force,' say—and let it go?"

But "kids get the point anyway," Powers concludes, and recalls the time when he, almost without thinking, asked his nine-year-old what the world would be like after a nuclear war. "It would probably be very smoky," she said, as if she'd pondered it carefully and at length, "and not many people, and lots of things ruined, and dark."

Even as teachers hope to respond to this knowledge, and answer the fear running in its wake, they worry not only about furthering students' uncertainty and apprehension, but also about becoming missionaries who thrust their truths down vulnerable young throats. As one teacher explained during a two-hour ESR discussion, "I have a personal desire to do something really quickly on the issue, but also feel it's wrong to enlist young people in the cause. So I use materials from PSR [Physicians for Social Responsibility] and Institute for Defense Analysis, but also from Committee on the Present Danger. I hope they'll choose PSR, but also hope the kids will be able to challenge my assumptions. As a citizen speaking to other adults, I can put my views forth, but don't want to have the kids just echo me."

Yet supporting diverse opinions doesn't mean embracing false neutrality. In the words of another discussion participant, "The best teachers I ever had were very committed to a particular point of view, a particular topic or particular authors, but not in a closed way. They were open to hearing other people. . . . and invited students to go through that process with them. . . . If there isn't any commitment, there isn't any education; there's just an accretion of knowledge." Shelley Berman believed teachers needed to convey not a monolithic viewpoint, but "a way of looking at everything in the world and assessing it and evaluating it," a sense of how they themselves reached their stands.

Shelley's stress on questioning emerged, in part, from memories of Vietnam-era in-fighting. He saw himself and others now concerned, not as factions contending for power, but as citizens becoming "elements in a change. . . . like Einstein and his talk about the species needing a new way of thinking to survive." Shelley worked towards this both in designing curriculums and in a teaching approach in which he focused on offering students complex enough material and sufficient emotional support so they could work through their own logic, facts, assumptions, and values—whether these led them to endorse nonviolent defense or a Star Wars shield. He even used a role-playing exercise in which students entered into another person's perspective—like Reagan, Gromyko, Helen Caldicott, or some individual committed to wholly different issues—and tried to discern strands of truth in positions with which they might ordinarily be in profound disagreement.

Obviously, Shelley said, certain solutions were both simplistic and dehumanizing. When United States-supported contras murdered Nicaraguan peasants in their fields, or Soviet helicopters did the same in Afghanistan, one had to call this evil. It was evil to lie, manipulate, or mislead regarding the consequences of our actions. "But kids can listen, make judgments, enter into the process of how Reagan thinks and see what's true, but also what's false. Evil isn't just maliciousness; Reagan doesn't consider himself evil, but the symbol of good, taking on the terrible barbarians. . . . One thing we need to recognize is that we all have a piece of it, which should make us a little more humble."

But controversy over nuclear curriculums goes beyond arguments over what should be taught. Many of those supporting our government's present course do not wish nuclear issues to be raised in any form, and view discussion as the stuff of rebellion, subversion, even treason. To a degree, Boston is a highly concerned community. MIT faculty and students gathered 3,000 names—including those of the school's eleven Manhattan Project veterans and four of its five Nobel

Laureates—for a petition supporting a Freeze, a no first-use pledge, and negotiation of a Comprehensive Test Ban Treaty. The *Globe* won a Pulitzer for its nuclear reporting. Over 100 local peace groups sparked an array of national efforts. But the area has also been subject to backlash and resistance.

Some of this backlash has come from the same elite institutions that produce much atomic dissent. Weapons strategists like Henry Kissinger and the researchers of Draper Labs are joined by Harvard professors such as Richard Pipes, historian and frequent Reagan administration advisor who suggested using military competition to force the Soviets into changing their political and economic system, or Samuel Huntington, who went from rationalizing massive bombing of Vietnamese civilians, to justifying a continued atomic arms race in his contribution to the book *Living with Nuclear Weapons*. These theorists have found more-practical counterparts among the technicians and engineers working for the ring of high-tech weapons contractors in sleek buildings on Route 128, and have joined them in helping give the greater Boston area nearly $7 billion worth of military expenditures per year—more than reaches the combined states of Illinois, Wisconsin, and Iowa. Resistance to the peace movement comes as well from those who resent the well-educated, well-bred Brahmins who make up much of the movement and so often seem to ask working-class Americans to shoulder the brunt of national sacrifice. Many individuals simply resist thinking about the subject.

In Framingham, a town of 65,000 located twenty-two miles west of Boston's city center, the school committee not only rejected bringing nuclear issues into the classroom, but barred a related in-service teacher training session, something generally given almost automatic approval. Shelley and I drove there on a clear spring day to talk with some concerned teachers, following a meeting with ones from Brookline who said efforts like ESR's made their jobs worth doing, and with a superintendent willing to back whatever they tried.

The concerned Framingham group was made up of nine women, mostly veteran educators in their forties and fifties. Shelley began by showing a videotape of various children, made by Bobbi Snow together with Eric Chivian, a young MIT psychiatrist who had been shocked when his fifth-grade son unexpectedly told him he thought there would be a nuclear war and everyone would be killed. In the tape, a six-year-old girl hugged herself and said, "Maybe I'd rather be dead so I could go up to heaven." A young high school man, half-tough and half-vulnerable, said he "wouldn't want to be one of the survivors," and a young boy added, "I get scared when a plane flies over." Some children giggled nervously. A fourteen-year-old girl asked, "If someone makes a mistake, why do we have to die too?"

After the video ended, the teachers told Shelley they were being attacked for wanting to put ideas into students' heads. The situation echoed earlier school committee actions vetoing sex education and resisting the teaching of black and Hispanic history. Schools, the committee had stressed, weren't in the business of "teaching love and brotherhood."

Though they taught at the same school, most of these teachers knew each other only casually. One had arranged a controversial lecture series during the Vietnam-era; the rest were new to political debate. They glanced around for ground to stand on, a sense that they would not be isolated and silenced. "Maybe we could hold a meeting in a church," said one woman, "somewhere besides the Unitarians, so as not to feed the stereotype." Shelley suggested separate workshops for parents and teachers, and said that dialogue is at the root of democratic citizenship. "We have the same teaching principles as before," he repeated. "The nuclear threat's just forcing us to live by them."

As in the sex education fight, many parents feared schools would prescribe an alien morality, yet worried as well where open-ended discussion might lead. The committee preferred, the teachers stressed, to stay with "reading, writing and arithmetic."

"What about contacting teachers directly," Shelley asked, "teaching without committee approval?" But they said that would be called a breach of guidelines. "Is the board educable?" he asked. The teachers thought not.

Perhaps the best hope was parental pressure, getting those who had been interested to come once more to some public meetings and voice their concerns. "I can speak up," said an older, grey-haired woman. I'm tenured, protected by seniority. Why do I always have to tread so carefully when they don't?"

Shelley agreed, and suggested, "If each of you could bring two people. . . ."

Yet the problem went beyond creating an initial opening. "We have to go further," said one young woman. "We can't just go into the schools, pop this up and say to the kids 'Aren't you scared?' Eventually we'll have to deal with the Freeze and questions of de-escalation." Others disagreed, said maybe just teaching conflict resolution would be appropriate.

Shelley told them how an ESR teacher in Avon, a small town twenty miles to the south, worked with administrators, students and other faculty to put together an elaborate Day of Dialogue presentation. After three members of Young Americans for Freedom attacked the discussions as unpatriotic, the community held a meeting. People argued until an older man in a worn leather jacket, a life-long local resident, said he had come to protest but changed his mind, seeing nothing in the least bit objectionable about ESR's material.

Shelley handed out more ESR brochures and information on a new Day of Dialogue. At times he resembled the peddler in Ray Bradbury's story, "Dandelion Wine," a courier of gifts who drives his wagon from house to house, gathering what people no longer used, allowing them to take, free of charge, whatever they most need or desire. Like Harold Willens with his business leaders, Shelley asked individuals to begin by simply reflecting on the nuclear issue; then left them to their particular responses. Like Bradbury's peddler, or some itinerant union organizer, Shelley passed on knowledge and inspiration as well: an idea here, a suggestion there, lessons from each group that continued to scrap and dream. He'd been working since 7:15 that morning. It was now 6:00 P.M., and he still had to attend another meeting, write a funding proposal, prepare a student workshop—an almost ordinary day in a parade of seventy-hour weeks.

Yet Shelley mistrusted the voice that insisted, "Look how good I am. I'm sacrificing everything to the cause." His ESR involvement offered ample rewards, like dialogue with fellow teachers, and a sense—whether when writing new curriculums or brainstorming about the Framingham School Committee—of working with others on something significant. Despite teaching one course a year to stay in touch with students' changing moods, Shelley missed "the relationship that you establish, watching them grow, getting to know them as they change." But he also liked leaving the classroom for the outside world.

For all the difficulties of organizing workshops, developing curriculums, and constant fundraising, Shelley found working for ESR easier in a sense than full-time teaching. In part because of America's political and economic priorities, committed educators constantly hit the barriers of overloaded classes, cramped preparation time, and lack of opportunity to collaborate with colleagues. "You can never do enough," Shelley said. "You always want to know more and do more. There's always one kid with something going wrong in their family, another going through some other hard times and you're thinking about it. If you do it right, the work rarely ends."

Shelley particularly valued support from an ESR steering committee that met every other week to exchange suggestions and toss around visions. Except through efforts like those spurred by the arms race crisis, teachers ordinarily never enjoyed this kind of exchange. Instead, they remained buried by day-to-day routines.

For educators to grapple with the most profound global issues is a testament that teaching matters. As Bobbi Snow said, "the general population often sees school as babysitting, unimportant, so the way students are treated follows. But you ask someone like Phil Morrison [the internationally known MIT physicist and Manhattan Project veteran] how he ended up where he is, you find out it was one pivotal teacher." Bobbi said these issues presented a chance to use all one's craft, vision, and courage, and to use them to address unprecedented stakes.

Granted, even the best nuclear curriculums by themselves can neither transform educational institutions nor shift an entire culture. Teachers can spew data on warheads and guidance systems until the subject becomes an arcane maze, denatured of any urgency beyond the need to memorize names and numbers for the next week's quiz. But by demanding complex thought and concern, and by refusing to suppress moral understanding for fear of social or economic sanction, discussion of these issues can make classes more than just innocuous Candylands or relentless preparations for future careers. It can change teachers from remote arbiters of right and wrong to individuals, vulnerable to a common threat, whose strength lies precisely in their fallible humanity.

Yet exposure to global issues by no means automatically makes people committed activists. Resistance in the schools comes from nervous administrators, fearful parents, teachers locked into habituated roles, and students embracing the patriotic bandwagon. Resentment can also come from fears that the educated liberal culture, which has defined so much recent resistance to the military state, offers only gilt-edged mechanisms of betrayal.

As Robert Coles, author of *Children of Crisis*, points out, middle-class professionals can easily slide into the trap of taking on the earth's grand crises, while blurring over worlds just down the hill or in the next town, the domains where everyone is not college educated, reasonably privileged, and assured from birth that their voice makes a difference.

As one of Coles' respondents puts it, after hearing Helen Caldicott give the graduation speech at Massachusetts' Salem State College, "we come there to see our son get a college degree—the first person in our family to get one—and she's telling us the world is sick, sick. She said it's 'terminal,' I remember. And she said we're sticking our heads in the sand—she didn't say that, she said something that meant that, that we're all numbed out, I remember. Everyone but her and her friends! How does she know? What gives her the right to think every single person in that hall isn't as worried as she is about a nuclear war? She talks down to you! She's telling us we should be like her in our ideas and what we do, or she'll call us 'sick,' and the whole earth dying. . . . And if we had the goddamned gall to want some other kind of message on the day our kid was getting his diploma, and getting ready to have the first office job of anyone in his family, I'll tell you then tough luck for us—and aren't we the dopes and the blind fools to expect that, when any day now the nukes will go off and that'll be the end, and here we are, whistling Dixie!"

The man made it clear that the issue concerned him, but he bridled at the arrogance of those who deem themselves morally superior for their involvement. "I was trying to get home," he continued, "and I'm going through this swanky town, and it's in the afternoon, and here these people are with their balloons, and they tell me we need a freeze. Great! Great for them! Meanwhile I'm covered with dirt, and I want to go home and take a shower, and I've been sweating it out on the line all day, and I'll tell you, to see them standing there, with those balloons dangling—it drives you mad, mad as hell!" Some people, the man once told Coles, have "so damned much" they can worry about the planet.

This is strong stuff, not easily answered. As James Lawson and Catholic Worker Jeff Dietrich point out, unless the movement addresses broader questions of power and equity, it risks appearing an effort of the pious and self-congratulatory affluent to protect a world already theirs. Granted, most movement participants are hardly rich; many, like Shelley, Marv Davidov, and even Harold Willens, came out of economic backgrounds similar to Coles' respondent. Teachers or social workers making $15,000, $20,000, or even $25,000 a year hardly live like Du Ponts. But the movement's core remains in the human service professions—those who echo the historic role of the Jews by serving as buffers and scapegoats for our present-day lords and princes—those who, whatever their wage levels, possess an autonomy in the workplace and a social standing that seems to place them in a world of relative privilege.

As a doctor, Caldicott inhabits a distinctly high economic class. Yet her prime mistake—Coles' respondent would call it her arrogance—lay in seemingly exempting herself, "her and her friends," from judgment and criticism. True, she runs herself ragged, pleading for individuals to confront the common threat. If everyone did a fraction as much, the planet might have a chance. But it is easy for any of us to project the entire world in our personal image; easy to say that because we fray and bruise our lives for the cause, others should do likewise, regardless of personal circumstances; easy to cast those not politically involved as less blessed and sainted than those out saving humanity.

The backlash Coles describes presents a paradox. Our culture systematically denies the reality of barbarism created in our common name. For an American peace movement to succeed, those like Coles' respondent must at some point participate. Yet, just as Charley, the former Greek Communist Party member from the New York bar, turned against those who called him to sacrifice, yet remained themselves insulated and protected—so many of those who resent the movement are turned away not only by institutional silence on the pending cataclysms, but also by calls to join and risk from individuals who seemingly drink from the golden cup.

The variance between differing class sensibilities emerged in the reactions of students at a Catholic boys' school, St. Dominic Savio, when they confronted nuclear issues for the first time in an all-day assembly. The events at Dominic Savio, located in a poor and scrapping East Boston neighborhood in the shadow of Logan Airport, embody both the movement's broadening reach and the resistance it hits when individuals attempt to bridge across chasms of class and culture. During Vietnam, things at the school were simple: priests blessed the new graduates and sent them off to war. Yet because an ESR history teacher interested some of his Dominic Savio students in the nuclear issue, and because peace currents were increasingly shaking the Catholic Church, the teacher's class pulled together an all-school gathering. They brought in a Physicians for Social Responsibility (PSR) doctor, a priest prominent in the Catholic peace group Pax Christi, a peace-through-build-up advocate from the Tufts University Fletcher School, and the local head of the federal civil defense agency, FEMA.

Although the school's students had been exposed to little previous debate, they praised PSR's Lachlan Forrow for his slide-show lecture describing the history of the arms race and a postatomic future of burns, radiation sickness, ozone depletion, and an uninhabitable world. Students called the FEMA spokesman's talk "pure bullshit," said he typified a government that "thinks of its citizens as statistics," and joked about how drivers couldn't even make it through the Callahan/Sumner Tunnel in the evening rush—let alone in the panic of an evacuation. Yet these same students also clung to the idea that weapons escalation would preserve American freedom.

These sentiments emerged in responses to the pacifist priest, Father McLaughlin, who students said "sounded like he was giving a sermon to a bunch of misguided kids." McLaughlin lived "in a dream world," they decided, because "man has had enemies since the beginning of time [and] he wanted us to have no enemies, live in peace, happily ever after." He told them, "those who live by the sword will die by the sword," said God would mourn terribly if we destroyed the world. They judged him soft, idealistic and weak. One commented, "Honestly, I really thought he was a Communist."

Had the students known McLaughlin well, had he been a familiar friend or teacher, they might have given his words greater credence. His talk of moral universals might have tied more readily into the accustomed discourse of a different community—one in which his moral premises (and not just their religious shroud) were comprehensible, a community that had at least discussed their difficult implications. To a degree, he simply communicated poorly, assuming shared trust in God would carry the day. But religion to the Dominic Savio boys was either the stuff of womanly sentimentalism, or a doctrine divinely blessing our nation whether in war or peace. McLaughlin's talk of universal brotherhood seemed like cant, babble, service to our Communist enemies—as much a fantasy as FEMA assurances that we'd all be saved by proper evacuation.

Like the friend of Coles, Dominic Savio students inhabited a culture in which respect for the president and military force were largely givens—even if their families also doubted the middle-class notion that government would heed the will of ordinary citizens. Because they lived close to brute power, to the hardscrabble competition at the butt end of the economic ladder, the students often projected such power as the sole means of surviving a rough, harsh world. In the same way some black parents worried that too much stress on peace might leave their children helpless on the streets; the residents of East Boston also feared both their children and their nation might be disarmed and made passive. Beyond this, the students felt global issues were taken care of by the official experts, and that if these experts found them intractable, ordinary citizens could hardly hope to affect their course. Acknowledging the pure horror of skulls and bones piled high, they judged the arms race an objective evil everyone should work to avert. But they were still afraid the Red hordes might slip in if the United States dropped its guard in the slightest. It was difficult enough to accept even a degree of American culpability, much less McLaughlin's contention "that it was our fault for the Cold War and that it was up to us to end it."

Students also feared personal repercussions if they acted. One boy, who liked McLaughlin and called Reagan "a bimbo who spends most of our tax money on bombs that we aren't even going to use, instead of for the poor and crippled," explained in response to a teacher's questionnaire: "If I had the day off [to work on the issue], I'd sleep because I break my ass at Wheels Plus and if I was to say something I would be called a liberal and get thrown in jail." Another, the one who repeated twice, "I swear Father McLaughlin really did seem like a Communist," supported further education on the subject; considered writing a letter telling "Ronnie Reagan" how disturbed he was by the questions raised during the assembly; and then suggested Reagan would react "by throwing me out of the country." The boy's sentiment was not the Animal House grunt of those who insisted the best part of the assembly day were the seventy-five-cent pizzas served for lunch, tarred McLaughlin as "a loser and a grub," or who

disliked Forbes because "his hair looked fake." But the fear embedded
in these and other similar responses suggested that while individuals
could gripe and mock, lightning would strike even the mildest direct
challenge to governmental choices.

Nevertheless, merely holding the forum brought critical dialogue
to an institution rarely exposed to these controversies. Even Mc-
Laughlin pushed a few students to ask what it meant "to destroy a
world of enemies we don't even know." And the majority of those
present—who sectored off enough of the discussion's implications
to respect both Forrow's support of arms race reversal and the Fletcher
School spokesman's Cold War rationalism—overwhelmingly judged
the day a success. Some students even thought about researching
the issue further, drawing up petitions, or "protesting on the White
House lawn." A few wrote letters, talked with their families, and
suggested directions for future forums. Given the previous silence,
no single event could do more than spark initial questions and impel
a few teachers and students to begin weaving their concern into their
own lives and the discourse of the school.

In Coles' judgment, children "in ghettos and in working-class
neighborhoods, or even in many politically conservative homes in
well-to-do neighborhoods," are rarely "overwhelmed or preoccupied
by fears of a nuclear war." Coles believes that if children don't hear
about the issues in their immediate environments, they don't particularly worry.

But the response of the Dominic Savio students suggests greater
receptivity and concern. True, many resisted the material's most
difficult implications. Yet they also recognized these were unprecedented issues, as did the black and Latino high school students of
an inner-city Oakland California teacher, who ranked the nuclear
threat by a five-to-one margin as even more urgent than racism or
unemployment. Similarly, the University of Michigan conducted a
national, cross-class study surveying 17,000 high school seniors during each of the past ten years and found that, since 1980, two thirds
said they worried about the threat of nuclear war, and roughly one
third agreed that "nuclear or biological annihilation will probably be
the fate of all mankind, within my lifetime."

Because the Dominic Savio community, like the communities of
South Carolina, was only beginning to confront the nuclear threat,
and its students lacked fully honed responses, it is easy to assume

they cared less than the intellectually agile and well-groomed Brookline fast-trackers. Levels of nuclear apprehension may have been, as Shelley Berman believed, roughly equal in these children of varied backgrounds, yet most Dominic Savio students seemed less ready to leap into direct involvement with the issue. Shelley agreed on the need to take seriously the role of economic coercion and the situation of those, in Coles' words, "for whom survival will still be an issue even after the last bomb has been dismantled." Shelley thought that compared to the reasonably affluent, most working-class children necessarily focused on simply getting by day-to-day, and were also far more likely to view the Soviet Union as the truly evil enemy.

This difference in reactions reflects our society's deep economic and cultural splits. Throughout U.S. history the labor movement has surged and receded as a source of new social visions—alternately upholding various images of a cooperative commonwealth and succumbing to entrenched resistance and the lure of a share in America's ever-expanding global reach. Yet since World War II, those engaged in direct production have largely abandoned the right to speak on issues beyond wages, benefits, and working conditions.

Part of this reticence is rooted in our society's division of labor. The closer one gets to the factory floor or the base of a mushrooming service sector, the more jobs emphasize largely operative reasoning. Workers are permitted to judge, at most, how to best approach particular tasks, but never to question what they build or produce. In the absence of a union tradition upholding far-reaching ideals, this fragmentation rebounds in a narrowing of perspective that limits moral reach to private life. A church cares for a sick member. A work crew resists a manager's overbearing demands. Individuals risk for family and team, for those with whom they are linked in tangible bonds. But issues more diffuse, such as the arms race, play on distant and invisible stages.

Granted, middle class professionals also find ways to avoid the core challenges of our time: including a pride in their missionary zeal and a politics that limits issues of peace and environmental concern so related questions of equity and social justice drop in benign neglect. But at least it is far more acceptable for those in the "helping professions" to address ethical concerns, than for those working in institutions whose sole goal is financial profitability success. Teachers, ministers, and nurses also receive a certain latitude in how they ply their trades, another liberty lacking on the factory floor. Because many middle-class activists have passed through the foundry of Vietnam-era activism, experiencing something beyond disenchantment and betrayal, their challenges to the military state at least have precedent.

Yet the very language these individuals use in attempting to save the earth is often seen as representing the hidden agenda, in Spiro Agnew's immortal words, of "an effete corps of impudent snobs." Caldicott's use of the Robert Lifton phrase, "psychic numbing," was received by Coles' respondent as an attempt to batter him down through superior knowledge, eliciting perhaps a very different response than had she simply said, "this is something we have a hard time facing." For all the accuracy of Lifton's term, the academism it echoes has traditionally used its power to name and define, to help mask our society's inequities. As a result, Americans often view the elite not as those who own most of our nation's wealth and guide both foreign and domestic decisions, but as those—possessing education but no massive affluence—who have the temerity to challenge ongoing policy.

Embedded in how we respond to broader concerns are questions of loyalty to our nation, culture and traditions, family, friends, personal vision, and fellow humans whose lives are at risk. The way these loyalties at times conflict and pull, and speak differently depending on the situation, is exemplified by the contrasting lives of Amanda Domingo, the daughter of the Navy medical corpsman, and an eleven-year-old Seattle girl named Rachelle Ackerman, who introduced a nuclear discussion group at her school.

Rachelle first marched in demonstrations when she was seven or eight, accompanying her mother and father; she was delighted to "run around yelling things, though I didn't really understand what an atomic bomb could do." Nuclear issues wove into dinner table discussion. One night, in the spring of 1983, Rachelle dreamed a bomb was falling. Her family fled in the car, holding scarves over their mouths and noses, until her brother dropped his and they had to go back. They reached an empty drive-in lot, and hid with others under old beds and upside-down couches. Then the mushroom cloud rose; the others died in a flash of light and heat, and Rachelle, numb with radiation poisoning, stared off into space, seeing nothing.

She made the dream into a three-page play that won a school contest, and her mother, who taught drama, directed several students in acting it out. Otherwise, Rachelle remained silent on the issue during the coming year, until one night, after a classroom discussion on nuclear bombs, she crawled into her mother's bed, and said, "I want to do something." Shaking inside, but acting cool as Walter Cronkite, Rachelle took a letter to her school's monthly parents' meeting, proposing a regular time when students could learn about the arms race and work on related projects. One parent thought the proposed group a wonderful idea, but said it was hard enough for him to face the issues, and he didn't think his child was ready; another suggested students below sixth grade be excluded. "We have to face these things," Rachelle responded. "Because they might happen if enough people don't do something." Children had "a right," she thought, to know about these issues if they wanted to. Some five- and six-year-olds understood more than some grown-ups.

One man who had considered transferring his son out of the school said softly, "If Summit creates kids like that, I'll leave him in." Others applauded, visibly moved, Rachelle thought, "because kids didn't usually talk that seriously to adults."

The group agreed to let all ages attend, as long as they got signed parental approval. I talked with Rachelle at her family's house as she folded a paper crane for an international project seeking to send 1 million of them to key world leaders on Hiroshima's fortieth anniversary. Both Amanda and Rachelle were thoughtful, inquisitive, fundamentally happy kids, who were also immensely concerned about the arms race. Yet Amanda faced far greater obstacles to continued future activism. Because the two came from different social classes, they were pulled by different loyalties. Not that Rachelle's family was wealthy—they scraped by on her mother's half-time teaching and scattered bookkeeping. But they inhabited a predominantly college-educated circle in which Rachelle's activism was admirable citizenship, a cause for pride as unalloyed as if she'd grown the star 4-H Club zucchini. And Rachelle herself framed the prospects of continued engagement quite matter-of-factly, explaining, to the back-drop of rocket fire echoing from her brother's Atari in the basement, that although she probably wouldn't do "anything real big—like I mean I won't be any Martin Luther King"—she liked acting directly "instead of just telling my family about my bad dreams."

Amanda could draw inspiration from ESR teachers and other "Peace Child" participants. Yet, although her family gave her emo-tional security and strength of character, the world she inhabited provided few models for peace movement dissent. As Ramon acknowledged, he'd worked for the Navy his entire adult life, in an environment that considered war imminent at any time. "Seeing that play makes you think twice. Because here you are. Your mission is to stop war—or fight the war. And seeing that play, you know, fighting for what? Maybe the kids are going to grow up for nothing."

Ramon said Amanda had asked about the Russians, and that he'd realized how little he knew, except from the papers and TV news. "I mean, I know when their president is sick, or they go up to space again. I know," he laughed, "that Moscow's a big city."

"And they have good ballet dancers," interrupted Amanda, who then ran back outside to play. Ramon continued, describing, with an ironic laugh, how he'd grown up being taught " 'Russia, it's Communist. It's bad.' And I guess I absorbed that kind of thinking. But I don't discuss it with my kids. I do with my wife."

Once Amanda had asked him, "What happens if a bomb falls?", and Ramon shielded her, saying only that it would be very bad and would kill people. "She's a really energetic kid," he stressed, "talking about going to college and stuff. But it's in the back of her mind about this war." She'd questioned him about his ship and nuclear weapons, and when I asked Nilda whether he and his fellow sailors discussed "Peace Child," Amanda broke in to say coyly, "I don't think my Daddy wants to tell them."

Ramon was proud of the play and thought more people should see it. But Amanda knew without asking that the peace movement might somehow be considered "going against Daddy." All his support could not readily erase this.

A scrapper in one context may be deemed a bad seed in another. When Rachelle defended her proposal, one parent exclaimed, "Good for you, Rachelle. You're a fighter. I want you on my side." Yet to speak out for peace in the Navy might invite social and legal sanctions. Children as well as adults receive the mandate for silence.

The notion that political involvement means abandoning one's personal loyalties echoes conflicts explored by Richard Sennett and Jonathan Cobb in *The Hidden Injuries of Class*. If someone from a working-class background leaves their community and becomes upwardly mobile in occupation or geographic residence, in a sense he or she betrays those "left behind." To draw our culture's full respect one must climb. But this action further stigmatizes others with failure, further locks them into situations accorded neither dignity nor power. Children like Amanda and the Dominic Savio students face parallel double binds. To take up what has been considered a middle-class cause both breaches accustomed definitions of loyalty and pushes boundaries potentially affecting economic survival. Yet precisely because of their situation's difficulty, their involvement and that of their families is an even more significant step—one that allows private faith and private solidarity to break out to a broader social realm. It embodies the beginnings of a peace movement diverse as our culture.

During the 1960s, West German theorist Rudi Dutschke proposed activists achieve their visions through what he termed "The Long March through the Institutions": working for fundamental change in each of the varied schools, offices, factories, and communities in which they settled. Parallel to village politics, and focusing specifically on workplaces and other domains of common life, this notion suggests any situation where people came together for work, play, comfort, or communication can support either debasing or humane values. Dutschke said our choices within these institutions could reinforce the separation of actions from their consequences, and the surrender of decision-making power from those directly affected to those commanding massive hierarchies and bureaucracies, or such choices could foster an understanding that coercion to "get the job done" inevitably carries a toll, and that human ends matter more than either technical invention or financial success.

This approach asks us to examine the web of work, community, and culture of which we are a part, to ask which values it serves and should serve, and to question how it feeds or resists those currents now threatening human survival. By taking on this role, ESR teachers differ somewhat from activists who put together demonstrations, vigils, and electoral campaigns. Wedded to their craft, they work within their institutions. They go beyond nuclear issues, as when Shelley coordinated a science curriculum using the question of toxic wastes as an entry to chemistry, biology, and ecology; or when he proposed that math classes examine how society uses statistics in advertising and in politics. Some teachers also work outside the schools, blocking weapons trains, canvassing for the Freeze, organizing around military bases and weapons contractors—drawing on whatever respect they are granted for the demanding task of shepherding our young. But their prime focus remains, above all else, nurturing thoughtful and committed future citizens.

Such efforts might not stop MX production, secure a Comprehensive Test Ban Treaty, or change the next congressional election. But because the nuclear threat is both a political issue and something rooted, at the very least, in the culture of nations that have spearheaded the arms race, we must address it on varied levels. Assuming we gain the time we need, it may be the teachers and other institutional workers who build the longer-term understanding necessary for a possible peace.

Distinctions between immediate and future impact often blur. Teenagers like Kathy and Sheila have voices as powerful as their adult peers. Shabazz inspired the broader Nuclear Free Zone effort in the surrounding community of Madison. Amanda raises questions for Ramon and Nilda, and Rachelle for the Summit School parents. For most students, however, the effect of nuclear education is diffuse, even if it may well seed the ground for future understanding and engagement. If they become involved—at age eight, thirteen, or eighteen—they do so out of individual responses to what their teachers have presented, and to ways the material stirs their personal vision. Just as PSR doctors stress the historical role of healers, and politicized churches act most strongly when their members maintain connection to their faith—so committed educators seek to both address critical political issues and fulfill their craft's most hallowed ideals.

Colleges have traditionally rationalized banishing the most urgent global questions not by referring to their students' vulnerable innocence, but by embracing professional specialization and value-free complacency. As Columbia's Seymour Melman explained to *Nuclear Times*, "two generations of young people came through the universities, trained [to think] there was nothing around but the arms race, or the regulation of the arms race—arms control," and the very idea of reversal got lost. Unlike Vietnam, which hit the campuses through direct draft calls and daily body counts, present-day horrors are deferred—as in the case of atomic cataclysms—or distanced even from the TV screens—as in the bombs currently raining on Central American peasants—and, therefore, carry far less tangible urgency.

As elsewhere in our society, a silence has prevailed over most university campuses, erasing knowledge of past history and its lessons. Multischool surveys conducted in colleges in 1983 and 1984 found that half their respondents had no notion the U.S. had ever used atomic weapons against civilian populations, and that students believed by even larger majorities that President Reagan favored a Freeze. In general, most freshmen, sophmores, and even seniors recall Vietnam and Watergate largely as vague historical names; know still less of Chile, the Dominican Republic, or the Congo; bury fears about a world flirting with annihilation beneath overriding concern for an economy in which it seems only the ruthless survive.

This absence of knowledge has been fed by a widespread disillusionment and the abdication from responsibility of so many who have pulled back from Vietnam-era engagement to inhabit the domain of Arendt's "inner immigrants." Without a tradition of recent activism, campuses nurture a generation with a divided sensibility: like a Seattle community college freshman who worried terribly about atomic weapons, criticized her father for working on the MX missile, and then supported Ronald Reagan because "if he is warlike and frightens other nations, no one will bother us"; or like a student government officer at the University of Texas, San Antonio, who dreamed of entrepreneurial stardom, proclaimed himself a staunch "young Reaganite," and projected a harsh, carnivorous world in which we had no choice but to ensure we ended up on top—yet also invited several arms race critics to lecture and worried about why his generation seemed so cynical and uninvolved, so quick to shunt aside broader values to grab for the dollar.

Granted, campus conservatism is to a degree overblown: although voters under thirty reelected Ronald Reagan in 1984 by roughly the same eighteen percent margin as did the general voting populace, full-time students (who had more chance for democratic discourse, and were perhaps less swung by the economy's last-minute deficit-manufactured upsurge) favored him by less than three percent. Yet, compared with their peers of fifteen years ago, the present college population embraces far more narrow visions.

But in the same way that the institution-by-institution march has brought in those involved in churches, secondary schools, and neighborhoods, previously silent campuses show steady signs of changing. At the beginning of the initial Reagan administration, the United States had little more than fifty college peace groups—mostly at elite schools like Columbia, Harvard, and Cornell—and about the same

number of related courses, mostly international relations classes that
as often as not rationalized current government directions. But just
as diverse individuals brought nuclear education to junior and senior
high schools, so university students and faculty members began to
push for classes, hold meetings, and present lectures and forums. In
November 1981, the Union of Concerned Scientists held a day of
teach-ins at 150 colleges nationwide, from which they spun off a
separate organization, United Campuses Against Nuclear War
(UCAM). Four years after its founding, the organization's networks
extended to over 600 campuses in every state and in Canada.

There was a parallel development in curricula. By the fall of 1985,
over 500 nuclear-related courses were offered in a wide range of
disciplines, from psychology to physics; from the University of Wisconsin's series of interdisciplinary lectures (which was broadcast on
Wisconsin Public Radio) to a New Mexico biologist's class on the
ecological implications of nuclear war, to a course taught by a University of Texas sociologist that grew to be the largest in his department. New York University founded a Center for War, Peace,
and the News Media. Schools as diverse as Dartmouth and Southern
Methodist University held campus-wide forums and town hall meetings. In the words of Robert Musil, coordinator of SANE's nationally
distributed radio program, "Consider the Alternatives," these courses
at their best approached the issues with "a sensitivity not just to the
facts, but the whole moral tableau—religious imagery and moral
questions, scientific calculations and medical effects, psychic numbing and guilt, the military uses of the bomb, incipient protest, and
more."

Although fear of manipulating vulnerable youth is far less of an
issue at the college level, teachers still disagree on where to draw
the line between honest partisanship and open inquiry: a young first-
grade teacher taking the highly attended Wisconsin lecture series
thought its coordinator strove far too hard for some mythical objec-
tivity, surrendering passion and diffusing the course's most important implications in a maze of boring esoterica "about how Uranium
has ninety-two protons, what year Marie Curie discovered radio-
activity, and which bombs had how many megatons." But teachers
have found a variety of ways to articulate their urgencies without
reducing their lessons to rhetorical sloganeering. Simple discussion
frequently spurs a general engagement, and students have formed

campus peace groups, researched weapons contractors, and developed their own lectures and slide-shows for the surrounding community. Beginning just after Reagan's reelection, concern over South African apartheid has raised related questions of moral responsibility to even larger numbers of students, through campus demonstrations from Florida and Berkeley. During one, at Cornell in early 1985, over 1,000 people were arrested. Although involvement does not yet equal Vietnam-era levels, an alternative presence from which to build now exists.

At Madison's nuclear-free Shabazz school, students played volleyball in the gym and shot baskets while a tape blasted out rap king Grandmaster Flash singing, "It's called survival." A black girl in a yellow sweater and matching leg warmers hit a volleyball spike no one could save, then turned a cartwheel in celebration. Outside Michael Brockmayer's classroom, a bulletin board displayed clippings from the Washington trip, photos of the students posing tough with the scrawled comment, "Ya Man, we is Bad," a Nuclear Free Zone certificate, articles on the arms race, and a comic, "Meet Mr. Bomb," that described postattack TV fare like "Little House under the Prairie."

Michael's class trickled in, sprawling on the Salvation Army furniture nestling amidst nuclear weapons charts and a photo of Einstein sticking out his tongue, with the caption: "Imagination is more important than knowledge." One girl wore a fur coat she found for fifteen dollars at Saint Vincent De Paul and funky boots a friend's mother had given her for babysitting. "I'm in a good mood," she laughed, eating yogurt while her friends vamped and flirted in the coat.

The students read in turn from the comic, *Barefoot Gen*, a partially autobiographical story written by an artist who was a young boy at Hiroshima; it had been serialized during the late 1960s in a Japanese children's magazine with a circulation of ten million, but was eventually pulled due to political pressure. The Shabazz students laughed at its farting jokes and at a fight between two workers depicted with the pop culture exaggeration of the battles between Batman and The Riddler. In one scene, Gen sang out at the table, "Koreans, Koreans, they wear funny shoes," and his father hit him for being racist. Michael interrupted to talk about Japan's Korean prisoners and Japanese opposition to the war.

When the bomb fell, Gen watched half his family die in the flames. "I hate you, I hate you," his little brother cried, as Gen followed his father's command and fled.

The Shabazz students joked briefly, calling the story "groady to the max," then grew quiet, dropping their heads, fiddling with their hands, knowing what was being talked of and what was to come. "God this is depressing," one said. "Sure does harden you quick," added another. Kathy Bryant wrote quietly in her journal. When the lesson of the comic ended, the images diffused. Sheila, who was taking different courses this semester, ducked in to say hello and try on the coat. Things were fine once more.

At Kathy's comfortable Madison home, where she lived with her mother and stepfather, Sheila told us a flip, fast story from a Frontier Airlines magazine about a young pilot who stopped a bullet with a Bible. "Where," she concluded, "among today's drug-crazed rock and rolling youth would you find this?" Poking at Kathy's optimism, she asked why bad music sold and good music didn't, why *The Progressive* and *Mother Jones* were small, and *Time* and *The Reader's Digest* were huge. "You've got the fairness doctrine, lets you put an ad for milk on at three o'clock in the morning. Great."

"Maybe you get to the people who put the media on," said Kathy. "Change them. They're just programmed like the tour guide, the robot. He could have been a smiling little kid until someone got to him."

"I'm just saying this," Sheila told me, ingenuously. "I could be saying what she says, and she could say mine. I just get into it." Sheila wore running shoes with blazing purple laces and a bright red scarf wound around her neck. She had danced six days a week before she got involved in the antinuclear work. "I wish I didn't think about this," she said. "I wish I didn't have to."

Kathy recalled a recent dream in which she woke up with her skin burned off and her mother dead: "I would have killed myself, would have died anyway. Learning this stuff's like going through emotional foreplay."

"Emotional foreplay?" Sheila laughed. "We're not talking about *that*." The mood swung and eased as Kathy laughed as well, went to the kitchen to make some tea, and sashayed back, presenting it on a tray with a flourish, karate kick, and mock torchy announcement, "Coffee tea or me. . . . you want honey, you got me baby."

The two played, drizzling honey from a plastic bear held a foot above the cup. Sheila sang the Ramones song, "I Want To Be Sedated."

"I want to live at least until my grandchildren," Kathy said, returning to seriousness.

"I want my grandchildren to live." Sheila responded, still riffing. "That's very good," she laughed again. "We work well together." She turned and repeated, "By me being cynical I'll force you to be an optimist. Then it will switch."

"But you do it too far," said Kathy. "I get mad."

Sheila defended herself, saying she wanted "to learn what people think." The cynicism was almost a game—testing me, the outside observer, testing their friendship, testing the remote chance that maybe nothing mattered and we would be better off not knowing or trying. If Sheila didn't believe Faith and Truth always prevailed, at least her play exorcised certain demons.

Kathy described her brother Dusty's attempts to be a musician, singing a bit "about war and how things should be," even though he balked at further political involvements. "Dusty's real into his friends and his music," she said. "He's starting to play around in town. I'd like to get Rick, his friend—"

"I know you'd like to get Rick," Sheila teased again as Kathy blushed. Then she apologized dramatically. "I'm a horrible person, I deserve to die." Turning serious, Sheila said the nuclear issue was so critical, "so fatal," so different from anything she'd been involved in.

The two thought people reacted to them differently because of their age: some becoming curtly dismissive, others drawing particular hope, like the seventy-five-year-old man who said Kathy was his child for fighting to save the world. Unlike Vanessa Kirsch's experience with the Cambridge Peace Commission, NUFFUM gave them full play in the group: Sheila had been made one of four members given the collective task of deciding whether the proposed Nuclear Free Zone ordinance would include atomic power as well as weapons. "Some people," Sheila said, "were shocked, impressed, felt guilty because we were so young. Because this is such a drastic and horrible thing that even people like me who have other things to think about are involved in it. Others discount—'They'll grow up.' NUFFUM put us in charge of schools but also brought us into other decisions. Now we spend Saturdays canvassing, speaking, attending meetings—even cynical me thinks it's better."

Sheila left to join her boyfriend. Kathy got some leftovers out of the refrigerator. Dusty and his friend Rick came up from the basement where they'd been playing music, and Rick asked her what good anything did if Congress was controlled by the giant corporations. She answered, believing it, "You've got to try."

"Sheila argues," Kathy said, "to see where the other position is. It's almost like she wants to get me angry because it's a joke to her. When she does that to people it makes them wonder if they're right. In some ways we've gotten closer, others further apart the last few years. I put lots of problems on her and I need to stop." Kathy thought "stepping into the movement" was the biggest change she'd ever gone through. "I'll have more later, you change and change, but I'm over the first one. I couldn't go back. I want to do this so badly, no way that I can stop."

A few weeks before she'd gone to see a play and run into a girl she'd known off and on since they were both first graders. "She said she saw me on Channel 3 and if someone her own age could fight for our lives—it meant so much, she was going to start something, a peace group, in her class. That was so neat. We weren't that close before, but I practically cried and just hugged her. You don't get that every day, but when you do it's the greatest complement."

In her book, *Despair and Personal Power in the Nuclear Age*, psychologist Joanna Macy recounts a letter written by a seven-year-old girl to the president. "Dear Mr. Regan," it begins:

> I think that you should stop making any kind of bomb just because I am in 2nd grade does not mean I do not care because I do. In the world we have unuf bombs to blow up the world 10 TIMES! You miht think that I am just a stupid little girl but I am not. It is so discusting that there was going to be a war whith us, I woild take a knife and kill my self. . . . You might not no what happened in Japan in 1945, but I do and I an thousands of other people do not want it to happen agian any were. . . . I am not being funny. I am not doing this because I head someone say that they did. There is a

time to play and a time not to and I am not playing. I am Sarah Kerlin and I want this to stop.

Even if cynicism has junior high students responding to teachers' questions by proclaiming fliply, "When I think of nuclear war I think of Cheerios," the young remain far less armored and more vulnerable than their adult counterparts. They are also less firmly locked into the roles and responsibilities that make adults hesitate to confront the crises of our time. Because much of the peace movement is profoundly conservative—acknowledging a world of limits, where the urge to invent whatever we choose has become potentially terminal—it also needs visions, like those embodied by Sheila and Kathy's pop culture banter, that are not always moderate, even-handed, and demure.

In this vein, a first-grade girl once explained to Bobbi Snow, "I know what to do about nuclear war. Take a vote. Everyone has to vote. If they want a nuclear war, we'd have one. If not, we wouldn't. I don't think," the girl said, hesitating a moment, "that they'd vote for it."

For a child to ask adults, the presumed actors in the world, "What will you do?" pushes us to engage these issues. Making exceptions for career climbing and romantic dreams, we see adult life primarily in terms of barriers and boundaries, but view young lives as being filled with opportunity, embodying promises waiting to be fulfilled. Because we connect with our children through the most intimate of human emotions, their voices remind us that we do possess choices regarding the future we create. Playing the role of common conscience, they can unearth the often buried urgencies we suppress behind our daily routines.

Inasmuch as children represent a universal future, one can, as Lifton cautions, justify any actions in terms of creating a world for them to inhabit: one can justify equally Martin Luther King's "beloved community," an America walled off behind palisades of warheads, even a Third Reich seeking "Lebensraum" for pure blonde Aryans. When Helen Caldicott culminates talks with the phrase— "There are no capitalist babies. There are no Communist babies. A baby is a baby is a baby"—she flirts with the dangerous notion that sinful, curmudgeonly adults are less worth saving than innocent infants; that the obliteration of complex webs of knowledge and culture, as well as diverse particular lives, might be a less heinous crime than the destruction of near-virgin souls. As an ESR psychologist explained, we have no right to "make the kids movement cannon fodder," to drop on them the burden of arresting a momentum that we, the adults, have by default let slide to its present velocity.

Yet Caldicott's notion of children as vulnerable conscience voices the truth that our successor generation may not take its rightful place in human history. And because the nuclear burden is inherent in our time, it is better, as Amanda said, for children to face it together than alone.

As Shelley Berman stressed, different teachers approached their peace work in various ways. In a sense, ESR required two groups: one a highly political organization mobilizing educators to act, as citizens, on issues like the Freeze and the militarization of their communities; another seeking to teach the most critical questions, to help students "develop the values, insights and commitments to make a difference in the world." Understandably, the same individuals were drawn to both courses, and national ESR debated, inconclusively, whether acting directly on political beliefs made it harder to bring peace curriculums to the schools.

Although educating, even on the most difficult truths, cannot by itself convert the weapons factories, dismantle the warheads, or move us to a world less fraught with needless cataclysms, the teachers' visions were unavoidably "political." Efforts like those of ESR set off ripples extending miles beyond the classrooms. Students like Kathy, Sheila, and Vanessa would go on to become engaged citizens. By placing nuclear issues on PTA and school board agendas, bringing them to the homely domains of PS 45 and Garfield High, concerned teachers could make arms race issues the concern of far more than just the beleaguered outsiders. Teachers could help legitimize more direct challenges, like those of the Honeywell blockaders.

At the same Brookline High where ESR was born, a CBS crew filmed the first Massachusetts use of the National Education Association's *Choices* curriculum. The class of a teacher named Ronnie Sidney had been chosen for this slot on the national news, but the reporters fidgeted while students discussed the less-than-juicy scheduled topic of conflict resolution. The crew had anticipated tales of

Armageddon, not modest lessons in turning down the heat; they waited until one of the students at last told Ronnie, "I don't think they want to film this," and she switched to discussing the roots of previous wars.

"Does the class scare you, or make you feel better?" asked the reporter, a short while later, almost as if testing new extra-strength Excedrin. They asked if the material advocated a nuclear freeze. Was it "anti-Reagan in its purpose?"

Class members agreed the learning carried a mandate, but said it was simply "to do something." Several voiced fears that "some computer will make a mistake"; one commented, "I was scared before, but now I'm more aware. It's hard to picture the whole world not being there." When a girl named Nicole suggested weapons money could meet other needs, they stopped filming, and she commented with disappointment, "Guess I was getting too political." A boy named Mark had said earlier we needed more weapons so as "not to get decked by the Soviets." Now he lent a friend his red white and blue windbreaker with the words USA—so the symbol would show prominently when the other student was interviewed on TV. With Ronnie's support, Mark had held his ground throughout the three-week unit, like a patriot besieged by hordes of insurgents, and insisted that peace required continued weapons build-ups. He repeated this theme in his own twenty-second clip, explaining "War scares me. This helps me understand how many close calls we've had. But if Russia keeps going then *we* should." And he said he thought the class was fair and interesting.

In 1943, as German bombs fell on London, Anna Freud wrote, "We shall know that peace has returned when nothing is left for the children to be afraid of except their own former ghosts and bogeymen." Since that era has not come, perhaps the best teachers can do is raise the fundamental choices offered in the situation we now inhabit—use the nuclear crisis, as Shelley put it, as "an entry to exploring ongoing questions of justice, global awareness, our own aggression and violence." Since it threatened "a final death, for everyone," Shelley thought it raised these questions "in an ultimate way."

Unlike teachers clinging to the verities of the three Rs, those involved with peace issues cannot know all the answers. Given that they are as vulnerable as their students to the potential cataclysms they discuss, their task is to use their knowledge, skill, and experience to make this common vulnerability spur learning and engagement—to confirm to those just beginning to confront both the adult world and its potential annihilation, that they are not alone. It is to help students address an era in which time-honored guarantees—for instance, that children of succeeding generations will sit and learn in classrooms such as these—can no longer be taken as givens.

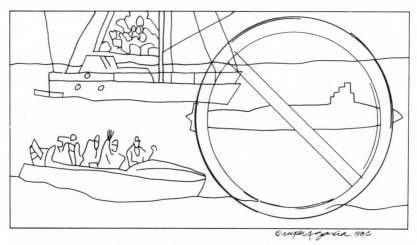

# 5. Washington State: Not Death or Glory

## The Saga of the Trident Blockade

T HE week before the Trident's arrival, the fifty-four-foot steel
ketch, *Pacific Peacemaker*, resembled less the flagship of a rebel
fleet than that of a Windjammer Barefoot Cruise. Soon, America's
first Trident submarine, the *USS Ohio*, would steam into its Bangor,
Washington base, twenty miles west of Seattle, and confront a small-
boat blockade. Forty-five women and men would take part, facing
sentences of up to ten years in jail. Yet now they sat, reading, chatting
with friends, and stretching in the sun, while overhead on the sail
a rainbow peace sign burned red and orange. Light filtered pink on
the water through patches of clouds. The earth seemed slow and
lazy in its turning.

Then people pulled on wet suits for a practice run, and boarded
the two-person rowboats *Peacemaker* would tow towards the *Ohio*.
The boat, which had sailed from Australia for this encounter, grew
quiet. Faces darkened. The sub's invisible presence drew closer—
the presence of a $2 billion machine possessing more destructive
power than 2,000 Hiroshima bombs. The apprehensions held until
the blockaders entered the water, at which point spirits eased and
lifted once more. Three people left their boats, using the buoyancy
of their wet suits to float on their backs. While his wife Lorraine

steered, skipper Bill Ethell and two other crew members fed out the tow line to the rowboats they earlier christened "the ducklings"; seven of them strung out behind the mother ketch, along with a motorized skiff and aluminum canoe named *The Children*. The erstwhile landlubbers began to find their sea legs.

They passed *The Lizard of Woz*, the bright yellow trimaran skipper Ted Phillips built himself before he emigrated from England to Canada, and its nine single-person boats, rowed for the most part by devout Christians like Ted. The boats, put together by Ted in his marine repair yard on Quadra Island, British Columbia, were called, along with their occupants, "the little lizards." Built of green fiberglass for lightness and maneuverability, each one displayed a plaque saying "with love from Quadra," and flew the blockade flag: a black submarine slashed by a red stripe made up of miniature people. Because the boats would tip if towed, the lizards rowed on their own. One rower moved furiously enough, intent as a champion racer, to almost match *Peacemaker*'s three-knot pace.

The exercise completed, *Peacemaker* pulled in its boats and people crowded around the galley, drinking wine, Jim Beam, and herbal tea. Dan Delaney, an ex-priest in his mid-forties, had come from Sacramento, where he lived with his wife Chris, and their son and daughter, as part of a Catholic Worker group that fed the poor, housed families visiting inmates at a nearby prison, and led pray-ins of housewives who blocked traffic into the local Strategic Air Command base. Thirteen years before this August, 1982 blockade, Dan and Chris founded the Los Angeles Catholic Worker house into which Jeff Dietrich would shortly move. Now Dan talked of learning in the Marines "how a bazooka stops a tank—not by massive force, but by boring a tiny hole with its rocket and then expanding." The people in the boats, "the crazies," made the initial breach in a similar fashion, so others who were more cautious could follow. Dan admitted employing a military metaphor was strange, but said even Gandhi used them. He'd been arrested six times, and recently jailed for fifty-five days after pouring blood on missile components at the Sunnyvale, California, plant of Lockheed Aerospace.

Dan laughed about a camp follower who said, "Oh, you're one of the Lockheed Four," showering him with hero worship. He thought people were always quick to erect new gods or single out individuals especially sanctified and blessed. "Groups with pious names like

'Christians for Peace' make me nauseous," he said. "You didn't see that sanctimonious crap when the early Christians were being arrested for preaching resurrection and defying the government's most powerful threat, the right to kill.

"Maybe you have to be a little crazy," Dan continued, "to risk doing two, three, or five years' time. I know I might be reaching that certain point where they stop treating you like one of their own, a middle-class respectable gone wrong, and instead haul out your computer sheet like they do with all the habitual offenders."

The blockaders numbered twenty-one women, twenty-three men and a nine-year-old boy. Seven were grandparents and over half had children. They came from California and Oregon, Washington, Minnesota, and Missouri, from Australia, Canada, Germany, New Zealand, and a half dozen other places in the United States. They included both hardcore reprobates like Delaney, and individuals who'd never run a traffic light. All faced the potential ten-year terms.

The *Ohio* was just the first of ten Tridents to be brought to the Northwest because the Hood Canal stays deep all year and the Bangor Poseidon base and nearby Puget Sound Naval Shipyard have extensive nuclear repair facilities. The site choice was also fed by Senator Henry J. "Scoop" Jackson's status as a Cold War ideologue with pork barrel clout. In part, the Tridents bring the world into a new era through their sheer power: each submarine possesses destructive capabilities greater than those employed by the combined navies in all the wars in history. Yet the threat of the Tridents stems from more than their massive annihilatory capabilities. Given that soon-to-be-deployed Trident II missiles will be able to land within 300 feet of targets 6,000 miles away, the subs will have the potential for a surprise first-strike attack against Soviet ICBMs in their steel and concrete missile silos. In a crisis, this prospect might well provoke the Soviets into launching their warheads first, to prevent them from being destroyed.

In 1973, Trident missile designer Robert Aldridge realized these implications and resigned from his job at the California Lockheed complex, where Dan Delaney would later be arrested. A group Aldridge inspired held the first civil disobedience at Bangor in 1975, and two years later purchased 3.8 acres of land directly adjacent to the base. After Aldridge's friends Jim and Shelley Douglass moved into a nearby house with their son Thomas, the Ground Zero Center

for Nonviolent Action became a matrix for both ongoing civil disobedience and complementary dialogue. Ground Zero brought in
weekly lecturers to lead discussions on peace, religion, and ethics,
and a few Bangor sailors even entered shyly and listened. The group
would later initiate the nationwide white train campaign, which tied
together communities along the tracks over which the atomic warheads passed. But for the moment their efforts were solely local;
joined by sympathetic supporters, they leafletted each week, handed
out printed literature and, on special occasions, added loaves of bread.
In the months leading up to the blockade, their efforts would lead
the Bangor base's chaplain and three other employees to publicly
resign.

"I don't want to go to jail for the *Ohio*," explained a former Montana
good ol' boy and ex-Navy sailor named David Host, as we talked at
the blockaders' temporary base camp. "I'm a very gluttonous person.
I like lying in the sun and drinking beer." He laughed, slapping his
stomach. "But going to jail tells people you're serious. Talk is cheap.
It's easy enough to stand by the Hood Canal with a sign in your
hand. Sure, civil disobedience can be a safety valve—letting you feel
effective and getting the dissenters out of the way. If you go in self-
righteously people will pick up the bad faith. But if you speak with
enough love and truth you create an alternative power."

"Any action," David continued, "can be a safety valve—pacifism
or terrorism, demonstrating or voting. But this reaches out without
restrictions. If I go petitioning, I address certain people—American
voters—and not others. If I join Physicians for Social Responsibility,
I'm parading myself as a professional, someone supposedly worth
more because my job has status. Some people have been suggesting
that nuns wear their habits and doctors their little eye magnifiers
when they march in demonstrations; we're supposed to emphasize
what sets us off from ordinary humans." Anyone, David emphasized,
could participate in civil disobedience, even individuals without access to legitimized, credentialed, and institutionally sanctioned power.
The actions reached out not to those who held levers of command,
but to whoever chose to respond.

But this potential reach and power didn't erase apprehensions.
Just as Erica feared the considerably more modest likely costs of her
Honeywell protest, and South Carolina minister Levon Hucks nearly
crashed his truck at the thought of simply attending the Florence

peace march, so the Trident blockaders worried about loss of reputation and career (a lawyer about to take the bar risked having his license withheld for "moral turpitude"); about leaving their children, seeing their gardens go to ruin, facing prospective violence and confinement.

In the words of Kim Wahl, a forty-five-year-old nurse and doctor's wife from an affluent Seattle suburb, those who rode the rowboats staked not only their freedom, but also "our property, our standing, and our respectability." Kim was inspired most by Raymond Hunthausen, the Catholic archbishop who won national prominence by advocating the withholding of war taxes. Hunthausen said people have to resist, regardless of the consequences, and that the atomic threat requires more than just the unseating of particular policymakers. Kim responded by placing her personal future at risk.

The blockaders hadn't initially planned to confront lengthy jail terms. They expected sentences a bit greater than those meted out to the 112 individuals who climbed the Bangor fence three years before, but never contemplated ten years. Then the Navy hauled out a 1950 Executive Order, giving federal authorities unprecedented discretionary control against "subversive activity." The government closed off eighteen miles of the Hood Canal and enacted a 1,000-yard moving security zone around the *Ohio*, buttressing these restrictions with threats of decade-long jail terms and $10,000 fines. They used the Coast Guard to deal directly with the blockaders, making the operation resemble (despite the invoking of national security statutes) an issue more of waterway safety than atomic weapons protest. Although the regulations were challenged by the American Civil Liberties Union, the National Lawyer's Guild and local church officials, a federal judge refused to strike them down on constitutional grounds.

No one knew what the actual penalties would be. The government might try to minimize the entire effort with relatively brief terms for most participants and longer ones for those considered key leaders or hardcore offenders; or it might view legal sanctions as a chance to teach people a lesson—to frighten them away from a growing movement, just as it had tried to do in 1960, when nonviolent activists who boarded the initial Polaris subs in New London, Connecticut, were given nineteen-month sentences. In addition to the risk of jail, the Navy took great pains to point out the dangers of getting close to the Ohio's massive eighteen-foot propeller, or of being run over when the sub could not stop in mid-course. Even if individuals avoided injuries and received sentences of only six months, what would the costs do to people with families, jobs, and ordinary human attachments?

Those jailed before already knew about separation from the normal flow of life; worries for physical safety; and hours, days, and weeks spent feeling bored. Jail would be an environment strangely similar to that inhabited by the Trident crews, who spent seventy days in a row underwater—one of claustrophobia, arbitrary command systems, and severance from the world.

Dan Delaney said prison, though miserable to be in, was a good lesson for middle-class whites, who would be "surrounded by all those weird poor people who frighten us so." Some of the protesters reassured themselves by talking with acquaintances who'd served time for civil disobedience, and by meeting other blockaders at decision-making retreats. Others made partial commitments, like the driver of one of the fast, maneuverable rubber boats known as Zodiacs, who decided he'd violate the security zone to do rescues, but wouldn't blockade; or like those who attended the retreats, then dropped back to supporting roles. Most acknowledged their fears and then continued on.

To the blockaders, the *Ohio* represented the beginning of a new and far more dangerous historical era. They hoped to not just maintain the present balance of terror, but to challenge the root forces that kept the world producing weapons like the Tridents. They believed, in the words of a grandmother from Ashland, Oregon, "that if we do spend two or three years in jail for something this honorable, people will get upset. They'll do something. It will be worth it."

Because this spirit of courage overrode the fears, the blockaders shared a joyful community. Individuals believed, as David Host said, that "If you're going to be out there risking getting jailed or beat up on the water, you have to be the kind of stupid fool who keeps getting your heart broken but keeps on anyway without holding back."

Yet people wanted not only to stand in witness, but also, at least briefly, to halt the sub. And just as the massive potential sentences escalated the action's possible costs, so the need to intercept the *Ohio* on the water funneled individuals' spirit and comradeship into what almost became a pacifist version of *Sink the Bismarck*.

Originally the venture was logistically simple. Echoing a Vietnam action of ten years before, in which people blockaded an ammunition ship, resisters in hand-built rowboats were to stop the sub at a narrow bridge near the mouth of Hood Canal. The Coast Guard would undoubtedly clear them out of the way. But the *Ohio* would not pass unchallenged.

With the closure of the canal, things changed. The rowboats were neither sufficiently fast nor seaworthy enough to get in front of the sub on open water. The blockade faced a major crisis until first the *Peacemaker* and later the *Lizard* decided to participate. But the involvement of two $100,000 boats meant the seamanship of Ted and Bill became nearly as important as the commitment of the "ordinary" blockaders. And paramilitary strategy at times almost overshadowed moral purpose.

By Thursday, August 5th, the blockade flotilla was based in Oak Bay, immediately north of the eighteen-mile Hood Canal restricted zone. The zone would not be in effect until announced, and the Coast Guard swore they'd give ample warning. But the blockaders only knew the *Ohio* had passed through the Panama Canal, that it was due in at any point, and would run on the surface and during the day. Worrying about preemptive arrest, and wanting to ensure the sub would not slip through unnoticed, they stayed outside the area the Coast Guard would close, posted spotters at key vantage points, used walkie talkies to communicate, and funneled information to an ex-Poseidon sailor for analysis. They created a communications center, a spider's maze of antennas and aerials, in the attic of a Victorian home in Port Townsend, a small seatown fifteen miles away. Inside, support people monitored Coast Guard air traffic and took media calls from Seattle and Los Angeles, New York, Vancouver, and Australia.

The ex-Poseidon sailor—who people treated with awe because he'd served in the devil's sanctuary—was far from the only person with maritime experience in a blockade where knowledge of winds and tides was at times as important as moral understanding.

Bill Ethell, the *Peacemaker*'s skipper, grew up in a northern England fishing port, in a home with seven adults, two children, and no inside toilet. His father worked with the other men on the local trawlers, facing arctic nights with force-ten gales, and rigging wires seven inches thick with ice. Half the men chopped the ice build-up so their ships would not keel over from the weight; the others gutted fish with frostbitten fingers, balancing on the wet and pitching decks.

Bill ran with a gang of children who, like him, watched their fathers pummel their mothers, usually in drunken frustration at humiliations levied by the respectable owners, magistrates and solicitors. Their schools only taught kings and queens, popes, prime ministers and generals—how Britain built an empire by civilizing the foreign savages. No teacher mentioned the history of trade unions or the Labor Party, massacres in colonial Africa and India—or how the British fishing industry belonged to a few wealthy men and had an accident rate four times higher than underground mining.

Bill and his friends passed their time fighting, stealing motorbikes, and dodging the police. But the endless scrapping got boring. Bill's father said if he stayed in the village he'd end up trapped like him. So at age fifteen Bill enlisted in the Royal Navy, hoping to see the world, learn a trade, and spend his free time water-skiing. The Navy turned out mostly to be endless miles of purposeless orders.

After nine years Bill bought his way out of the twelve-year contract and moved to Australia with his wife Lorraine, a veteran of the Women's Royal Naval Service. He became a bricklayer, and got involved in union politics. In 1976, the United States proposed establishing a Trident support base close to the home the Ethells had built near Perth—suddenly placing them on the atomic front lines. Bill and Lorraine started working with local peace efforts, then took on the broader goal of a nuclear-free Pacific.

Ted Phillips also joined the Royal Navy, volunteering at age seventeen in 1951, similarly hoping to get away and find a career. He wanted to protect England against the kind of tyranny that killed his two brothers during the World War II. Ted's wife Eve spent two years in the women's branch. The blockade group included two other Navy veterans, a commercial diver, and several others with maritime backgrounds. Ted might not have come forward had he been unable to offer his particular skills and twenty years of experience. The demands of the sea proved to be both a challenge and a bond.

It was perhaps because of this experience that Ted and Bill came to be viewed as experts not only on sailing and navigation, but on every aspect of the blockade. "They call me captain," Bill said, "or ask, jokingly, 'What shall we do now skipper?' We talk a lot about democracy, equality, and participation. But we're awfully glad to surrender choices to anyone who we think knows better than we do. It's something a lot of middle-class people still haven't gotten over."

Although the *Peacemaker* had a good many nuns, former priests, and other religious individuals on board, its blockaders were at first somewhat condescending towards the pious lizards. Some teased about the Christians drinking grape juice following afternoon practice, while they downed Jim Beam. Though Bill respected Ted's marinership and courage, at times he wondered "If he's gotten rid of all the Royal Navy blood and iron."

Aboard Ted's bright yellow trimaran, the lizards painted names on their boats—signs to inspire and sustain them. Jim Douglass, cofounder of Ground Zero, named his after the Trappist monk and nonviolent theorist Thomas Merton, others after friends and inspirational figures. The mood here was more serious than on the *Peacemaker*, more concerned with honing vision and spirit to the keenest possible edge. The lizards drank less and prayed more, although they also joked about heading to the Bahamas, and one floated happily alongside on an innertube. *The Lizard* was an ideal boat for any South Sea sojourn, with a forty-eight-foot main hull of foam and fiberglass, and, separated by a nylon trampoline, two outrigger floats. Ted designed every space, including minute storage niches and a drying rack that used excess stove heat to air out damp clothes. He built the boat in an English fishing village called Lizard, then sailed with his wife Eve and their two sons along the trade winds route, through the Panama Canal, and up the coast to British Columbia, where he set up his own marine repair yard.

Ted hadn't intended to directly blockade, just to build the little lizards and ferry them down. A dozen years before, he was finishing his twenty-year sojourn in the Navy and dismissing those who marched each year on Britain's Aldermaston atomic weapons lab as Communists, cranks, and pseudo-intellectuals, who failed to recognize the harsh world in which Hitler had invaded Europe and Britain had almost gone under. Yet Ted was moved when he saw mothers pushing babies in their carriages in demonstrations; he learned enough from the papers to attend a massive anti-Vietnam rally and read the sheafs of leaflets distributed by a hundred radical groups. It outraged him that the United States dropped far more bombs on North Vietnam alone than on all of Europe during World War II. He began studying social change, drawn to Che Guevara because of Guevara's passion for justice, then decided that violent revolutions inevitably turned on the ordinary citizens they ostensibly sought to serve. In Canada he wrote letters and attended meetings of Vancouver Island's Campbell River Peace Group, and it was at a Campbell River meeting that he saw a videotape of rowboats being constructed for the blockade.

Ted called Jim Douglass and said he'd make ten boats in his Quadra Island marine yard. Eve said, "You won't do anything stupid will you?" Though he assured her he would not, when he reached Hood Canal and saw participants from across the globe and all walks of life, he decided to risk his liberty and *The Lizard*.

To prepare dinner for Ted and for herself, Eve went to the local supermarket and bought pork chops, eggs, milk, mushrooms, and peppers, all of which the Coast Guard could confiscate—along with the boat—if they weren't consumed by the time the *Ohio* arrived. But Ted wasn't worrying about the excess food, or any of his belongings or tools. *The Peacemaker* crew, seeing no reason for their possessions to disappear down the gullet of Uncle Sam, unloaded everything they could. But Ted left his future to the fates. If the Coast Guard took it all, they'd have to write receipts for the eggs and chops, for his sweaters and socks, books, binoculars, wrenches, razors . . . and for a $100,000 fiberglass trimaran.

While Eve fried the pork chops, Ted showed me the oval doorways, rear sleeping quarters, cabinets squeezed in every free corner, and instruments carefully positioned to safeguard them from the spray of the sea. The vessel's interior decoration was spare—a bark rubbing of a flower, a pennant from the Lizard Regatta in the town where the trimaran was built, and a cloth banner with the words "Resist Trident," the outline of a dove, and calico rowboats blocking a dark submarine. In terms of elegance and function, Ted's vessel was immaculate, and he told me how awed he was by another machine, one "which can send missiles from under the sea into the heavens, then drop them halfway around the world within a few hundred feet of wherever we choose." Aside from Trident's terminal implications, he thought that not even the finest racing car possessed more technological beauty.

When a Canadian journalist came aboard, Ted chastised the man for headlining his article "Peace Guerrillas" and attributing to him the journalist's own metaphor about the little boats being "bullets from God."

"Look, I'm a straight guy," Ted kept repeating. "I just want people to be straight with me."

The journalist defended himself and said he didn't write the headlines. Ted repeated, "I'm happy to have you aboard. You're welcome to a beer. But I just want to tell you I'm angry."

The problem, Ted explained, was that the military metaphors confused things by linking the blockade with violent acts. He'd always admired Che Guevara, still did, but Che "was a gentleman guerrilla, not like these people who blow up old ladies on trains." And Ted definitely didn't like getting confused with them.

Ted quoted Christ's statement that the hurt suffered by the least of his brothers was suffered by him. "You know, I'd really like to get to know Darla," he said, referring to a twenty-eight-year-old blockader on *The Lizard* who'd been paralyzed from the waist down in an auto accident six-and-a-half years before. "I think she'd have a lot to teach me." He mentioned the statement of some philosopher, "I don't remember who, but he said we know a society best by visiting its prisons, hospitals, skid rows, and all those other places the comfortable never see.

"That's why I didn't like Disney films," Ted laughed. "They're this imitation having nothing to do with life. I remember when I was a kid watching Bambi and wondering why I didn't feel anything when his mother died, and the big tears rolled down his face, bloop, bloop, bloop. Then I read some left-wing magazine saying Disney was responsible for more fake images than anyone else in the world. I decided they just might be right."

This irreverence towards Disney was unexpected from a theological fundamentalist whose bedside table contained not only one of Jim Douglass's books on liberation theology, but also the newest work by Hal Lindsey, author of the apocalyptic classic "The Late Great Planet Earth." Even some of the *Peacemaker*'s nuns joked about Ted's holy crusade, but no one questioned his sincerity or directness.

His religion mattered, as did pride in craft and marinership, belief in work, honesty, and compassion. As with Bill Cusak and Mary Mills, Marty Coleman and Levon Hucks, faith pushed him to challenge a worldly authority he had once accepted.

Because Canadian TV was coming and he'd been wearing nothing but blue running shorts, Ted said "Guess I'd better put on some underwear to look respectable," and went into the rear cabin to change.

When the TV crew arrived, Ted asked them their feelings about nuclear war. They said it frightened them, but they had to be objective on camera, and they'd come down because the blockade would be an excellent picture story. After citing specifics on the *Ohio*'s first-strike capabilities and destructive power, Ted called the sub "the embodiment of Satan."

Granted, he'd just finished explaining in a very nonapocalyptic fashion how the blockade was only one small action, and how the important thing was "that Ground Zero will be out there, just as usual, leafletting in front of Bangor next Thursday." But when he said, "there is so much spirituality here I just don't know what might happen," it was as if the waters of Hood Canal might part.

On Friday, August 6th, thirty-seven years after Hiroshima, the community breakfasted at 8:00 A.M. Volunteers used donated food and donated money, and cooked the meal inside a large portable yurt pitched on land lent by a sympathetic local resident. After eating eggs, oatmeal, and toast, people gathered in a circle, like Quakers in a spontaneous prayer meeting. They talked and read support letters from Scotland, Australia, and Holland, and one from the Trident Nein, a group who'd entered the Groton, Connecticut, Electric Boat yards, poured blood, and sprayed USS Auschwitz on the *Ohio*'s sister sub, the *Florida*.

Later, on the *Peacemaker*, Lorraine and Bill described how the idea for the boat was first suggested at a Nuclear-Free Pacific Conference in May 1980, which Bill attended as a delegate from the Building Workers. Working with a core group of other activists, they mortgaged their home and borrowed money from friends to raise an initial chunk of the $100,000 they needed to buy and outfit the boat; then spent nine months frantically scraping together further loans and contributions, and selling $250 shares to labor unions, churches, community organizations, and even groups of neighbors, workers, and students who chipped in $10 or $20 per person to do their part. Thousands of people owned the vessel.

In *Peacemaker's* first confrontation, in Waitangi, New Zealand, the police nearly threw Bill overboard. The crew sailed up an inlet to where governors, admirals, and other dignitaries were commemorating the transfer of native lands. The Maoris considered the treaties less a cause for celebration than for mourning. *Peacemaker* brought aboard several Maori leaders and broadcast their comments over three huge loudspeakers and over live radio, which beamed the event to all of New Zealand. The police boarded and made a few initial arrests, but backed off and let the *Peacemaker* go when told the boat's sponsors included Australia's major unions, largest religious denominations, and the deputy premier of New South Wales.

After meetings with groups up and down the New Zealand coast, the crew headed to Moruroa Atoll, where the French had been testing atomic weapons since 1966, after massive protests prevented them from using a site in the Sahara Desert. Boats had protested in the area before, including voyages into a nearby U.S. test zone twenty-five years before—which helped spur the U.S.-Soviet ban on aboveground atomic explosions—and a recent Greenpeace action challenging the French. But no one had entered the heart of French territorial waters or directly confronted those presently in charge of testing. *Peacemaker* sought to deliver a bilingual letter inviting the admiral responsible to come aboard for dinner and discuss nuclear tests in the region. Gendarmes from a French cutter refused to accept it. Therefore, *Peacemaker* continued sailing into one of the most radioactive areas in the world, reducing the risks by drinking only bottled water and thoroughly washing each pot, pan, and utensil against invisible contamination.

A short while later, a second cutter stopped them and warned against going further. They continued anyway, broadcasting to Australian radio via a live hookup. At night, helicopter searchlights raked their deck. The crew ate dinner on the stern, and the children waved at the French. The next day, just three miles from the atoll, a boat four times *Peacemaker's* size veered close, swung a huge crane across their deck, and severed the mizzenmast in two.

Quite likely, the goal of the attack had been to cut off the radio. But the aerial the French wanted was attached to the main mast, and they only knocked out the citizen's band and an old color TV. The French cutter then towed *Peacemaker* outside the twelve-mile limit.

After an hour and a half spent cutting rigging and dodging the wildly swinging broken mast in steep pitching seas, the crew continued safely into Tahiti harbor, where their boat was promptly seized by French police. Australian unions retaliated by refusing to move or unload the French freighter *Kangourou* as long as *Peacemaker* stayed captive. Postal workers threatened a ban on handling French mail, and the Pacific Trade Union Forum threatened boycotts on all French goods throughout the Pacific. In the meantime, Kangourou lost $28,000 a day in dead time and dock fees, and was risking its perishable cargo. After twenty-six days, French authorities capitulated and levied a token $200 fine, which was paid by a Tahiti minister. *Peacemaker* was freed to set course first for Hawaii and then for Bangor.

Win Olive, a sixty-four-year-old Australian, became part of the vessel's core crew when she retired, after forty years as a clerk and shop steward with the Metal Workers Union. Vigorous and tanned, with a lined face, close-cropped hair, and a deep unabashed laugh, Win wondered why we were "always run by what we dread instead of by what we want." She thought joining *Peacemaker*'s journey was "much more delightful than sitting down worrying about the nuclear future," and said a planned film of the voyage should include "dolphins, Maoris, swims, songs, nude bathing on deck and all the things that bring this society down—but not quite quick enough." In New Zealand she stayed up all hours dancing "to punk rock" at a club with Bill, Lorraine and several other crew-members. Interviewed on "Good Morning Sydney," she scolded herself afterwards for "looking so serious, never cracking a smile." She said, laughing, that she never had gotten used to Australian leftist meetings, "even though I've been going to them for forty years. They always outline the same impossible aims in the last five minutes, even though they do seem to be achieving a few." Comparing *Lizard* and *Peacemaker*, she explained that she wasn't too religious, and didn't "like to put labels on belief."

"It seems lots of them have a very strong faith," she continued, "and there've been so many very dedicated people who've done all that prison time. I don't know about all their prohibitions or saying you're coming here for sacrifice and death. Maybe that almost invites it, which doesn't appeal to me, even though there are a lot of them who have such maturity and commitment. I feel I'm in it more for the feeling we had at Waitangi: standing up to the military and being part of something with other people who support you. I've never been arrested and I hope my nerves hold when it happens. But I'm doing this because I bloody well enjoy it."

Bill returned to the helm, eating a sandwich and wearing a blue vest given to him by a Seattle Machinist's local. He described how much this voyage differed from his time in the Navy. There, work had seemed eternally purposeless, so he logged his hours, served his time, and risked as little of himself as possible. Here, even during storms that flayed and soaked him, with waves crashing over the bow and the wind hammering torn sails like the fire of a light machine gun, he loved it because the journey mattered.

He described how he first got involved in politics through an old Jewish radical in the Australian Building Trades union. "I used to worry about burnout," he said, "but I'd talk with that guy who'd been doing it for fifty-five years. The lesson here is tenacity, not death or glory. Throwing yourself on the deck of a Trident doesn't mean much unless you do it again and again."

Bill often referred to activists a hundred years ago, who—at least in the noncolonized European world—ended the horrors of four-year-olds working sixteen hours a day in lace factories, brass foundries, and cotton mills; and who opposed the sweat shops, brutal mine-pits, and rotting houses where children died of consumption before age ten. People talked these days about apathetic populations, and being too beleaguered to fight, but what apathy and resistance did the early agitators face? If they could make inroads against this extreme misery and degradation, Bill thought, surely we, possessing far more choices and far greater comfort, could put up with confusion, anxiety, frustration, and fear in order to change a situation in which, given the proper circumstances, "one lunatic can send the whole of Eastern, Western, tribal, nomadic, underdeveloped, overdeveloped—the whole bloody lot of human civilization up in a puff of smoke."

Yet Bill's concerns went beyond abstract talk of a need for peace. He still asked who took the bruises and who got fat; he saw the atomic threat, for all its universal implications, as one in which some made fortunes producing mechanisms of mass annihilation and others, "the bricklayers, boilermakers, and candlestick makers," ended up "on the front lines to get the chop." He remembered being a fourteen-year-old Sea Cadet in a chapter founded by a man whose father owned one of Britain's largest fishing fleets. The founder, a man named Basil Parks, began the group during World War II but, like the rest of the major industrialists, stayed far from the front lines, and made further millions running the show back home.

When Parks visited the chapter in his silver Rolls Royce to review the sons of his workers, Bill thought of how casually this man's company decimated the town each time they decided the market wasn't right and cut back their fleet, and of an uncle who'd died shortly before, when the ship he fished on went down with all hands. Bill wanted to kick Sir Basil in the balls.

Later Bill found an essay by nineteenth-century critic Thomas Carlyle that articulated his rage at these polite respectable individuals who barely noticed the lives they stunted and destroyed:

> To my own knowledge, there dwell and toil, in the British village of Dumdrudge, usually some 500 souls. From these . . . there are successively selected, during the French war, say 30 able bodied men . . . They are shipped away . . . some two thousand miles . . . And to that same spot are [brought] thirty similar artisans, from a French Dumdrudge . . . Straightaway the word fire is given . . . and in place of sixty brisk useful craftsmen, the world has sixty dead carcasses, which it must bury, and anew shed tears for.
>
> Had these men any quarrel? Busy as the devil is, not the smallest! . . . How then? Simpleton! Their governors had fallen out; and instead of shooting one another, had the cunning to make these poor blockheads shoot.

It seemed, Bill said, that the governors no longer needed to send the villagers a thousand miles to kill and die. Instead, they sent the bombs, and no one could evade them. But the Sir Basils and their emulators continued to rule much as in Carlyle's time: living high while breeding cataclysms from World Wars I and II and the Stalinist purges to Vietnam, South Africa, and Trident's annihilatory threat. Parallel systems of power kept people blinded and subjected. And unless individuals were willing to directly challenge the social orders through which these men enact their will, Bill felt that all talk of peace, gentle living, and universal communion would be so much self-indulgent dreaming.

Bill wasn't sure what would stop either the atomic era's ultimate violence or more muted carnage like that which drove his father and the other Lancastershire fishermen to their drunken rages. Perhaps the Sir Basils would have to be kicked, threatened, and confronted before they'd surrender the wealth, privilege, and property amassed through the labors of others. He admired Gandhi's achievements, yet thought most pacifists and spiritual activists judged class and labor politics to be too messy and ungenteel, preferred to smooth over direct-interest conflicts. He joked repeatedly about being "a meat-eating atheist among Christian vegetarians." But Bill also acknowledged the need for change to be "more than just the emotional revenge of the oppressed." Although he savored spy novels and thought he'd make a pretty good technological terrorist, his point was to make people understand Trident, not physically attack it. He retained compassion for the *Ohio*'s ordinary sailors, because he remembered "being a young raw kid in the Royal Navy."

"No way does the Coast Guard know what we'll do," he concluded with a broad grin that recalled dodging behind walls and hedgerows to outwit the Lancastershire police, "because we don't ourselves. They can handle either Ted's discipline or our unpredictability, but with both together they'll never stand a chance."

The communications center interrupted to announce an unusual number of Coast Guard boats off Dungeness Spit, a long point thirty miles towards the entrance of the sound. "Be calm, more information forthcoming," the radio voice continued, but nothing developed. *Peacemaker* was stripped now, the crew's personal belongings stored in the garages of sympathetic Port Townsend residents. "We're almost like the Doukhobors," explained Dan Delaney, and told me about the Canadian religious pacifists who burn their houses and strip themselves naked when the authorities try to levy taxes. He talked as well about Archbishop Hunthausen, now almost an activist celebrity in Washington State. Though Hunthausen's demeanor was more that of a kindly grandfather than an angry Jeremiah, his moral passion and positions on the arms race had elevated him from an ordinary resister to a symbolic shepherd whose role was to point the way. People wore buttons, displaying miniature hearts, saying "I love Hunthausen." The archbishop became an international figure when he called Trident "the Auschwitz of Puget Sound" and made public his tax-resistance decision.

Hunthausen's actions and the attendant ripples came only after years of dialogue with local church people, including Jim Douglass—who he visited and offered mass for during one of Douglass's numerous jail sentences—and fellow blockaders Jon Nelson and Charley Meconis. Jon, a husky Lutheran minister with a silver beard and booming Norwegian laugh, had been jailed twice for Trident actions, and had to leave his family of eleven children, five of whom were adopted. He relaxed now on the *Peacemaker* deck, talking with Dan Delaney and Charley Meconis, a thirty-seven-year-old former priest who taught comparative religion at a local Seattle college, headed an ecumenical peace group called SERPAC, and held a Friday afternoon "Bogart bar" to commemorate the spirit of *Casablanca* and help friends and fellow activists stay sane. Charley had already been jailed for four months for going over the fence at the Bangor base, participated in a 1972 draft board raid, and written a book, *With Clumsy Grace*, on the Catholic left. He listened while Jon talked about Hunthausen's strength and integrity—beginning in the Vietnam era when, as Bishop of Montana, he ignored the polished silver and polite jazz masses of the official University of Montana Newman Center, and instead went out to talk with demonstrating students.

"He talked with the students," Jon repeated, "and got the university's Catholic president to oppose the war. Instead of the place being torn apart, they turned it into a peace and justice learning center." Now, Washington State activists were building an equivalent community, and local Lutheran ministers had recently voted two to one to support nuclear civil disobedience. "That isn't like church leaders who make fire and brimstone speeches about peace, and then suggest bilateral disarmament as their grand solution," Jon said. "They don't crank it all up for a little drop of rabbit turd at the end."

Jon laughed a lot for someone who'd clearly receive one of the heaviest sentences. He said in jail he felt uncompromised, "because on the street it's far easier to cheat." And that it was ironic "that if we fail to reverse the threat there'll be no one left to say 'I told you so.'"

Jon continued, describing Jubilee, Isaiah's Old Testament vision of a moratorium every seven years, where debts were forgiven, land returned to its original holders, slaves freed, and fields left fallow. It was a model of revolution, of the peaceable kingdom, of Martin Luther King's "beloved community." Christ, according to Luke, said it could be brought about by vulnerability, love, and learning to suffer—as Nelson said, "by little children praying in the Birmingham, Alabama, streets against the fire hoses of Bull Connor."

"I don't know," said Charley. "Sometimes I feel we're in a race between this unchecked technical rationality—and Trident is an amazing achievement—and our ability to develop new forms of nonviolent resistance. We tried a bit in the sixties, but not like this. It's an almost desperate effort to prevent the world's two greatest empires from bringing the whole house down."

"So what do they have to fear?" laughed Dan. "That we will out PR them to the American people by challenging their 560-foot submarine with twelve-foot wooden dinghies?"

Charley wasn't sure, but thought those with a vested interest in the military state were beginning to worry they would lose the uncritical support "of troublesome sectors—labor, churches, whatever." He didn't like using military analogies, but felt those engaged in civil disobedience were "the commandos hitting the beach and taking the heat." Groups like his religious action coalition, SERPAC, had spent the past ten years trying to build bridges between the few who'd climb a fence or block a sub and the many who might back those actions with milder, less risky work.

This bond was being forged in Seattle's religious community. The lawsuit against the security zones had been brought by nine interfaith leaders; other plaintiffs included the American Civil Liberties Union, several Hood Canal residents, and the Church Council of Greater Seattle. The day before the blockade, witnesses on a support boat included not only Hunthausen, but also the local heads of the Lutherans, American Baptists, United Church of Christ, Washington Association of Churches, and Washington State Catholic Conference, as well as nationally prominent rabbi.

Like the South Carolina Presbyterians who argued whether they had a right to work for peace in more than just "the self, family and congregation," Seattle's religious leaders faced a choice between opposing the weapons or ignoring their implications and sequestering the highest ideals of their faith. A hundred years ago, American labor activists used similar religious language to sanction their challenge to an entrenched economic order. Union papers stressed how Christ drew his disciples not from the wealthy but from common fishermen, carpenters, and sailors. The Industrial Workers of the World (IWW) called Christ "Jerusalem Slim," making him the prototype itinerant organizer. Even the conservative American Federation of Labor described Jesus as "scattering the table of the money changers in the temples . . . going down in the poverty-stricken alleys of the robbed industrial slaves, and raising up [the] victims."

Biblical messages will always remain ambiguous: just as the Eastminster elders pushed Congaree to confine peace-making to its narrowest definitions, so nineteenth-century business leaders insisted moral and personal considerations were entirely separate from economic activity, and even claimed that those possessing massive wealth were divinely ordained. The dominant theology spoke largely of enduring earthly travails for a later place in heaven—the sentiments mocked by IWW poet Joe Hill in his classic line, "You'll get pie in the sky when you die." Yet, as historian Herbert Gutman says, religion often provides the activists with common vision, by offering "values that transcend the particular social order they criticize."

This vision, however, was not one always taken up by church institutions. More frequently in U.S. history, the *Bible* and the gun have marched hand in hand in taming the frontier and subduing the savages; faith's most visionary call has drawn only a small group of individuals willing to embrace what Dietrich Bonhoeffer has termed the cost of discipleship. Yet in an era when humans face potentially terminal threats—and the end of all creeds, moral beliefs, and promised futures—churches are being drawn increasingly towards at least nascently addressing human survival.

Ground Zero's Jim Douglass writes of journeys into powerlessness, and quotes Jesus saying that "anyone who wants to save his life will lose it; but anyone who loses his life for my sake, and for the sake of the gospel, will save it." Douglass cites this passage as a call for the radical change of mind and heart termed *metanoia*, a renunciation of both our grasping and ego-bound selves and of external idols like the goods of a runaway consumer society, or the security of atomic weapons that some have called "Gods of Metal." Although many of the religious blockaders undertook their own "long march through the institutions," working in particular churches and congregations, they retained a notion that institutional support might always be transient and ephemeral—that what mattered more was following the acknowledgedly demanding paths of truth and faith. In a book entitled *Resistance and Contemplation*, Douglass quoted the judgment of Thomas Merton that "we can no longer rely on being supported by structures which may be destroyed at any moment by a political power, or political force. . . . They are good, and they should help us, and we should do the best we can with them. . . . [But] if everything is taken away, what do you do next?"

Merton's questions echo ones raised by Bonhoeffer in an essay, "Who Stands Fast," written from a prison cell while awaiting execution in Hitler's Germany. Bonhoeffer described the common failure of the responsible people who "think that with a little reason they can bend back into position the framework that has got out of joint"; of those who rely on an abstract force of conscience, who are approached by evil "in so many respectable and seductive disguises that [their] conscience becomes nervous and vacillating"; and of those who trust private virtue, keeping themselves "pure from the contamination arising from responsible action," and end up shattered by internal disquiet, or entrenched as "the most hypocritical of Pharisees." True strength, Bonhoeffer said, came only from "the man whose final standard is not his reason, his principles, his conscience, his freedom or his virtue, but who is ready to sacrifice all this when he is called to obedient and responsible action in faith and in exclusive allegiance to God."

Just as Bill Cusak broadened his notion of salvation to suggest that vision and sustenance could come not only from specifically Christian language, but from acting "in the Jesus way," one might consider Bonhoeffer's statement a call less for a particular theological creed than for some trust in a broader transcendent whole. His words warn of a need for resisters to root themselves in forces larger than their individual lives—or risk succumbing to the awesome powers they seek to confront.

Even among the committed Christians, beliefs varied from person to person. Some envisioned an all-powerful God, a being who could respond to particular prayers and act directly in the world. Others, like Charley Meconis and Jon Nelson, believed God moves in history, but through human agency, truth, and conscience—not, as Charley put it, "like some heavenly phone operator" responding to individual petitioners.

For those for whom God is truth, religious traditions offer hope, "not from God coming down and cleaning everything up," as Charley explained; but rather, "from a promise that if we answer the call of conscience our actions won't go for naught."

This feeling sustained Charley during an earlier jail term—four months in the federal prison at Lompoc, California, for climbing the Bangor fence in October 1979. Charley hadn't intended to be an in-prison resister, but when he looked at the packing crates from the furniture factory where he was assigned, he discovered they were headed for—of all places—Bangor. To support the very base where he'd been arrested seemed unconscionable. Like Jeff Dietrich facing jail for the Anaheim Arms Bazaar, Charley thought about Christ's statement, "Father, if it be possible, let this cup pass from me; nevertheless not as I will but as thou wilt," and its mandate to uphold true ethics whatever the costs. He explained to the prison officials that he could not make the furniture, and waited, knees shaking, for the penalty.

But Charley's action did have an impact. When the warden asked in worried tones if he was planning to lead a strike, Charley realized the authorities were more frightened than he was. They relegated him to the pig farm, the only white they'd ever placed there, but its black Muslim prisoners vowed to protect him and even had him address their group on nuclear issues. Where once the inmates had viewed Charley as the freak who entered prison by choice, they now began to respect him.

Charley was sustained in his act by the belief that faith would be answered, though probably not in any direct fashion. For secular activists, no forgiving (or judging) presence will respond to their act of witness. They ground themselves instead on their connection to human community, to the complex order of the natural world, and to the interdependence embodied in Bob Willard's notion that "it seems wrong to eat the grain but never water it. It feels better to participate." They act from what Marv Davidov called "a hunger for justice," the moral and political commitment necessary "to be a dignified human being" in an age of global barbarism, and because in Win's words, involvement is ultimately "much more delightful" than denial or retreat.

But whether the blockade participants were secular or religious, their efforts were not undertaken in isolation. They received emotional backing from the Australian unions, whose organizers reminded Win that *Peacemaker* was in part their boat, and promised they'd help again just as they had following Moruroa; from Trident Nein and other groups who broke statutory laws in the face of a higher urgency; from kinship with a global activism that challenged the global threat. Help came in more immediate ways as well, from people who worked to keep the lizards and ducklings on the water.

Supporters from Vancouver, Seattle, and California cooked in the yurt camp and brought food down to Oak Bay each morning and night. In Port Townsend's cooperatively run Salal Cafe, cards on each table advertised a nearby support rally. Workers at a local bakery covered the shift of the blockade's media center coordinator. Citizens never involved in dissident politics found ways to participate.

But it wasn't only Port Townsend residents who helped. Despite a twenty-five percent local unemployment rate brought on by the collapse of the logging industry, people throughout Washington's Olympic Peninsula donated or lent walkie-talkies, wet suits, and life jackets; brought meat, eggs, and vegetables to the yurt camp cooks; and greeted *Lizard* and *Peacemaker* with brownies, coffee cakes, and freshly cut flowers. A Navy wife washed and ironed the *Peacemaker* laundry. A blue-blood Republican lent a portable heater; and a teen-ager pumping gas at a marina chipped in $2.50 to help fuel the tank of a Zodiac. Even the woman whose Volkswagon van displayed a large "Welcome Ohio" sign gave bread and water (Oak Bay had no drinking fountains) because she felt it her "Christian duty."

This left the blockaders free from routine claims and distractions— even though one lizard dropped his wallet while circling an incoming Polaris sub and had to call VISA to explain that his credit card now rested at the bottom of Oak Bay. But even as they sought to affect and preserve human history, they became exempted, as if on a holiday, from some of that history's mundane pull.

From one perspective the involvement of the blockade supporters was a waste. What massive human energy was expended just to delay the *Ohio* fifteen minutes in the channel. But the effort did not play on the field of accountants' balance sheets, but on that of prophetic conscience. It drew people who previously feared dissent, connected them with the blockaders and with each other. It spurred further thought and action.

Although media coverage from the blockade at least briefly reached viewers and listeners across the country, the action had the most profound impact on those possessing personal bonds with the lizards and ducklings. As with the Honeywell arrests, friends, neighbors, relatives, and fellow employees were forced to ask why individuals they knew and respected risked loss of status, jobs, and liberty. Here on the Hood Canal, the stakes were acknowledgedly higher: months or years of jail, and a consequent separation from everything constituting the blockaders' ordinary worlds. One's acquaintances might not choose to respond on the same level of personal risk; might rather treat the action as a call to work, for all they were worth, in some other fashion. But habitual distancing mechanisms—turning the page, changing the subject, trusting opposing experts, or escaping to cynicism—could occur only at the cost of at least a small personal betrayal.

Much as the Oak Bay mariners proceeded apart from many day-to-day concerns, to the degree they were rooted in their communities, their actions created a pull similar in its intimacy to more conventional village politics—created this pull as a general call of conscience. But could most Americans jeopardize their freedom to the same extent as the *Ohio* blockaders? For all their diverse backgrounds— for all their ties to children, grandchildren, and complex webs of human culture—most blockaders either led a somewhat precarious economic existence or, like ministers Meconis and Nelson, had substantial discretionary control over the conduct of their work. One could conceivably spend a two-week vacation from Boeing or Honeywell on Hood Canal, but a jail term or even a trial would hardly help career security. Civil disobedience is far more costly in a society in which most people are hired employees, profoundly circumscribed as to how their time and skills are used; in which, by contrast to societies like Gandhi's agrarian India, friends and family cannot pitch in to tend the crops when one is jailed. The only solutions are to accept repeated moves from job to job, to be self-employed, or for unions or other occupational organizations to win the right for members to take time off for prison.

This last demands, once more, that ordinary workers be able to speak on concerns broader than wages and hours. Much as Bill Ethell considered his union leaders overwhelmingly bureaucratic drones, labor organizations purchased over a third of the *Peacemaker* shares, and the vessel was launched by the head of his national trade union council. Australia has a heritage of major strikes over broad political issues, including the 1938 refusal of New South Wales dockworkers to load pig-iron destined for a militarily expansionist Japan; the 1946 refusal to load Indonesia-bound ships and help the Dutch suppress a nationalist uprising; and the "Green Bans" levied by the Builders and Laborers Union on projects judged environmentally unaccept- able. The newspaper of Win's Amalgamated Metal and Foundry Workers ran stories on Chile, Greenham Common, and acid rain. Major unions waged a protracted fight against uranium mining and exporting, employing a variety of boycotts, bans, refusals to handle machinery destined for the mines, and even a nationwide rail strike.

The notion that institutions should support individuals who resist illicit governmental action was raised in a different context when Jon Nelson asked that his expected jail term for the Trident protest be considered a half-pay sabbatical from his post as a University of Washington campus minister. His church had recently sanctioned civil disobedience against atomic weapons, and Nelson received the backing of local Lutherans and the five-state Northwest Synod. But the national body, the Lutheran Council USA, refused both direct support and Jon's modified request for a token $10 salary to represent an ethical commitment. After much debate, the council explained that, while they supported Nelson's "personal act of conviction," they could not see the blockade "as a corporate act of the ministry."

When Daniel Berrigan heard about the decision, he sent Jon a $200 check with a note saying, "The oligarchy of the church has reneged; here is some non-reneged support." Other people found out through ecumenical publications or word of mouth, and money and pledges of help came from groups and individuals in Houston and Boston, Albuquerque, Cleveland, and Chicago—from cities and towns in twenty-five states. Support came from sympathetic min- istries in Brazil, Sweden, and eight other countries; from a congre- gation in Hiroshima; and from one of Nelson's former jailers, who promised, with his wife, to canvass their Seattle neighborhood. Jon received over $4,000 in direct gifts, and enough pledges to last through whatever sentence would be imposed.

Archbishop Hunthausen has stated that wealth separates our cul- ture from the fundamental human truths; he also suggested that the government would inevitably impoverish those who seriously op- posed it. Kim Wahl, the nurse and doctor's wife, thought at length about what this meant in terms of risking middle-class respectability. She grew up in Chicago, then worked as a military nurse in Walter Reed Hospital in Washington, D.C., where she tended the brash paratroop lieutenants and dignified generals. After moving to Seattle, she raised her children and assisted her husband in his medical practice. She thought little about politics until, in 1978, she came across Robert Jay Lifton's book on Hiroshima survivors, *Death in Life*. She read works on Vietnam and Hemingway's *A Farewell to Arms*. She learned about the Honeywell cluster bombs—designed to so maim the Vietnamese that National Liberation Front soldiers would have the burden of carrying their wounded—and wondered whether her Walter Reed generals, so aristocratic even in their hospital gowns, had ordered them commissioned.

Kim's new knowledge paralyzed and disturbed her. She discussed her reading with her husband and their son, who was exploring much of the same material through an international studies program at college. For a while they did nothing more. Kim felt almost as she had during the final days of Vietnam—sympathizing with the marchers, yet holding back to remain no more than a shy observer. But now her urgency was greater, even if it brought in its wake periodic surges of helplessness. When disarmament forums began to proliferate, and Kim and her husband received invitations to the events of Physicians for Social Responsibility, she began to attend. Kim soon set up her first community meetings, apprehensive about the response in her comfortable suburb where it seemed half her neighbors worked on high-tech weapons components for Boeing, Honeywell, and the scores of Silicon Valley-style subcontractors. She displayed nuclear literature at the medical office she shared with her husband, and circulated Freeze petitions at shopping malls.

In January 1982, Kim attended a Catholic retreat at Ground Zero. Hunthausen spoke, and Jim and Shelley Douglass led workshops describing their community's ongoing outreach to Bangor employees and local residents. Kim watched a Hiroshima film and listened to the talk of a visiting hibakusha. Touring the base perimeter, she was photographed by security guards inside. Though the Douglasses briefly mentioned the blockade, Kim didn't think much about participating.

But Kim's commitment grew with her involvement. The previous year she kept finding excuses to avoid demonstrations—the last when two visiting priests convinced her to stay home and cook them dinner instead. Having sworn she'd never hold herself back again, she started talking with all her friends, pushing her church for peace education workshops, serving as a pro-peace delegate to the state Democratic convention, and even witholding a modest amount of taxes to protest military spending. When she and Bill drove to Seattle for a blockade meeting, they froze when reached the cafe where it was held, and instead of entering, stared through the glass, wondering what thresholds they flirted with crossing. A few days later Kim listened to a tape of Hunthausen speaking. He talked of the choice between the Kingdom of God—a nuclear-free world—and annihilation, of how humans could fight for life in the midst of preparation for holocaust, and of how responding to the atomic threat would require far more than a change of political leaders. She visited a friend, a single mother with a thirteen-year-old daughter, who had served two months for going over the Bangor fence. She thought of her neighbors, and how they prayed for peace in Lebanon, Asia, or anywhere their sentiments could be safely distanced. She feared the violence of jail, losing her nursing license, and separation from her family.

By the time Kim attended a June blockade retreat, she knew she was close to participating. Her last hesitation was that because she wasn't a star athlete or experienced mariner, she might endanger someone else on the water. But Jon Nelson called and asked if she wanted to be in the *SS Plowshares*, a motor launch that would carry Jon, Charley Meconis, Lutheran deaconess Grace Baranski, and Jon's mother, Ruth, with whom Jon would later participate in the initial Honeywell blockades. Remembering Hunthausen's admonition that evil had to be resisted regardless of consequences, Kim decided to accept the risks and go.

The blockade confounded stereotypes by mixing ministers and suburban nurses with activists who took life on the social and economic margins for granted. The group's two senior members could hardly have had more disparate pasts—sixty-four-year-old Win Olive and seventy-eight-year-old Ruth Nelson. Whereas Ruth carried a respectability commenserate with her 1973 title of National Mother of the Year, Win had always been a rebel bohemian. Ruth's brothers were governors and congressmen; Win joined the Australian Communist Party (she quit after "spending all my time fighting party bureaucrats"), and only later settled down to raise three children. Ruth believed in the family, holy matrimony, and the virtues of limits and restraint; Win wasn't "sure whether monogamy really does make sense," believed religion too often yoked and bound people, and felt lust was "actually quite a nice thing." She'd even spend four days, just before the blockade, resuming a torrid World War II affair with a man who now lived in Los Angeles.

But the ideals that drew Ruth and Win together overcame the variances in their backgrounds. Ruth had her own style and strength: becoming the first woman inducted into the Athletic Hall of Fame at Minnesota's Gustavus Adolphus College; meeting her minister husband by defeating him in a three-mile swimming race; helping integrate their Washington, D.C. church at a time when that was wholly unthinkable. Jon Nelson recalled her resolving a quarrel he and his sisters and brothers had with a neighbor woman, "by baking a bunch of brownies and sending us down with it. We kids were not happy with doing this, but it was amazing to see how disarming a tactic it was." As early as Hiroshima, Ruth knew "the thought of going out and obliterating people" had become "very obnoxious" to even imagine. And after visiting Jon in jail, "a very traumatic experience" that left her heart pounding, she realized why she had to join him in the next round.

At first Jon tried to dissuade her, but she said she'd risk being thrown into the cold waters of the canal. "I had to put my life on the line," she later explained. "That's the way I really felt. If I had to go to prison, I was willing to do that to say *no* to what the Trident represented." And when the government increased the sentences, she once more stated her refusal to be threatened or cowed.

It was this steadfastness that moved Marv Davidov to consider Ruth such a beacon of courage. Like Win, she believed it a gift to act for a cause that mattered so much. The two women talked about their children and grandchildren—Win's in Australia and Ruth's at the blockade—and the people who'd inspired them, like friends of Win's who were jailed in Japan for cutting loose a net to release 500 dolphins. When Ruth saw Win knitting, she said, laughing, "I wonder why I'm not back home where it's familiar and comfortable." They both had come far to risk so much.

On the day of the action, a Coast Guard sailor would aim a water cannon at Ruth and others in the *Plowshares*. Looking straight at him, she would point her finger and back him down, admonishing with all the prairie spirit she could muster, "No, no, young man. Not in my America, you wouldn't do that."

As Bill put it, the blockade included "both mystics and mechanics." The mystics, based largely on *The Lizard*, believed God's peaceable kingdom was postponed largely because people desired too much, and viewed Trident as this desire taken to an ultimate madness. They wrestled with their own ego and pride; strove to trust a spirit greater than themselves; and hoped to overcome the worldly seductions that blind us to the fundamental moral callousness of our course.

The mechanics acknowledged the same historical responsibility, but focused more on pragmatic political impact: writing press releases, building ties with support communities, and ensuring that strategies meshed with the needs of the moment. Worrying less about the rigor of their souls, the mechanics sometimes wondered, as Win said, whether those who talked of the happiness of individuals "persecuted in the cause of right," did so, at times, not only to explain their sources of sustenance and strength, but also to almost savor martyrdom as proof of true faith. Bill toyed with the ambiguities of revolutionary asceticism in an entry in the *Peacemaker*'s open journal, written between Waitingi and Mururoa:

> I've just put the dinner on, American corned beef hash with peas, followed by Michel's rice desert. Preceded by sherry, beer maybe, a dry white wine. Finishing up with port—then brandy and cigars for the women and a light red for the men as they wash up and put the kids to bed. I must get that washing done tomorrow. Lorraine would do it but she's researching the international bullion market and its effect on the North/South dialogue. Gai is composing a sonata and Mei is analyzing the political significance of contemporary radical Maori feminist poetry in relation to the developing consciousness of white middle class do gooders. . . . the Kinder are preparing an infant anarcho-syndicalist commune just above the mast, under the gaily colored banner of the 7th March revolutionary peoples liberation front of Neptune's 4th Republic. . . . It's one long round of self-sacrifice, this bloody protesting.

Bill liked his sensory pleasures, even if the voyage wasn't quite as idyllic as his tongue-in-cheek portrayal. He questioned the mystics' stress on our universal sin, guilt, and violence—what they called "the Trident within us." Compared to the Reagans, Thatchers, and Sir Basils, the blockaders and others who did their best to chart a different course were hardly the ones leading the planet to the edge of destruction. Bill chafed as well at the "middle-class notions" of many who considered themselves spiritually committed that things would be fine if we all learned to swim with the dolphins, listen to the whales, and find a personal peace.

Yet the mystics' witness was no inward retreat. "If one perceives, loves, and dies in private," Jim Douglass has written, "without protest and resistance to murder, then the public dimension is given over without contest to the rule of the technicians, and without dissent to everything their rule implies." Similarly, influential theologian Henri Nouwen has cautioned activists against "becoming so dominated by their fear of tomorrow that they miss the gift of the hour."

However, because the religious blockaders assumed some divine presence would respond to their commitment, and saw change coming through leaps of human spirit, they placed pursuing the path of truth above seeking to affect the latest congressional vote or political coalition. They hoped to reverse the course of weapons build-up through individual conversion, and through connecting with the fundamental forces that move the world. Jim Douglass cited a statement Philip Berrigan wrote from a jail cell: that he believed the "lowliest of draft resisters, buried anonymously in some federal prison, forgotten by everyone but parents and one or two friends," contributed "more to the building of peace than the most spectacular dove, who makes headlines and rallies supporters, and whose exhortations are heard with apprehension even in the halls of government." Douglass said the blockade should occur whether or not it got even a minute of media attention.

Just as the religious blockaders sometimes wondered whether their secular counterparts would be able to maintain their moorings and continue with strength, vision, and compassion when the task became hard and the penalties severe, so the mechanic's sensibility might judge notions of spiritual leaps as nice, but hardly enough on which to stake the future of the earth. Although NBC should not have the power to define public discourse, what would risk mean if no one heard?

Although those with transcendent faith might particularly be attracted to acts of witness, the Trident's blockaders fit few narrow categories. One could consider their differing cultural visions as embodying a spectrum of discontent with threats that would annihilate equally the sacred and profane. The actions of Douglass and other Ground Zero people spoke not only to God but also to the Bangor area community, with which they'd worked for over five years. And for all that the mechanics focused on popular outreach and political impact, sailing a steel ketch 11,000 miles to blockade a submarine could hardly be done without some vast leaps of faith.

Several nights into the blockade, the northern lights illuminated the sky. The moon shone orange and full above the firs and pines, surrounded by bright white stars. The blockaders watched as milky bands of ghost light danced and swirled, hanging in vertical streaks and rippling as they ascended through the dark. By Sunday, August 8th, the Oak Bay group had spent nearly a week on the water, and some began to joke whether, as Dan said, the *Ohio* was something "we made up the way some people still believe we never went to the moon." It was strange to focus so much effort on something they'd never seen, something whose potential impact they understood at most through the mediated images of films, histories and casualty projections. Yet those made uneasy by the weapons' implications might find a quite concrete inspiration in the extraordinary actions of this group that now risked ten years in jail.

Though the blockaders were eager to confront the *Ohio* directly, each day the Navy waited seemed in itself an interim victory. Continuing to read the signs of approach, people monitored the radio, tallied rumors from base employees, and sifted through various phoned-in tips. The Coast Guard brought forty boats off Dungeness Spit, and for a brief time everyone thought the *Ohio* would come that day. A local resident said Hood Canal was closed, but it turned out to be just a rumor. The Navy ordered 136 pounds of dress slacks to be pressed by Wednesday, and a sympathetic laundress passed on the word.

Meanwhile people waited. When a modified Polaris passed through, a two-person motor boat called *James Jordan* circled it, and *Peacemaker*, *Plowshares*, and *Lizard* came close; two sailors even waved. It felt strange letting pass unchallenged a sub whose loaded missiles could destroy millions, while the one people intended to stop would be empty. But the *Ohio*'s first-strike potential represented a new level of threat, a new escalation of an already terrifying era. And no one wanted to be picked off prematurely.

So they waited beneath a tropical sky, and Bill told of a blockade in Auckland harbor, where a man rode a surfboard onto the bow of a U.S. atomic sub.

By Monday, August 9th, with the *Ohio* due any day, a Bronx-born musician and actor who lived in Berkeley, staggered up at 5:15 A.M. exclaiming "Good morning, good fucking morning. That damn submarine better be coming in today or I'm going to be pissed."

Then he laughed, sang the old Rolling Stones song, "This may be the last time. . . . baby, the last time, I don't know," and told me, "My parents keep asking 'Isn't there anything else you can do?' "

Later that afternoon, aboard the *The Lizard*, someone asked Ted what would happen if the Coast Guard shielded the *Ohio* with log booms. "Lizzy can go over them with enough built-up speed," he answered. "We'd break our propeller and rudder, but under full steam we'd get through ok. . . . I don't want to attack Naval property, though," he said, pausing and grinning. "I want to go in front so they'll have to either stop or ram me."

"It's important what we do if we get in the water," Jim Douglass said, sitting quietly in an alcove. "There'll be men with carbines on deck and it's our chance to speak to them."

Bruce—who rowed everywhere in a lizard named after St. Dominic, and seemed as happy as anyone there—said he'd jump and swim if *Dominic* was seized. "At least there won't be guard dogs like at Livermore," said a former English graduate student from San Francisco. Other lizards joked about the CIA arming porpoises.

Terry, Darla's husband, wanted to board the *Ohio* by its slanted bow, and then offer the sailors communion bread.

Jim worried, "The submarine people may fear we have explosives."

"This is a zone of death," Terry insisted, "a place of darkness that I feel called upon to reclaim as a peaceable kingdom. There's always the chance of being shot. I would hope, though, that they'd see the truth and understand."

Ted thought it was "not a very nice gesture" for one mariner to board another's boat without permission.

The discussion continued, and David Host said people "shouldn't storm aboard like on the sands of Iwo Jima. . . . Maybe Terry could give a statement of intention, telling them 'I'm a Christian. I'm led here by the spirit,' explaining 'I'm coming aboard to break bread.' "

"I don't need to ask permission," Terry responded. "The Berrigans didn't knock politely before going in to the King of Prussia missile plant."

Darla whispered angrily to Terry that his obstinacy was disrupting the group. They tabled the issue after David cautioned about "seeking peak experiences."

Then Darla announced she'd be going in the water. There was more shock: because she was paralyzed, people said she risked drowning or being flayed by the eighteen-foot propeller. But she planned to wear both wet suit and life jacket, didn't expect to even get close to the sub. She wanted mostly "to give them one more person to deal with."

Not everyone prized the endless discussions. One quiet lizard felt he'd wandered into a therapy group. Dan Delaney said spiritual catharsis was great, "but after you stir up your ready-mix excitement you still have to come back down." For most, though, the talk seemed to strengthen resolve.

Bruce was in fine spirits at the evening campfire. He said he'd been thinking "that we leave and come into the the world naked, but I feel like right now we're clothed in some kind of grace." He repeated Jesus's final words, "Forgive them for they know not what they do," and said, "I don't think the Trident crew knows what they are doing either." He felt he was here "for love and truth and forgiveness."

Love and truth again. But how better could one express a desire for mutuality and caring—that encompasses even those presumed one's adversaries? Could better metaphors describe actions uncowed by fear and taken without expectation of reward?

Despite an American legacy stretching from the Boston Tea Party and Thoreau, to the 1960s Civil Rights Movement, nonviolent civil disobedience is a concept alien to most in our society. As a Coast Guard sailor said on the day of the *Ohio*'s arrival, "This isn't a question of peace, it's a question of authority." Or, if nonviolent protests do banish the specter of lawless chaos, resisters become viewed as prissy saints, presuming themselves holier than individuals less engaged.

Yet the aim of the blockade was not to take the stance of the eternal good kid, but to challenge a misplaced reverence. "What does America put its faith in?" Dan Delaney asked. "In missiles and warheads.

'God's nice,' they say, 'religion's nice, but you know realities are realities.' "

If the blockade opposed anything, it was this "nuclear idolatry," this blind trust enshrining our present course as an eternal future. Accepted forms of irreverence—like getting drunk and howling at the moon—only detach people from broader concerns, and remain purely personal and idiosyncratic. At their best, the blockaders rejected the presumed inevitability of weapons like Trident and refuted the notion that individuals threatened by governmental sanctions must inevitably succumb. Yet they also remained far from sanctimonious about their own role and mission.

At present, few will risk ten-year sentences, even when they believe atomic weapons will quite likely annihilate the world. Marv Davidov struggled over whether the crisis created by the Tridents and other new first strike systems was so grave and pressing that survival called for individuals to undertake more costly, felony-level, nonviolent disobedience. "The Berrigans may be right," Marv said. "All of us may have to turn to that too. I ask myself, am I afraid to do one year or five?" But he also listened to the voice that said he should continue working to involve as many people as possible— trying to spark the broadest, most massive possible nonviolent resistance campaign. At present, Davidov has made the latter choice, while treating the most costly actions as an inspiration and call. He had in fact preceded the initial Honeywell Project blockade by bringing Daniel Berrigan to address a 1,300 person audience at the premiere of a film based on his trial, along with his brother Philip and six others, for pouring blood and smashing missile nose cones inside the General Electric plant in King Of Prussia, Pennsylvania.

In his book on Solidarity, Lawrence Weschler quotes an unsigned *New Yorker* editorial explaining how the Poles took on, as a new principle of action, the task of creating for themselves what they wanted for their society. They wanted free elections, so they freely elected individuals; wanted free speech, so spoke freely; wanted a trade union, so founded one; began, through this process, to dissolve the foundations of an unwanted regime. Weschler goes on to describe how leaders of KOR, the workers' support movement, risked job loss or even prison by printing their names and phone numbers openly on the back of each mimeographed sheet describing incidents of police harassment against then-unknown activists like Lech Walesa. "It is as if," Weschler comments, "KOR were calling out to everyone else, 'Come on out! Be open. What can they do to us if we all start taking responsibility for our true dreams.' "

Although the coercive mechanisms that keep the United States a feeding ground for corporations like Rockwell, Boeing, and Honeywell differ somewhat from those maintaining the power of the Polish bureaucracy, our society is also dominated by forces profoundly resistant to democratic control. Like the Solidarity activists, the Trident and Honeywell blockaders acted directly, without endless appeals to entrenched authority, and challenged immense institutions of power. To end Honeywell's weapons production, they sat at its gates; to stop the Tridents, they blocked their passage. No instant victories would be achieved, any more than the Polish people could in a single moment throw off their internal colonization. Yet the participants in both efforts raised, without equivocation, their highest visions, and did so through stating that, in the face of whatever coercion, they would not be deterred.

As the *Ohio* approached, mornings became a time of action. People camped out on the boats—hauling their sleeping bags on board each night, then unloading them each morning so they wouldn't be confiscated. They breakfasted on scrambled eggs delivered to the vessel by the yurt camp cooks and on coffee cake and fruit donated by in-town supporters. Sympathetic sailors reported when other subs were moved in their berths to clear space. A locksmith mentioned fixing a broken Navy safe so incoming crew could be paid. Even the citizens' band patriots escalated their pace—breaking in to sing "God Bless America" when the *Peacemaker* and *Lizard* were talking; commenting testily, "It's not the *Pacific Peacemaker*, it's the Pacific Troublemaker"; whispering, "The Trident's coming. The Trident's coming. It's going to get you," in silky voices at 3 A.M.

Tuesday, August 10th, was foggy. People worried that the sub would not be seen, that it might slip by invisibly; then they decided its commander wouldn't risk running it on the rocks. In the afternoon the fog burned off, and thirty-nine Coast Guard boats staked a perimeter up the channel, while others circled the blockaders. The Coast Guard brought in their first helicopters, but the blockade now had its own plane, volunteered by a sympathetic pilot who, if he saw the sub, would dip his wings as a special signal.

Early in the morning, a Japanese monk named Suzuki rode out on a Zodiac, with his head shaved bare, and wearing a bright green nylon running suit. Pounding a stick on a flat skin drum, he chanted a resonating dirge. His mantra echoed through the mist. A dozen support boats stood in the harbor, with sails down, masts surrounded by the fog. The *Peacemaker* could have been Henry Hudson's ghost ship, *The Half Moon*.

"Na Mu Myo Ho. Ren Ge Kyo." The chant carried over the muted Zodiac motor. Suzuki had come with other monks to build a peace pagoda at Ground Zero. They'd erected others throughout the world, but this would have been the first in the United States had it not been halted, half built, because the Kitsap County Commissioners prohibited further construction. The pagoda remained a skeleton chapel of poles, wooden platforms, and rebar steel. The reason, the commissioners explained, was that it was "incompatible with its neighbors to the west"—the Trident base. The monks also built a geodesic dome, a ferro-concrete structure to be used for meetings and sleeping. One night vigilantes poured gasoline and torched the dome. The broken shards of a Buddha and a Christ now rested inside the Ground Zero house, shattered and twisted, their iron burnt red as dark salmon flesh.

Earlier, when people still stayed up late talking, Dan Delaney began a midnight discussion on nonviolence. People miss the point, Dan explained, "when they see black marchers on TV getting beaten up by the cops and say, 'that's a great tactic.' It's not a tactic, it's a way of life.

"Christ, and Gandhi follows his tradition, set up his crucifixion. The day before the biggest feast he trashes the temple and throws all the money around. When the priests come asking by whose authority he did this, Christ says by the same as John the Baptist, who they couldn't disavow because he had too large a following. They'd built a whole game where people had to buy animals for sacrifice, just like souvenirs. Jesus went right in and broke it up.

"The temple was the key to power," Dan continued. "Christ goes in and trashes it all. At one of their meetings, they said they had to kill him. 'One man must die for our country,' was their phrase, which is exactly what they're still doing—sacrificing human life for the military state. If Jesus had come today Christians would be wearing miniature gas chambers around their necks."

Dan talked about standing up to fear—how, when the British taxed all trade in India and forbade home manufacture, Gandhi led his march to the sea for the highly illegal action of gathering salt.

"Without making a big thing of it, I have six priors, and depending on how it goes, the media and everything else, someone like me will probably get at least six months to a year."

He laughed and sipped a beer. "It's no big thing really, just a chance to stick your tongue out at them."

When asked whether these risks and costs were worth it, Dan compared the blockade to the military, as he had once before. "There's an old feeling about valiant soldiers. People revere bravery, risking one's life for friends, fighting for a purpose. I remember I was counseling a draft resister who said 'I don't believe in dying for my country; I'm going to make the other motherfucker die for his country,' and it revolted me. What happened to heroes and courage? Why can't people act to inspire each other?"

Ironically, the Trident sailors inhabit a world not of Errol Flynn heroism, but of grey routine. And maybe the blockaders were the real heirs to the qualities of camaraderie and honor, of loyalty, spirit, and even the patriotism we so admire in the men who put up the flag on Iwo Jima. The blockaders expressed their ideals directly, without bolstering them by demonizing an outside enemy. In part, their heroism was that they were very ordinary people taking extraordinary risks. And, as Bill said, throwing yourself on the back of a Trident didn't mean much unless you were willing to do it again and again.

In a sense the blockade's community was ephemeral. No matter what happened, most of its participants would never see each other again. The flip side of their internationalism was their transience. Yet they would remember whatever "beloved community," whatever "Kingdom of Heaven," whatever model of a possible future they had built here. And this could sustain them long past the Trident's arrival.

By the night of Wednesday, August 11th, the *Ohio* was clearly imminent. Final confirmation would come from the spotters or from the Makah Indians, who promised to keep watch while fishing on the Straits of Juan De Fuca. The canal was not yet closed. But high dignitaries had been invited to a Bangor reception Thursday afternoon. The magistrate who would arraign those arrested canceled pending appointments. Coast Guard boats were everywhere. People staffing the media center were so busy playing Jimmy the Greek on arrival dates, they barely had time to explain the blockade's moral purpose.

Back at camp, Bill was ready for his arrest with a fresh shave and haircut. He and the actor from the Bronx danced an arm-in-arm jig before dinner, singing "Today's the day the Teddy Bears have a picnic." Some young local men came down with a keg of beer and a van with a sign on the side saying "Welcome Ohio" and showing a sub with huge jaws eating the *Peacemaker*. Because the camp was out of beer, Dan said "Hey, let's go on over." The men greeted us by asking "Where are you from?" and "Which side are you on?"

When Dan explained we were on the side of good beer, a guy in a jean jacket asked, "Have you ever worked?"

"I'm on food stamps," Dan said, jutting out his jaw. But the joke didn't take. We left quickly without our beer. Later on, two of them came over to apologize for the confrontation, and talked with Dan and with Win Olive about Trident, their Vietnam days, and the blockade.

Although people would get up at 4:30 A.M., campfire singing went on until late. When it ended, I walked with Bruce to his boat. As usual, he would row quietly out to *The Lizard* rather than ride a Zodiac. I carried his oars and two cartons of eggs for breakfast. He told me about Gandhi's notion that successful movements simultaneously broaden and deepen—reaching out to more and more people, while continually strengthening the commitment of those involved. This strategy had ultimately freed India, and Bruce saw the same process in the blockade.

Before he left, we agreed that, no matter what happened the following day, those here had already achieved their purpose. Without this resistance, the *Ohio* would have sailed in unquestioned: quietly and unnoticed, or perhaps with Vice President Bush, champagne, and exotic dancers. The Navy had still imported a rear admiral, a marching band, and relatives of the crew. But pomp and circumstance are different when defended by barbed wire fences. Or when the star attraction is hustled in on the sly like a third-rate politician charged with graft.

From inside the blockade, the action seemed the center of the world. Outside, for those who knew no one involved, it was diversion, entertainment, or at best, provocation: a story in the newspaper or images on a screen. The blockade made people more aware of Trident's existence and those who challenged it; when Phil Donahue held several Seattle shows, popular requests led him to bring on

Charley Meconis and a University of Washington Cold War advocate. But more immediate impact depended on the blockaders' human connections.

The blockade affected the Navy and Coast Guard as well. Their members could trash it with cynicism, condemn it as treason, or laugh it off and go about their business. But its message directly questioned their day-to-day activities. On the day of the *Ohio*'s arrival, a Bangor base worker quit his civilian job because of Trident's implications. A Coast Guard man visited Ground Zero. An *Ohio* sailor told a courthouse meeting of blockade participants, "A lot of men in the crew really appreciate what you're doing."

But as the blockaders kept repeating, the impact of their actions could neither be quantified nor guaranteed. Compare the effort to the California Freeze, which Dan Delaney said asked Jerry Brown "to go to Reagan, like an orphan out of Oliver Twist, and plead 'If you please sir, could you limit nuclear arms.' " Freeze activists could count the votes they received, and use them to prove that others cared as well. Military appropriations might be rolled back through letter-writing and lobbying. Yet while the blockaders didn't altogether disdain these approaches, they sought to confront not only weapons systems, but the systematic surrender of individual responsibility which fostered their proliferation and that more "legitimate" political mechanisms often implicitly fed. As David Host acknowledged, projects like the Freeze might gain time for work embodying more deeply rooted visions. "But if we have only short-term efforts, and keep living in a society where 'security' depends on a worldwide threat of terror, sooner or later we'll blow ourselves up."

In a 1982 *Village Voice* review of a Chilean exile's poems about torture, English critic John Berger wrote:

> During the 18th and 19th centuries many protests against social injustice were in prose. They were reasoned arguments written in the belief that, given time, people would come to see reason, and that, finally, history was on the side of reason. Today this is by no means clear. The outcome is by no means guaranteed. The suffering of the present and the past is unlikely to be redeemed by a future era of universal happiness. And evil is a constant ineradicable reality. All this means that the resolution—the coming to terms with the sense to be given to life—cannot be deferred. The future cannot be trusted.

The moment of truth is now. And more and more it will be poetry, rather than prose, that receives this truth. Prose is far more *trusting* than poetry; poetry speaks to the immediate wound.

The Freeze, the peace candidates, and the other respectably circumscribed campaigns perhaps take the model of prose; the blockade, of a far less rationalized poetic vision. Its direct community and direct challenge may speak far louder than attempting to legislate hope through bureaucratic labyrinths. It may, at the least, provide a vision to spur more pragmatic efforts and to sustain the sensibility Antonio Gramsci called "pessimism of the intellect, optimism of the will," which allows individuals to act without illusions in an era where hope may well be uncertain.

By declaring martial law on Hood Canal, federal authorities had already brought Bangor's normally invisible implications into high relief. At 4:00 A.M. on August 12th, spotters had at last confirmed the *Ohio's* passage through the Straits of Juan De Fuca, and Bill woke everyone aboard the *Peacemaker*. When Win asked him if they'd have breakfast, he answered, "of course," and they served tea and buttered toast, hard boiled eggs, apples, oranges, and watermelon. Meanwhile *The Lizard* headed out into the channel, perhaps slightly afraid the *Peacemaker's* less devout group might not arrive in time.

But the *Ohio* was not even in sight when Coast Guard cutters approached *The Lizard* and ordered it to stop. Ted veered sharply away and continued towards the area where the still-distant sub would enter the Hood Canal channel. The cutters opened up with water cannons, sweeping the deck and knocking him down from his position at the wheel. Ted got up, was knocked down once more, and got up again. The cannon bashed him repeatedly against the side of the cockpit. It turned on the other lizards, who first took refuge beneath their green fiberglass boats, then launched them into the water. The Coast Guard now aimed at these fragile vessels, scattering them like leaves on a wind-blown pond, finally upending them and dumping their occupants.

Ted maneuvered all the while, weaving between the Coast Guard ships, banking more and more tightly to avoid them. Then a large cutter, the *Pt. Glass*, cut directly across *The Lizard's* bow (they would later say Ted rammed them), and men with M-16s boarded the vessel from a Zodiac. The Coast Guard rounded up the remaining lizards, though some kept swimming towards the *Ohio* until being pulled in with grappling hooks. A young sailor put a cocked pistol to Ted's back and held it, his hand shaking, while Ted and his wife Eve told the boarding party they loved them, then knelt, together with Jim Douglass, to say "The Lord's Prayer." Later, after *The Lizard*'s crew had been handcuffed and transferred to a nearby Coast Guard cutter, Jim and Darla's husband Terry tried to stand up and jump overboard. A Coast Guard sailor knocked them down, added leg shackles to the handcuffs they already wore, and bound everyone face down on the deck.

The two mother vessels originally intended to head out simultaneously, but with *The Lizard* intercepted, and the government brandishing a ninety-nine-vessel support fleet (including a Navy mine sweeper) and five helicopters overhead, the *Peacemaker* decided to withhold its challenge until the *Ohio* was closer. With Lorraine at the helm, they sailed steadily along the land-spit leading to the Canal entrance, towing the ducklings not at the three knots of their practice runs, nor at the four or five they'd hoped for, but at a full nine knots—faster than remotely imagined. At first the Coast Guard came by and handed them a warning:

> The commander, thirteenth Coast Guard district, has issued an order under the authority of the Ports and Waterways Safety act. . . . Having found that a planned small boat blockade of the *USS Ohio* will create a hazardous condition, he has authorized me to issue the following direction:

But the space below was blank, so that Coast Guard officers could write in the appropriate directives and halt any vessel however they chose. The pronouncement concluded by threatening five-year jail terms for those violating its orders.

Bill pulled the boat over at first, but then resumed. A sailor in a Zodiac tried to cut the tow rope; a *Peacemaker* crew member lifted it high out of reach. Again, men boarded with automatic weapons. With *Peacemaker* captive and the tow line finally cut, the ducklings tried unsuccessfully to row to the *Ohio* on their own. (One Coast Guard man said, "you'll never make it," then, without sarcasm, wished them luck.) Some returned, milling around their mother ship, slightly lost. Coast Guard boats seized the oars of other ducklings—including the canoe—and left them to drift until rescued by friends in witness boats.

When the *Pt. Glass* was about to leave and tow *Peacemaker* into Bangor (*The Lizard* was now empty, guarded by two silent Coast Guard men wearing orange vests and carrying rifles), a nun in one of the ducklings grabbed hold of the tow line between the boats. From the deck, a few feet above, the Coast Guard hosed her down. She hung on against the stream until two more blockaders replaced her, aided by four others who bailed out the boats with half-cut plastic milk jugs and bleach containers. They held on so as not to abandon their friends, and because the locus of the blockade had shifted from the sub itself to the men and guns seeking to erase their challenge. They held on against the hoses until they could hold on no more.

By 8:30 A.M., *Peacemaker* was being towed towards Hood Canal. A slow parade of witness boats followed behind; Bill's mother Ivy was on one, having flown in from England to look after the children. Because Ivy was turning fifty-one that day, the handcuffed *Peacemaker* crew began singing "Happy Birthday," as if to both honor her and mock their bondage. The remaining support boats flew their blockade flags, and their parade resembled that of survivors at a New Orleans jazz funeral, playing all the harder to prove the spirit still moved. The *Plowshares*—the launch with Kim Wahl, Charley Meconis, Lutheran Deaconess Grace Baranski, and Jon and Ruth Nelson—chased the long, low sub but couldn't catch it. They followed it into Hood Canal, flanked by cutters, until at last they were stopped and arrested. The young sailor who handcuffed Charley asked him, "Didn't I see you on TV?"

One boat made it through the ninety-nine-vessel flotilla guarding the *Ohio*. It was the *James Jordan*, a three-person launch driven by a quiet, bearded man who used to teach physics to Naval personnel. The cutters stopped the *Jordan* once, were offered communion bread, and then inexplicably let the boat continue on. So the *Jordan* homed in, passing cutters seemingly reluctant to leave their fixed posts, and driven faster by the propeller wash of military helicopters. It circled the *Ohio* once, nearly twice, then at last was left behind. The remaining blockaders rowed slowly in.

As the Coast Guard made only fourteen arrests, the blockade ended for most participants almost before it had begun. Most of the lizards and the entire *Peacemaker* crew, except for Bill and an Australian filmmaker, were taken to the Bangor base and then released. They balked at leaving, wanted to stay in solidarity with their friends. Guards roughly dragged them into a van, then dumped them outside the gates. Those booked were released on personal recognizance.

For a few days the selective arrests produced confusion and division. The blockaders had felt at the center of history, and expected to pay commensurate costs. Now, most were left behind, let off the hook, cast adrift while the planet went about its business as if the entire saga had never occurred. Some felt singled out and ignored—as if they'd somehow failed. The sub had steamed in, yet they were free. There was almost jealousy towards those facing charges.

But the constriction quickly broke, and most blockaders began to move on to new projects following a Sunday meeting at the yurt camp. The Port Townsend supporters said they were proud to have been involved, but would need time before doing it again. People watched TV replays treating the blockade as a sporting event in which—outside of the single score of the *James Jordan*—the underdogs were totally crushed. A rear admiral repeated, on every network, "If the *Ohio* never fires a shot in anger it will have achieved its mission." Ground Zero members explained how others could join their ongoing projects. People planned vigils, educational meetings, and a later successful project in which American activists would purchase the *Peacemaker* and continue its journey.

For most, the awkwardness was largely a momentary transition; a time when people blinked to adjust to a different light, then continued their previous pursuits. Kim Wahl returned to her suburban home and spent a day staring at bills and wondering how they connected with the fate of the earth. Then she weeded her garden, picked lettuce, carrots, leeks, and the season's first tomatoes and herbs, baked a plum and blueberry pie, and felt relieved to be home. A few days later she visited her conservative Catholic church, fully expecting to be ostracized. When members of the congregation had talked nuclear politics at all, it had been to criticize people like Archbishop Hunthausen. The pastor had refused her request to lead peace education workshops. How would they react to her blockade of the sub?

But instead of condemnation, she received thanks. People hugged her and said she was their witness, representing them out on the water. The pastor came as a supporter to her arraignment. A local underwater sports shop tore up the bill for a wet suit she had rented. The community embraced her with pride.

In many ways this welcome was fleeting. Though Kim received warm letters, friends and neighbors quickly felt uneasy about the implications of her actions. Before she had just been active; they could put her visions in a box and hope she wouldn't mention awkward subjects. Now, in itself, her presence posed difficult questions. Hoping her friends would change along with her, Kim mourned as they clung to a denial that treated her every act as an accusation. She retreated to her family, the few friends who stayed, and the new community of others who were equally engaged. She felt she'd charted an irreversible course.

For more rootless blockaders, the transition was harder still. One group sat talking on the courthouse lawn when a support person began a conversation with a young bus driver who'd been involved in Vietnam protests. "You get involved step by step," she explained, as if a teacher elaborating on a lesson. "First sign a petition, then write a letter, do support, and the next thing you know you're blockading. You should join our next blockade."

"Right," said a listening blockader named Chris, very quietly. "And then the Coast Guard is shooting you with water cannons."

Chris was not cynical, just shaken by the Coast Guard violence and perhaps by a feeling of being in over his head. He'd given up his San Francisco apartment, sold his books, left a graduate program in English, and prepared himself for jail. Now he was uncertain where to go. So, along with David Host and Bruce, their fellow lizard, he took off for a fruitless attempt to establish what they called Ground Zero Canada at Ted Phillips's Quadra Island home. To the degree that they believed in a God who directly answered prayers, the Trident's passage into Bangor either meant God was stopping the sub in ways beyond human understanding, or that their love and commitment had been imperfect. Severed from the community that had both sustained them and counterbalanced the most isolating extremes of their vision, they held a grim vigil, huddled on a Victoria breakwater, to protest the passage of the next Trident sub. And they handed out leaflets full of caring, but leaden with rhetoric. At least for the moment, their faith became less a promise than a shield.

Because civil disobedience trials could become major forums, those facing charges looked forward to the chance to present their views in a context that, as one of the ducklings said, might create an impact as powerful "as the Chicago Seven trial without the crazies." But a week later the government dropped all charges.

Part of this was due to a flimsy case: people were arrested well outside the stipulated exclusion zones (Coast Guardsmen boarding *The Lizard* broadcast the question, "Ok, now what do we charge them with?"). But the government seemed to fear equally a further escalation of publicity that had already generated international coverage.

So the authorities pretended the blockade never happened and trusted its effects would quickly disappear. Since the first Trident came only once, they pulled the shroud of silence back over it, and hoped the protest was just a one-time event.

But, as Douglass says, nonviolent action can possess a ju jitsu quality. Massive power, like that of the military state, can overreact and stir public opposition. Acts of conscience pull in support and commitment. Seemingly helpless individuals have an impact beyond their numbers. In this case, if government representatives had imposed draconian sentences they would have risked creating massive sympathy; yet by releasing people without penalty, they risked weakening future threats. Though this action built no more than a foothold from which to take the next difficult step, its impact could not be erased. That the Coast Guard launched their preemptive strike, and that the courts dropped their charges, were measures of the power of the blockade.

The night before the sub came, people sang old songs around the campfire. And they added their own verses—playing guitars, harmonicas, and drums made of pots and pans. One, to the tune of "Down by the banks of the Ohio," proclaimed, "Tear up that income tax return. You'll buy no bombs with what I earn. If you want money, then you should know. That I won't pay for the *Ohio*."

Then a Seattle folk singer led another song. "We're here to say we're going to be here tomorrow. We love this world and we won't let it burn. We're choosing life in all of its wonder. We promised the children that they'll have their turn."

Each generation implicitly pledges to the next that the world they are born into will continue. If, as poet Wendell Berry has said, we have shifted from colonizing territories to colonizing the future, then weapons like Trident are the farthest extension of this shift. And if

Trident can close off human history to those who by all natural right should inherit it, then people may well have to risk more than ever before.

# Obstacles and Visions

# 6.　Stones in the Pathway

## Politics of the Void

A year and a half after the Trident blockade, one year following the California Freeze initiative, and shortly after Erica's Honeywell jailing and the October 1983 Florence peace walk, a dozen Seattle neighbors watched the nuclear holocaust film, *The Day After*. The diverse group gathered at the home of a retired elementary school teacher, and included three teenagers, a retired airline stewardess and her husband, a former local union official, a nurse, a geology graduate student, and two other teachers. All of them lived on the same quiet residential block. Because none of the participants were arms race experts, the teacher also invited a hiking friend involved with Physicians for Social Responsibility.

These assorted neighbors watched along with others attending formal and informal viewing sessions throughout the nation. Initially, they joked about how the previewed scenes of destruction resembled the run-down house on the corner; they became slightly edgy in apprehension of what might be presented for them to see; mostly they savored the convivial mood. They grew quieter as foreshadowings of war interrupted the TV characters' familiar concerns of going to work, raising children, watching football, and fighting their ordinary battles. When U.S. missiles arced over the pastoral Kansas cornfields, the viewers stared mutely, echoing the stunned gaze of the characters on-screen and glimpsing briefly the shadow of the cataclysm that constantly hangs, a bare half-dozen minutes away, over our lives and our world.

By the end, the group was vulnerable, angry, and shaken. Some were so outraged about the common jeopardy that it seemed they might begin to learn, speak, and act with others to challenge the web of politics, economics, and culture that keeps the arms race escalating. If nothing else, the film jolted their complacency.

But no sooner did Jason Robards finish stumbling through the ruins of his former world than we returned to the counterfeit balm of those who have always portrayed the global danger as hardly being real. A special segment of *Viewpoint* featured an expert panel, including Henry Kissinger, William F. Buckley, Robert McNamara, MX committee chair Brent Scowcroft, and (in a separate preceding interview) Secretary of State George Schultz—as well as a brief humanist counterpoint provided by Carl Sagan and Elie Wiesel. Certain of their positions, the experts lectured in rational and positive tones, which Ted Koppel contrasted with what he considered to be the movie's simplistic emotionalism. Deterrence worked, they insisted, and would always work—provided we avoid the twin perils of rashly using the weapons or leaving ourselves, in Kissinger's words, "morally disarmed."

It was for humane reasons, Kissinger emphasized, that the United States had developed the policies of flexible targeting, which allow for responses short of wholly annihilating an opponent's society. Schultz said the film's lesson was that nuclear war was impossible. And Scowcroft said it was in order to preserve security that we were building MXs, because the Soviets would always be our enemies. Aside from brief comments made by Sagan, McNamara, and Wiesel, the program's dominant thrust was that we dare not diminish our arsenals.

The film had pushed viewers to question: If indeed we are not protected, if indeed our lives are fragile, then perhaps we should be less willing to hand over our common future to those who claim we have no choice but to trust them. But by the end of *Viewpoint*, nearly an hour and a half later, those watching had retreated into isolation, helplessness, and exhaustion. Gut knowledge believed the threat. The message of the film was the ultimate horror of the pending annihilation, but the panel's stern parental voices defined as illegitimate the very unease necessary to make us begin to confront our present situation. The wounds barely opened before they were clamped and sealed by the experts.

In November 1980, when Ronald Reagan was first elected president, the atomic disarmament movement was near-invisible: a small core of dissident scientists; pacifist groups like Fellowship of Reconciliation, the War Resisters League, and American Friends Service Committee; and scattered others who raised these issues wherever they could. A more diffuse body of individuals attended the occasional march or rally, then faded back into ordinary life. Organizations like Palmetto Alliance stirred up related challenges to commercial atomic power. But the nuclear weapons were largely shrugged off and ignored.

Since that time, we've seen a blossoming of concern perhaps unprecedented in its breadth of reach. Marches occur in small South Carolina towns. Preachers like Bill, Levon, and Ernest Thompson raise global issues from the pulpits. Students, from Kathy and Sheila to the boys of Dominic Savio, question whether there will be a world for them to inherit. Scientists, physicians, teachers, lawyers, and even a few of Willens's business colleagues work to bring discussions of the arms race into their respective institutions. California joins eight states in passing watershed Freeze referendums. MacDonalds' heiress Joan Kroc runs full-page peace ads in ninety-two major city newspapers, and the National Mother of the Year helps blockade Honeywell and Trident.

Together, these choices have broken a prevailing public silence, and spurred a popular awareness unthinkable just a few years back. Yet, even as concern reaches remote corners of our land—even as over eighty-five percent of Americans have said they would favor a bilateral atomic weapons freeze—we have also seen a continuing build-up of the arsenals; congressional support for destabilizing systems like the Pershing, cruise, MX, and Trident; escalating wars from Central America and the Middle East, to Angola and Cambodia; and the massive electoral victory of a president more heedless of the developing human crises than any since the first bomb fell on Hiroshima. In 1980, the *Bulletin of the Atomic Scientists* clock stood at seven minutes to midnight; as this book is being completed, in spring of 1986, it hovers at three.

Given these setbacks, and the continuing power of an entrenched weapons culture to mold public opinion, have the choices of individuals like Erica Bouza, Bill Cusak, Shelley Berman, Harold Willens, Kim Wahl, or Rachelle and Amanda mattered in the least? Is the concern they represent a mere backwater eddy in a torrent of militarist revival, a passing moment when our society blinks, looks up, and then nods off to apathy once more? Can a citizens' movement sustain itself for the efforts necessary to reverse over forty years of atomic weapons buildup?

Because the arms race is not only a technical process, but also a set of relationships between individuals and their cultures, this book has focused on those who've come to grapple with its threat. Unless ordinary citizens act and continue to act on an unprecedented level, our species has little chance of emerging from its peril. Yet these actions take place in a broader context. And although the peace movement's success cannot be determined by simply tallying scoreboard results from each electoral campaign, military vote, or administration power struggle, we still need to ask how individual choices can affect the decisions of state that have produced our present crisis. We need to examine both why our government continues with its ultimate folly, and how we might keep commitment and resilience for as long as is needed to reverse its course.

The institutional strains fueling America's support of an endless global arms race are not discretely isolated, like bacteria in a petri dish. They complement one another: from dependency on Pentagon dollars to trust in all-knowing experts; from the strength of entrenched elites to the fickleness of electoral mechanisms; from individual cynicism to a political life steered increasingly by an all-powerful executive branch. As a microcosm of obstacles that the peace movement faces, we can look first at Reagan's reelection—a profound setback after the movement's initial renewal and bloom.

November 1984 has clearly helped set a tone, for much of the culture, of acquiescent jingoism. Yet evidence that the voters crossed an ideological watershed is contradictory. Whether from apathy or disdain, nearly half of those potentially eligible never registered or made it to the polls. In Illinois, Massachusetts, and Iowa, the majority of those who did vote elected both Ronald Reagan and three senators as resistant to blind jingoism as all but a few in recent years—Vietnam Veterans against the War cofounder John Kerry, prime intervention critic Paul Simon, and SANE national board member, Tom Harkin. Washington State's rural Skagit and Whatcom counties went by almost fifty-six percent for Reagan, yet at the same time passed Nuclear Free Zone ordinances by nearly two-thirds margins. Even if these last votes could be considered direct self-protection—citizens not wanting reactors or bomb plants in their own back-yards—they spurned pork-barrel dreams and went beyond merely urging Freeze negotiations to directly challenging the path of the arms race.

The fact that Reagan carried Whatcom and Skagit counties and the rest of the United States was in part because voters shunted concern over atomic escalation to the domains of impossible dreams. Reagan's victory was based on lower OPEC oil prices, distaste for Walter Mondale, and deferment of social, economic, and ecological costs to the future. Fundamental issues were washed away by an abstract and self-referential notion of "leadership," which consisted largely of acclamation by images: a picture of the president and the Pope that the Republicans ran as an ad in nearly every Catholic paper in the country; Reagan's praise of Bruce Springsteen in New Jersey (even after Springsteen refused to endorse him); marshaling of the ghosts of Truman, Kennedy, and Roosevelt.

Like Richard Nixon, Reagan has cast himself as a populist outsider, even as he has extended the most authoritarian aspects of the state. And since his shift to selling Star Wars through the rhetoric of disarmament, he has steadily incorporated peace movement symbols. When Mondale called Nicaragua "a Marxist dictatorship," and nei-ther asked core economic questions nor challenged basic Cold War premises, but merely suggested we proceed a shade more circum-spectly, he was easily cast as a "wimp." He knew the United States' cause was right but so feared breaking the rules that he dared not risk to win the global game. And, ironically, Reagan took moral high ground for manifesting toughness and strength.

We might ask why, despite Mondale's support for destabilizing weapons, his lineage of red-baiting, and salient lack of inspiring vision, numerous peace workers so prized his presumed ability to mobilize the traditional Democratic machine, that they helped him fend off Gary Hart (who was, admittedly, also compromised) in the primaries. Or we might wonder, as did minister Jim Lawson, why more activists did not back Jesse Jackson's campaign: one that jarred imagination and conscience by giving a message "that the struggle is not lost, not over—that there is a higher morality that is not being looked at, and that is the real alternative."

Jim questioned why the majority of the white peace movement tarred Jackson permanently for sins (such as the "hymie" remarks) for which he later clearly apologized, while shrugging off Mondale's continued financial support from major military contractors like Honeywell, and his red-baiting, which even extended to calling Hart soft on Central America. Jim said the point was not whether Jackson could have necessarily captured the nomination, much less the general election: "the peace movement has not had as its primary rationale for being that we can win. We've always fought against the odds." Immersion in electoral in-fighting could certainly have diverted effort from other critical work, yet the campaign's discourse might well have changed had the Democrats, in Jim's words, "made the primary and the choice of candidates a debate on fundamental questions." A candidate with more vision and courage might have emerged from a convention with a few more contending voices, or Mondale might at the least have taken stronger stands.

In its broadest sense, we can call Reagan's reelection a politics of the void—a void that allows the dominant public voices to support an increasingly militarized culture. In a society in which democratic community has substantially eroded and alternative voices are largely muted, it is easy to grab false hope, shrug off our leaders' callous distortions as endearing idiosyncrasies, and convince ourselves that nothing can be done.

When, during Reagan's initial term, the peace movement directly reached individuals—like those touched by the chains of invitation and engagement begun in Leo Baeck temple, Congaree Presbytery, and communities from Florence to Shabazz High—lives were changed. But for those who merely read of the Freeze, saw the marches on TV, or heard a few abstract questions, concern could readily be set aside once the president shelved talk of winnable nuclear wars and echoed the chorus for peace. As with Nixon's secret plans to end the Vietnam War, it was easy to believe assurances that the morning was in bloom and the nation was renewing its pride—that if we just trusted our leaders everything would turn out fine.

## Electoral Mazes

Because America's formal political institutions determine which weapons we will build, which countries we will invade, and how we will use a major share of our nation's capital and resources, activists face inevitable dilemmas. And the choices between conventional politics and the direct challenge of the Trident or Honeywell blockaders are not always hard and fast. Even as Jim Lawson proposed direct citizen action comparable to that of the civil rights era, he also acknowledged a need to get individuals with wisdom and vision—like Mark Hatfield, Ron Dellums, or former Senate Foreign Relations chair William Fulbright—into Congress and into the legislatures. Cities as diverse as Chicago, Philadelphia, Portland, and Atlanta have recently elected mayors with relatively compassionate visions. Yet, at least on the presidential scale, electoral campaigns rarely give a sense to those who stuff the envelopes and post the door-hangers that their personal hopes, beliefs, and dreams matter at all in the grand process we call politics. Because there is never enough time or money to articulate complex visions, discussion squeezes into narrowly foreshortened frames—whatever will change the votes and get out the bodies. As Bob Willard said, reaching ten people no longer means anything: "You need thousands." With Mondale's ample doublespeak coupled to four years of Democratic pliancy before even the most blatant Reagan administration outrages, the 1984 election could not help carrying the taste of a protracted bitter fever—hardly an encouragement for ordinary citizens to act on broader concerns.

The contradictions of our political system do not disappear when the elections are over. Congressional representatives can be called, written, and visited, and at times this pressure makes a difference. But as Jim Lawson pointed out, activists can rarely match the Rockwells, Honeywells, and TRWs in sustained lobbying power. To focus solely on petitioning, to make the legislators final arbiters, is to forget the climate that elected them, to allow debate in the spheres of ordinary life to erode by default, and to abdicate chances to directly offer alternative social and political visions and to confront weapons-culture institutions. Moreover, such abdication leaves elected representatives all the more vulnerable if they take the risk of rejecting military build-ups.

Few situations better exemplify the morass of legislative trade-offs than the wrangling over the MX missile, which has wound on throughout the past decade. Jimmy Carter backed this weapon so the Joint Chiefs of Staff would approve SALT II; then it became Reagan's miracle "bargaining chip" against the Soviets. The MX scheme has survived through a process of plea-bargaining in a Congress where few embrace its merits.

In a *New Yorker* article following the spring 1983 House vote on this weapons system, Elizabeth Drew detailed key mechanisms that have moved this and other destabilizing technologies steadily forward. "It is a story," Drew explains, "of well-intentioned people acting on a combination of their own sense of what it means to be 'responsible'; their own sense of what they needed to do to 'position' themselves politically or lay the groundwork for political advancement; and political fear."

Numerous Democrats viewed the MX vote as a way to redeem their credentials as team players and members of the vital center; as a way to atone for mildly dovish votes on the Freeze, on funding only part of Reagan's massive defense budget increases, and on questioning Kenneth Adelman's nomination as director of the Arms Control and Disarmament Agency. In fact, the 1983 vote was intentionally delayed so that those who, in eventual-supporter Les Aspin's words, "begin to get a little uncomfortable if they've gone too far one way and start looking . . . to pop back the other way" would have a change to repent and make compensation.

In this search for neutral and inoffensive ground, issues affecting whether or not our species will survive are treated like those of any other debates where representatives position themselves carefully with constituents, key financial interests, and the government's internal bureaucracies; the issues can equally be the MX, timber leases, or standards of weights and measures. Add to this equation career advancement and ingrained Cold War assumptions; a Congress that is constitutionally mandated to determine foreign policy now ends up at best belatedly checking interventions initiated by the executive branch. Yet to wholly ignore the electoral sphere may be to leave it to those who sytematically exclude human consequences from their calculations, and who may make us all expendable bargaining chips in a game of unprecedented stakes.

At times electoral campaigns and lobbying efforts can build autonomous community. For all of its high-tech gloss, the California Freeze campaign furnished ample domains of engagement for Jo Seidita's door knockers, precinct walkers, and petition circulators. A follow-up Los Angeles Jobs with Peace initiative not only carried by a sixty-one percent majority against the November 1984 Reagan tide, but also spurred a grass-roots network that remained afterwards, able to coordinate meetings, pressure elected representatives, hold demonstrations, and foster the dialogue necessary for a sustained political movement. By electing a populist mayor who brought in Tony Bouza as police chief, Minneapolis citizens helped the Honeywell blockaders avoid what had often been brutal governmental responses.

The point is not to wholly disdain electoral paths, but to recognize that by themselves they guarantee neither wisdom nor democracy. Just as ordinary citizens shrug off misgivings about the arms race by trusting the experts, so elected representatives make the same surrender, the same deferral. Shortly after the fall 1983 Florence march, I talked with the district's first-term congressman, Robin Tallon, a man who had taken political risks by supporting the Freeze and opposing MX deployment. Although Tallon was clearly concerned about the arms race crisis, he supported MX research and development, believing we should keep all options open, and explaining that the president had called him in and said our nation needed the weapons. Tallon also backed European deployment of cruise and Pershing II missiles, citing previous NATO commitments and the political power of the Reagan administration juggernaut; yet, at the same time, he acknowledged that the Pershings' location—less than eight minutes from Moscow—seemed to clearly shorten the atomic fuse, as did the ability of the cruise missiles to fly beneath most radar screens, their dual nuclear-conventional status, and the problems they create for verifying their numbers. Tallon was at least somewhat sympathetic to the peace movement; he cared and risked significantly more than he had to—yet in the end he shelved personal misgivings to join the official team.

Along with the pressures cited by Tallon, weapons escalation is fueled by media definitions that reduce and blur the implications of the arms race and other critically pressing issues. Certainly, compliant media aided Reagan's reelection by endorsing him overwhelmingly on newspaper editorial pages; focusing far less on the issues than his prospects for a fifty-state sweep; and glossing over even blatant official misstatements. Yet more important than specific campaign coverage are the frames that shape our general political discussion. Presidential candidates who even hint at questioning ongoing Cold War assumptions (individuals like Fred Harris, Eugene McCarthy, George McGovern, and Jerry Brown) are automatically tarred as naïve, sentimental, and unrealistic. We are the only Western democracy without a single acknowledged socialist, of any variety, serving as a major columnist or TV commentator. The terms of acceptable foreign policy discourse allow Nixon and Kissinger to be considered respected elder statesmen, while those who opposed Vietnam are increasingly told their efforts constituted shameful whining and complaining.

This is not to portray American media as monolithic. Although the year before the major Freeze campaigns the subject of arms race opposition was nearly invisible, national TV and radio interviews have since broadcast the visions of activist leaders, breakaway members of the atomic priesthood, and ordinary citizens ranging from Erica Bouza to the Trident blockaders and the June 12th marchers. But such dissenting images still appear primarily as a marginal counterweight to the endless repetitions of those directing our present course, and all too often end up circumscribed and trivialized—as when Philip Berrigan appeared on a major Seattle TV show, followed by a segment on dancing bears. Although discussion of nuclear issues continues at a level unthinkable before the peace movement resurgence, coverage of the activists themselves has more recently dropped off to the point where, unless citizens have alternative conduits of information, it is easy to believe the American populace is once again gladly delegating its concern to the men in Washington and Geneva.

## Addiction and Dependence

Fundamental to this containment of dissent is the sanctification of experts. Before anything else, Cold War dissenters are attacked for being naïve outsiders, ignorant of the true complexities available only to the atomic priesthood. Because Jonathan Schell's *The Fate of the Earth* articulated the new movement's insistence that our present course led only to annihilation, critiques of his book quickly stressed that popular action, whether in the United States or in "totalitarian" societies, could only muddy issues better left to official experts; that it was a naïve dream to believe the weapons or political forces that brandish them could ever be eliminated; and that we must live in the real world of armed self-interest—within the traditional structures of deterrence—and not seek to reinvent a new one. The year after Schell's book was released, the Harvard Nuclear Study Group—including prominent Vietnam strategist Samuel Huntington—published, in *Living with Nuclear Weapons*, their own prescription for why we have no choice but to continue our present course. When Schell released his follow-up work, *The Abolition*, Lord Solly Zuckerman, former chief scientific advisor to the British Ministry of Defense and a moderate arms race critic, dismissed him in *The New York Review of Books* as a chic know-nothing newcomer—despite the fact that Schell had been writing about issues of war and mass annihilation since his first book, fifteen years before, on a Vietnam village the United States destroyed in order to save.

*The Day After*'s experts also took this patronizing stance: a similar relegation of ordinary citizens to a pat-on-the-head world; a similar assertion of jurisdictional privilege. At times these experts proclaim their toughness in the face of the task, as when Harry Truman exclaimed—after J. Robert Oppenheimer talked of his guilt regarding the bomb—"I never want to see that cry baby in here again." Or when Kissinger wrote, regarding the United States' right to intervene and initiate the process leading up to the Chilean coup, "I don't see why we need to stand by and watch a country go Communist due to the irresponsibility of its own people." Just as—according to U.S. Senate historian Richard Baker—not a single congressman or senator's son was killed in the Vietnam war, the decision makers' power distances the costs of their actions.

Beyond this insulation, the notion of a nuclear priesthood helps cast the arms race as a technical problem, where we need only develop Star Wars, the Peacekeeper missile, or some other magic system, and we will be granted happiness and security forever. Ordinary activists, few of whom can refute every last official statistic or assertion in one-on-one debate, come off again as naïve innocents, unknowing pawns of Soviet manipulation or of an insidious "adversary culture." The projection of military opponents as illegitimate meddlers extends even to the all-too-rare challenges presented by Congress, as when, following its initial refusal in spring 1985 of military aid to Nicaraguan contras, Reagan stormed, "We have got to get where we can run a foreign policy without a committee of 535 telling us what we can do."

Legacies of Vietnam, Watergate and an array of citizens' movements have left Americans far more mistrustful of government leaders than they were during the years of the earliest movements to ban the bomb. Yet even those who now challenge the weapons course may retain lingering doubts on whether our global jeopardy might indeed be too complex to be resolved by any but a specialized elite. Or they may, as did many in the late-1960s New Left, combine a general reaction against the bomb's "looming shadow" with a notion that even the most callous technocrats would be rational enough not to initiate global annihilation. This deferring of responsibility is vastly accentuated in facilities and communities dependent on the military economy, where it supports not an abstract, distant process but the employees' day-to-day world. Gordon Adams, of the Center on Budget and Policy Priorities, has described an "Iron Triangle" linking the military, major weapons contractors, and congressional representatives eager for pork-barrel largesse. Boeing's fifty-five-person Washington, D.C. delegation spends more money to support its lobbying than the costs of the combined offices of all eight Washington state congressmen. During the 1984 election, the top twenty military contractors contributed $3.6 million to campaigns, particularly those of senators and congressmen on key weapons-related committees.

To say that the military-industrial complex helps fuel the arms race is a truism, even if it is honored most often with an indulgent shrug. We expect home district contracts to be traded like baseball playing cards. But beyond the weapons producers' direct lobbying power lies a more subtle shaping of political climate. Military workers and those dependent on their salaries inevitably see curtailment of the arms race as a threat to livelihood. They feel the fear that touches us all when we envision being jobless and alone. But this dependence also builds on nonmonetary ties, such as loyalty to coworkers: for to shut down the plants is to destroy what the group has built and shared, and a pride vested in a common creation.

The men and women who manufacture the MX components, serve on the Trident subs, assemble helicopter gunships destined for El Salvador or South Korea, and research the Star Wars laser weapons, do so for comprehensible reasons. Many believe they're serving their country. The work can offer learning and advancement, new frontiers to effect one's will in the world, or, as Robert Oppenheimer put it—in describing the creation of the H-bomb—a challenge that is "technically sweet." Even if one wants to leave weapons-related work, it is less than easy when there are few jobs in a highly specialized field, and half of one's resume may be classified.

Dependence also brings what a Los Alamos study called the "halo effect," by which "the prospect of additional economic well-being . . . can be expected to more than offset any qualms about radiation exposure risk or other fears." Or workers can retreat into cynicism by judging the entire military-industrial enterprise a cost-plus con, but project this same mistrust outward, asserting the best we can hope for is a world of carnivorous hustling.

Amidst resurgent citizen concern, the military and its subsidiary industries suppress discussion that challenges their role, and prevent even asking which weapons are necessary to secure national integrity and which invite imperial adventurism and brinksmanship. Public debate largely curves around these institutions as if they were islands in a stream.

In Washington's Hanford complex, which has produced half the plutonium for U.S. warheads, even the most modest arms race challenge is an unconscionable threat. When a nascent peace group began in 1982 in the adjacent community, led by the wife of a skilled microwave engineer, her husband's superiors soon began asking him about her public statements. Coworkers fearing aspersions of disloyalty stopped joining him at the lunchroom tables. Where security, in accordance with routine procedures, had previously searched his car perhaps twice a year, now he was inspected nearly every week. Administrators fired another peace group member for wearing a company badge at a vigil. The names of local activists were sent to security officials in Washington, D.C., and their one-time friends now parked away from their homes so as not to be thought involved in unacceptable dissidence. In Amarillo, Texas, the United Way cut off all funds to Catholic Family Services because Bishop Leroy Mat-

thiesen had suggested workers who assembled the final nuclear warheads at the adjacent Pantex plant consider the moral implications
of their work, and because an order of priests gave a grant to counsel
those with qualms.

We are tempted to dismiss actions like these simply as human
nature, as inevitable as the distinctions between the Florence newspaper editorial praising local peace marchers and one in the paper
of a town adjacent to the Savannah River Plant, which called participants in a planned protest "shiftless failures as human beings."
Of course the weapons communities defend their own, and their
elected representatives support each new warhead system. It is easy
to understand why peace organizers in Charleston, South Carolina,
fear even to discuss nuclear issues at their jobs, or to display Freeze
bumper stickers on their cars: a third of the local economy depends
on the massive naval complex serving as the Atlantic Fleet's home
port. Do we expect peace leaflets lining the bulletin boards of Long
Island's Grumman plants or the Minnesota facilities where Honeywell produces cluster bombs? No more than we expect even sympathetic members of Congress to accept former Texas Senator John
Tower's flip annual challenge to critics of military spending: begin
the cutting in their own home districts. In the same way that erosion
of democracy and popular control makes it less possible to address
broad issues like the arms race, so every additional dollar spent on
the now $300 billion annual military budget, every deployment or
weapons contract, extends the domains in which social, economic,
and sometimes legal sanctions prohibit necessary political questioning—and in which employees are quarantined from external debate
by fear of job-loss and a security mystique.

Beyond this, the weapons culture links the loyalty of those under
its most direct sway with loyalty to the nation. In an echo of the
notion that only the Kissingers and Weinbergers know enough to
judge our course, military workers alternate between deferring to
the "men who know best" and asserting that their own proximity to
the weapons gives them a unique perspective—arcane information
denied those on the civilian side. At the same time, sophisticated
military technologies themselves distance actions from their consequences. The atomic warheads exist only as products of vast industrial and scientific enterprises, where responsibility is inevitably
diffused. Most participants in the weapons chain never remotely see

their targets. When asked how they could shoot peasant women and children, the Vietnam helicopter gunners explained cynically, "You just lead your fire a little more slowly."

One need not condemn weapons facilities workers to recognize that the institutions they serve leave scant room for addressing the fundamental issues of war and peace civilians are at last beginning to examine, or to recognize as well that the shroud of enforced silence extends beyond these facilities and bases to the communities dependent on their subsidiary economies. Why should individuals risk ill-will by involving themselves in public dissent? It's easier to comply and keep misgivings private. Given the constraints on thought and action faced by those who staff our varied weapons complexes and live in their shadow, it is little wonder they hang back from questioning.

## Power and Vulnerability

As political scientist John Gaventa points out in his study of a resource-rich but economically devastated Appalachian valley, power is not only a question of who prevails in bargaining over contested issues, but also of the rules and institutional structures allowing access to debate to begin with; the climates that determine how individuals shape their perceptions of areas of potential social conflict; and the mechanisms that "prevent conflict from arising in the first place." In this sense, military dependence, bought and compromised political mechanisms, media images that circumscribe our vision, and deference to God-like experts all exemplify less than democratic strains of American society.

In October of 1982, a United Electrical Workers' local at a non-military General Electric turbine plant outside of Charleston, joined with a South Carolina Freeze group to sponsor a 200-person peace march. They'd planned to publicize it through a special arms race insert inside the paper they routinely handed out to all their members. But company management, perhaps sensitive because GE was the third largest atomic weapons contractor in the nation, said the insert didn't pertain to plant or union affairs and that they wouldn't allow the already-printed papers to be distributed. Beleaguered by the loss of members recently laid off, the union couldn't afford to strike over the affair. They accepted the action with only verbal protests.

The UE local's engagement was hardly fruitless. They distributed as many papers as they could outside the plant, and inspired some workers to attend the rally; later they drew on the sense of community they had created to initiate a plan for technical conversion when GE decided to shut down the factory. But immediate dialogue was suppressed by a broader context of powerlessness.

We see the sway of unaccountable power in the unwillingness of most reporters and commentators to even question the prevailing assumptions of war and peace debate: that governmental leaders have the right to make life or death policy decisions for the world; that we must endlessly play global policeman; that the United States acts only in the service of righteousness and justice. We see it, as well, in the more direct suppression of dissenting visions: as when, in the 1950s, the United Electrical Workers union got red-baited out of Honeywell; or when, during Vietnam, a junior professor at the University of South Carolina was censured and saw his salary frozen for holding up a sign saying "Westmoreland, Doctor of War," at a ceremony in the general's honor. We see this power in various governmental actions like the McCarthy-era loyalty oaths, Nixon's Cointelpro burglaries and organizational disruptions, and the acknowledged infiltration of present-day peace groups. Finally, we see it in the quiescence of cultural institutions ranging from schools silent on the most critical global questions, to churches speaking only of private salvation, to a consumer culture implying personal and global wounds will be healed if only we drive the right cars, wear the right cuts of clothes, and apply the perfect beauty secrets.

When the revived Honeywell Project scheduled its first civil disobedience in November 1982, the action was preceded by the premiere of "In The King Of Prussia." In this film, Daniel and Philip Berrigan, along with six others, were tried for entering the General Electric plant in King of Prussia, Pennsylvania, pouring their own blood on missile nose cones, and smashing warheads with hammers. Honeywell Project and other local peace groups pulled out all the stops to help draw the 1,300-person audience to hear Daniel Berrigan, film director Emile Di Antonio, and actor Martin Sheen, but the director of one of the event's two official co-sponsors, a group called Film in the Cities, balked a couple days before the showing. He explained he hadn't known Honeywell Project was going to be involved, and that this unacceptably blurred the lines between art and politics. "We can't have you at the press conference," he told Marv Davidov repeatedly. "We can't have you speaking." The director read a disclaimer at a public press conference and pleaded with Marv to prevent Berrigan from mentioning Honeywell.

The Film In The Cities director believed his organization was doing more than enough by bringing in important and controversial films. So did one of his board members, who called her old friend, Honeywell CEO Edson Spencer, apologizing for their having inadvertently involved themselves in politics. They didn't want to jeopardize financial support for ongoing work by being identified with actions like the sit-in. They were not an advocacy group.

To Marv, however, the moral links were obvious. What, he asked, was the film about except the responsibility of corporations like General Electric and Honeywell for toying with global annihilation? Daniel Berrigan was not appearing as an entertainer.

In the end, Di Antonio invited Marv up from the audience to announce the Honeywell action—and made clear, as did Berrigan and Martin Sheen, that he would stand as a supporter the following morning. The director didn't lose his grants. But Marv had clearly sinned by going beyond fine talk of how nice peace would be, to pinpointing institutions that fueled the arms race course.

Arbitrary power maintains its sway largely through a general climate of fear—as in the St. Dominic Savio student's notion that if he spoke out in the least, "I would be called a liberal and thrown in jail." Those who wield this power label certain visions—like notions that wealth might be popularly controlled—as irredeemably subversive, and damp citizen engagement with critical public issues in general. We also feel this power as a generalized economic pressure: if the costs of living are skyrocketing, we devote more time to simply providing for our children, leaving less for shaping our society in accordance with our dreams. Because distant corporations so dominate our nation, the command structures even of ones not involved in weapons work inevitably reinforce a generalized sense of powerlessness.

The arms race continues in part because maintaining power becomes its own end. In the words of the British historian and peace movement leader, E.P. Thompson, "the cruise and Pershing missiles have got to come [to European deployment] because they are symbols of America's hegemony over its clients and their acceptance is demanded as proof of NATO's 'unity.' They must be put down in noxious nests in England, Germany, Sicily in order to hold the old decaying structure of life-threatening power together. . . . Nuclear weapons are not for the continuation of policies by other means; they are the suppression of politics and the substitution of the symbolism of extermination."

Accepting this suppression of politics takes its toll. In the words of Brazilian educator Paulo Freire, "the culture of silence grows among those denied the democratic experiences out of which critical consciousness emerges." In this context, politics means more than merely the formal mechanisms—the right to choose between Mondale and Reagan: rather it means the chance to accumulate what Gaventa calls the "resources of challenge . . . organization, momentum, consciousness" that enable individuals to act and continue acting for their deepest beliefs.

For all of us lacking an alternative to America's dominant culture, the atomic arms race can become simply one more sordid proof that we are ultimately helpless. We can deny our own hopes, decide awareness only brings pain, and seek instead our purely private sanctuaries. In his book *The Minimal Self*, historian Christopher Lasch examines such a retreat of American culture to narrowed concerns. Acting less from a clear ideological stance than from an absence of vision, this minimal self avoids broader responsibilities and participation in a "public or common world," and clings instead to family, friends, and the most immediate spheres of life. Dreams degenerate to those of becoming rich in the pending bad years, or more often, echo to those of Kafka's beleaguered burrow creature—merely getting by day to day and month to month. Individuals lose what Lasch calls the traditionally sustaining webs "of human associations and collective memories," as well as the ability to form political movements to address their ills' root causes. As broad issues fade away, responsibility ends, as Bob Willard said, at the door to one's home.

With enough vision, individuals can fend off official lies and betrayals by keeping their hope and trusting instead the admittedly fallible dreams of their fellow ordinary humans. Our culture's ills can breed resistance as well as fatalistic cynicism. But the very illicit actions of state can also be seen as easy, bitter proof that nothing can be done.

We see this process of resignation in the high school students interviewed by the national University of Michigan study, over half of whom believed their actions mattered little in the world. And we see it in the near-deification of corporate entrepreneurs, the young upwardly mobile who serve as their junior stewards, and others who resolutely pursue private interest while letting its messy social and economic effects fall where they may. Resignation is embodied as well in reactions like those of the reactor director at a plutonium production plant in Washington's Hanford reservation when he explained how he feared atomic weapons and thought the more we had, the more risk of nuclear war—then he insisted that if government experts judged the warheads necessary it was his job to continue helping produce them. The same resignation surfaces in the gallows humor that had Vietnam marines mocking their expendability through a song, a letter to a generic mom, which went, "Tough shit, tough shit, your kid got greased. But what the fuck, he was just a grunt."

In part, this cynicism stems from a general isolation. We have become ruled by America's traditional get-what-you-can individualism, and dislocated by an economy that simultaneously promises entrepreneurial glory while shunting more and more of us into bottom-rung jobs as orderlies, clerks, and MacDonalds' cashiers. We are left with few notions of common good beyond those embodied in the rhetoric of national security militarism, pork-barrel dependency, and corporate paternalism. Lacking even the vocabulary to express cooperative visions, we instead pursue our classic tendency, described by Alexis De Tocqueville, for "each [American] citizen to isolate himself from the mass of his fellows and withdraw into the circle of family and friends." Particularly for those of us working for institutions that allow scant space for our voices and our dreams, it becomes easy to project a Hobbesian world where power solely means armed might.

Beyond our fears of losing what we have, the erosion of our values and sense of community by market forces, and our generalized feeling of helplessness, we may be haunted by the ambiguities of being what theologian Ronald Sider termed a nation of *Rich Christians in an Age of Hunger*. We sense, with half-buried vision, that a good chunk of our affluence may ride on the backs of nations and peoples beyond our borders, believe that we may have little choice but to preserve— as a later-repentant George Kennan wrote in a key 1948 State Department document—"a pattern of relationships which will permit us to maintain this position of disparity."

But this pattern—of endless economic expansion in a world of always receptive global markets—ends up being another name for what historian William Appleman Williams termed *Empire As a Way of Life*. He explains: "Once people begin to acquire and enjoy and take for granted and waste surplus resources and space as a routine part of their lives, and to view them a sign of God's favor, then it requires a genius to make a career—let alone create a culture—on the basis of agreeing to limits."

Because it is frequently seen in a context of fatalism, complacency, and cultural atomization, the bomb can become even more of a reason for helplessness. "When you're dead, you're dead," we rationalize, deeming atomic weapons no more destructive than conventional bullets or bombs. Why worry about nuclear war when there are already toxic wastes, acid rain, and people killing themselves on the highways? Made aware of nuclear horrors by the peace movement, we may embrace them—as did Secretary of State Shultz in his commentary on *The Day After*—as a guarantee that deterrence will continue its tightrope balancing act. In the phrase of Amanda Domingo, we change to another channel because we're scared.

Like the weapons themselves, this psychic numbing becomes a constant, a pull like the wind and tides, capable of being ruptured by popular outcry, yet so present that its sway, unless continually challenged, will inevitably return. The late-1950s and early-1960s ban-the-bomb movement faded away at precisely the point at which it halted above-ground nuclear testing and created the climate for the initial SALT and nonproliferation treaties. Even as the actual rate of testing steadily increased and weapons systems modernized to increasingly precarious levels, the threat became more invisible and distant. On a day-to-day level, routine life tends to mask and lull us. As Modjesca said, people end up caring about "what song is on the radio or what they're going to buy, not about what kind of world they're going to leave for their children."

There are ways to break out of this inner retreat and begin to act for dreams of global peace, the "beloved community," or simply the continuance of ordinary life. But to do so requires grappling with possibilities, both dire and redeeming, that are not constantly thrust before our eyes: reaching beyond the minimal self to imagine a world linked, if nothing else, by common necessity.

## The Expendable Human

As a beginning, the necessary change requires overcoming a notion that can be called "the expendable human": the assumed right to sacrifice individual lives for a presumed greater good; the acceptance of a world, as Albert Camus said, "where murder is legitimate." Unlike the Nazis with their *untermenshen*—subhumans—we don't entirely relegate our enemies to a separate species. But even when we resist branding them as gooks, krauts, or chinks, they become faceless as we annihilate them. "Let the rats squeal," proclaimed a Vermont congressman, heralding the dropping of the Hiroshima bomb. "We have no scorched-earth policy," stated Guatemala's U.S.-supported dictator, Ephraim Rios Montt. "We have a policy of scorched Communists." Ronald Reagan explains how Americans "have a different regard for human life than those monsters do." In the words of a 1950s U.S. Army manual, "the Communist soldier is a weapon, not a human."

Of course we are neither the first nor the only society to condemn massive numbers of unknown lives. Vietnam-era responses—such as those illuminated by polls in which more than half of those asked refused to believe the My Lai killings occurred, or stacks of letters attacking *Life* magazine for printing pictures of the naked corpses in a family publication—find a counterpart in Soviet citizens turning a blind resigned eye towards Hungary and Poland. We inhabit an age when, in the words of novelist Hans Koning, a professor can "think up a plan while brushing his teeth, have it typed in six copies with nice margins, send it to the President, and presto, a hundred thousand Vietnamese" [read Salvadorans or Chileans, Afghans or Czechs] are "pushed out of their beds or cots or whatever they sleep in, trucked five hundred miles," and shot or bombed if they fail to comply.

As psychologist Sam Keen has shown, images of the demon other—beasts, vermin, barbarians, faceless puppets or robots, and despoilers of women, children, religion, and the hearth—remain remarkably consistent on all sides of nearly whatever modern war one chooses to examine. Yet our willingness to make other peoples expendable also feeds on projections of our own particular hurt. Indochina frustrates our will, so we send in "Rambo" to finish the job; multinationals toy with our lives, so we envision a world of red subjugation. In all cases the enemy wants our liberty, property, and life. Because they would gladly exterminate us if left unchecked, we must anticipate by preparing to kill them all. In the words of former Senate Armed Services Committee Chair Richard Russell, "If we have to start all over again with Adam and Eve," we should make sure these survivors end up "Americans and not Russians."

Even where the acknowledgedly innocent are involved, the deaths produced by the arms race are deemed regrettably necessary. Leaving aside economic devastation and the atomic fallout now diffused throughout the globe, the list of those made incidentally expendable includes the over 200,000 atomic veterans: marched into Nevada test zones while chaplains told them the atomic fireball would be "a wonderful sight to behold"; designated, with minimal supervision or training, to clean up highly radioactive ships anchored near the Bikini Atoll H-bomb explosions; sent into Hiroshima and Nagasaki almost on the heels of the bombs. Years later, cancer linked these soldiers and sailors as fellow victims with residents of the small Utah towns raked by downwind radiation, with exposed weapons facility workers, and with the peoples of Tahiti and the other Micronesian islands who were in the way of U.S. missile launches and French atomic tests. A recent study by scientists at the Oak Ridge atomic complex proposes that, because of the long latency period between radioactive exposure and the development of cancers, the United States could best survive an atomic attack if older people did the jobs and ate the foods that would carry the greatest risk of contamination.

Elie Wiesel has suggested that "we are all now Jews" in facing the nuclear age. Whether for ourselves, or for anyone on the planet, our acceptance of human expendability is core to the damage done to vision and spirit, even as the warheads rest in their silos. As Marshall Frady has written, describing the effects of slavery on white Southerners:

> That curse consisted of all the deliberate little deadenings of his heart and mind—the numberless small violences, like self-mutilations, against

his own soul that were necessary to bear the natural outrage of slavery and then its camouflaged sequel, segregation. Possibly the only true capital crime is the assumption of an aptitude for converting the personal into the impersonal, the human into the abstract; from that subtle decadence all other sins derive.

That we prepare daily to instantly obliterate our fellow humans' unique webs of dreams, memories, and hopes on a scale unimaginable in any previous time marks the extension of Frady's "subtle decadence" throughout our culture. Yet, by pushing us to reject this expendability, our situation can also offer a glimpse of a different path; it can force us to ask, as did Mary Mills, whether a person in jail, Central America, or the Soviet Union matters in the sight of God as much as we do. We can discover a world not of implacable opponents, but of fellow frail humans.

## Real Security

Rejecting the notion of the expendable human does not necessarily mean taking on a stance of absolute pacifism. Roger Fisher, of the Harvard Negotiations Project, proposes graduated step-downs, while half-seriously suggesting we counter our numbing by implanting the codes required for ordering a nuclear strike in a capsule next to the heart of a volunteer who the president would personally have to kill with a butcher knife before launching the weapons. At the least we must understand the present and potential costs of our willingness to annihilate entire populations for a presumed greater good. We must recognize how much we debase our culture even in preparing for this possibility, and begin to act in a manner, as Camus once suggested, that will make us neither tacit victims nor tacit executioners.

Acknowledgment of our shared vulnerability may offer common ground with those our government presently portrays as our enemies. Yet American citizens often accept the arms race not only because they demonize the Soviet people, but because they fear the warheads presently aimed at our cities and silos, and fear as well a legacy of genuine barbarism stretching from the Stalinist gulag and crushing of dissent in Czechoslovakia, East Germany, and Hungary, to the ongoing war in Afghanistan. Although it would be false to cast this fear as the sole reason individuals do nothing about the growing peril, neither can it simply be dismissed.

We can respond to these apprehensions without getting lost in endless fights about technical abstractions. We need not attempt to match the NORAD computer in charting every maze of probable action and possible intent, but need rather to understand the direction our nation must head and to recognize that—as Richard Barnet once said—there exist an array of reasonable paths towards reversal of the arms race, all better than our present course.

These paths have been amply examined in studies of the atomic threat's historical, technological, and diplomatic facets. But it seems useful to explore at least a few aspects of the process that must occur. The Freeze Movement attempted to anticipate mistrust of the Soviets by proposing an immediate stop to new testing and deployment, and by requiring the security of bilateral agreement. Clearly, the message was made more salable—by asking only, as the California ads said, that "our leaders should sit down with the Russians and figure out a way to stop the arms race." This approach avoided the attacks, like one by Leon Wieseltier in *The New Republic*, that—raising the specter of our nation instantly weaponless—tarred unilaterialism as "a disgraceful notion, produced by people who think so little of themselves that they believe in nothing except life." The Freeze succeeded in challenging the belief that strength lies in having ever-increasing numbers of warheads, provided a forum to demonstrate the superpowers' essential strategic parity, and offered an alternative to trying to oppose the arms race by attacking the weapons systems one at a time. Most of all, it asked, in a manner millions of citizens could comprehend, that the endless cycles of escalation be halted.

But because it so stressed bilateral agreement, the Freeze allowed the Reagan administration to diffuse much of the growing disarmament consensus with Geneva talks and the promised technical fix of a Star Wars shield. The same congressional representatives who approved its legislative passage could promptly turn around and pass the MX, the Euromissiles, research for an array of space-based weapons, and the largest "peacetime" military budget in U.S. history. Given that national governments rarely move in synchronicity, and that one side's deterrence is the other's provocation, institutionalized forces in both the United States and the Soviet Union have used the rhetoric of peace, stability, and strategic balance to propel the arms race steadily forward for over forty years. With such a legacy, we must ask whether the wait for bilateral agreements is more of a trap than a salvation.

In the words of Herbert York, an eminent physicist who worked on the Manhattan Project, directed Defense Department research and engineering, and served as science advisor to President Eisenhower:

> We have repeatedly taken unilateral actions that have unnecessarily accelerated the race. . . . Just as our unilateral actions were in large part responsible for the current dangerous state of affairs, we must expect that unilateral moves on our part will be necessary if we are ever to get the whole process reversed.

Abandoning what Robert Borosage has termed "the bilateral box" does not necessarily mean dropping all cherished assumptions of deterrence. Given how our actions and those of the Soviets trigger each other, we can initiate the equivalent of a challenge-grant halt, by working directly towards reversal, then waiting, at any given de-escalation point, for a reciprocal response. In 1961, University of Illinois psychologist Charles Osgood developed just such a formula for structured unilateral moves. He called it GRIT, Graduated and Reciprocated Initiatives in Tension Reduction, and proposed that the two nations alternate in taking direct steps to curtail the steady growth of their weapons arsenals. GRIT's principles were used by President John F. Kennedy, when he initiated a unilateral halt to atmospheric testing, Khruschev reciprocated, and the 1963 Above-Ground Test Ban Treaty was formally negotiated and signed.

In part because the Reagan administration now threatens to upset the traditional balance of terror, former arms race shepherds like Robert McNamara and McGeorge Bundy have recently taken on opposition stances. The current peace movement both trades on the legitimacy of these individuals and is constrained by embracing their stress on deterrence, mistrust of unilateral action, and desire to regain an equilibrium now profoundly unsettled. But the movement is shaped as well by those who have been called the new abolitionists, those who judge atomic warheads and perhaps all weapons of mass destructive power as simply morally unacceptable.

Activist sentiment differs as to the most appropriate reversal programs, and even individuals' internal judgments contain uncertainties. Bill Cusak separates his personal belief in a Jesus who would not shoot a Russian even to save his life from his public focus on the Freeze's modest bilateralism. Individuals cast in the role of spokesperson stress specific de-escalation programs, like Willens with his five-step plan for initial rollbacks. Others, like Shelley Berman and his committed fellow teachers, primarily seek to raise broad questions about national choices in a critical time. Some, like the Trident and Honeywell blockaders, focus on specific weapons systems or the corporate webs that support them—leaving negotiation of the final treaties as a secondary concern.

How can the movement reconcile these diverse approaches, and allow individuals with radically different visions to join in rolling back our common jeopardy? Can these differences aid, and not hamper, attempts to shift the fundamental course of our culture? We might begin by recognizing the fundamental choice between believing we can live forever with atomic warheads, managing them perfectly, through technical escalations and global crises, for longer than any social arrangement has existed in human history; or between taking a path perhaps as challenging as any our species has had to travel, yet at least heading towards the warheads' eventual elimination.

If we take this latter course, we can hold in abeyance the decision of whether or not to relinquish our last ten, fifty, or even one thousand presumably protective warheads; can maintain the threat of annihilating 20 or 200 million Soviet men, women, and children if their government should choose to attack us first; can begin the process of reversal, while laying aside differences as to how we will traverse the final stages of our journey. It is perhaps useful to envision the dismantling of the arms race as a time-line, extending between our present crisis and a desired future in which our planet would be secure from these annihilatory threats. Beginning at our present level of weapons buildup, with Reagan's $300 billion military budgets and 30,000 strategic and tactical warheads, we might respond to direct Soviet initiatives like the unilateral halt in weapons testing begun on Hiroshima's fortieth anniversary, or like recent, and far more comprehensive proposals for a mutual rollback. Or might initiate our own unilateral halts in destabilizing systems, returning to "the other side" the moral and political burden of taking the next step. In the judgment of former Massachusetts Institute of Technology president Jerome Weisner, if Moscow built more weapons for decades and Washington did nothing, we could still mount a pulverizing retaliatory response.

Other proposals for cuts distinguish aspects of military strength that deters direct attack from and those serving to buttress global

intervention. George Kennan suggests immediate fifty percent re-
ductions in all atomic arsenals, with each superpower determining
which weapons would be turned in and destroyed—a proposal he
says could "be implemented at once and without further wrangling
among the experts, and [could be] subject to such national means of
verification as now lie at the disposal of the two powers." We could,
in the process, return to the levels of the Nixon and Ford eras,
perhaps keeping single-warhead submarine missiles for maximum
invulnerability. Or even return to the 500 deliverable warheads that
a study commissioned by Robert McNamara, during the early-
1960s, decided would be enough to kill a third of the Soviet citizens,
destroy nearly two-thirds of their industrial capacity, and thus ensure
deterrence as much as the grandest arsenal. As Kennan said, regarding his fifty percent proposal, "whether the balance of reduction
would be precisely even—whether it could be constructed to statis-
tically favor one side or the other—would not be the question. Once
we start thinking that way, we would be back on the same old fateful
track that has brought us to where we are today. Whatever the precise
results of such a reduction, there would still be plenty of overkill
left—so much so that if this first operation were successful, I would
then like to see a second one put in hand to rid us of at least two-
thirds of what would be left."

At some point we could even go beyond McNamara and Kennan's prescriptions, perhaps undertaking Jonathan Schell's proposal
in which atomic weapons would be eliminated but remain capable
of being rebuilt should one side or the other end up cheating. Or
we could shift to a reliance on primarily defensive weapons—mines,
antitank guns, and precision-guided munitions versus a global network of nuclear deployments.

The point in laying out these possibilities is not to expect instant
agreement on the farthest reaches of arms race reversal, but to recognize that, as Kennan says, de-escalation means accepting "the minor risks in order to avoid the supreme ones." The range of possible
solutions reflects the diverse voices in the movement, and the strength
possible if individuals can both express their particular visions and
work together on common ground. It will be far more productive to
debate whether to abandon the last 500 or 1,000 atomic weapons
when they are all that remains, than to say that, because some wish
them entirely abolished and others disagree, we must forever follow
the track of endless escalation.

Yet the nuclear crisis involves not only weapons technologies, but also relationships between nations and individuals. The peace movements challenge not only the MX, cruises, and Tridents, but also a climate of mistrust that feeds the escalation's reach. This does not imply sentimental naïvete—about either the Soviet capacity for repressiveness or America's imperial streak—but a recognition, once more, of our shared stake on the earth, and an understanding that all actions—whether of nations or individuals—either reduce the jeopardy or fuel the fires.

Given this, we should at least begin to consider whether nations can be securely defended without the use of weapons. Harvard political scientist Gene Sharp proposes what he calls civilian based defense—the training of entire populations to resist external aggression without force of arms. Sharp's three-volume study, *The Politics of Nonviolent Action*, was hardheaded enough to draw praise from not only Margaret Mead and Coretta King, but also from a colonel at the U.S. Army War College and a Navy captain who said it should be required reading at Annapolis. The book detailed examples ranging from the stamp act boycotts and Boston Tea Party of the American Revolution, to Norwegian teachers who, after their country was occupied by the Nazis, refused to accept fascist education guidelines for teaching their children and successfully resisted even after 1,000 of them were taken to concentration camps and threatened with death. The Nazis at last capitulated, as they did in another situation in which Aryans with Jewish wives or husbands stood outside the deportation center and demanded their loved ones be released. Sharp suggests integrating these and other nonviolent resistance models into planned defense strategies, whereby nations would train special forces and equip them with communications devices, printing presses, mobile broadcasting stations, and other tools for facilitating mass noncooperation. He suspects these forces could defend national integrity with far less loss of life than conventional military approaches.

Again, civilian based defense is not something we need to rely on immediately; it is merely a direction to explore and point toward. The other pole, of fear and suspicion enshrined as eternal virtues, is exemplified by the context in which martial law crushed Poland's Solidarity movement in December of 1981. The government's repressive response was prompted not only by the nation's internal chaos, and by Solidarity's threats to institutionalized bureaucracy, but also by pending European deployment of cruise and Pershing II missiles, and a general tone of Western belligerence. Afghanistan, which has helped blur American memory of Vietnam, was invaded, not in a time of U.S. "softening," but after NATO announcement of the same planned Euromissile deployments, after Senate hostility to SALT II, and amidst a general collapse of detente—justified then and now through rhetoric nearly identical to that used to rationalize U.S. interventions in Vietnam, Chile, Guatemala, the Dominican Republic, and the Philippines. Just as the Soviet's 1948 Czechoslovakian coup helped deflect the profound worldwide concern growing in the wake of Hiroshima and Nagasaki, so the repression of Solidarity severely damaged current Western European peace efforts, for the moment abruptly checking, in E.P. Thompson's judgment, "a hope that had been growing . . . of healing our split continent by the convergence of popular movements."

Similarly, one can trace at least a certain share of Russian paranoia to the 1918 intervention, when U.S. troops landed in Archangel and Vladivostok and for two years joined the forces of Britain, France, Japan, and the Czechs in supporting White Tsarist armies against the nascent Soviet revolution. Even Stalin's brutal hold over Eastern Europe was in part a consequence of Roosevelt's failed promises regarding the opening of an early second front in France: a choice, made over the objections of Generals Marshall and Eisenhower, to let the Soviets continue to do the bulk of the dying. The Russians suffered a total of 20 million casualties versus 400,000 U.S. dead, mainly because Roosevelt limited our European contribution to ninety divisions. When the Soviets rolled beyond their borders to destroy the German forces, they received further proof their citizens were deemed expendable by Western powers, and stayed to consolidate control—much as the United States did in crushing dissident forces in nations like Greece and Turkey.

More currently, U.S. proxy wars in the Middle East and Central America provide testing grounds and impetus for research and development on "near-nuclear" weapons like the advanced cluster munitions—derivatives of those Honeywell produced during the Vietnam War—which combine with "fuel-air explosives" to offer destructive power as great as small atomic weapons. Thus, these wars not only erode the nuclear threshold, but also further buttress Soviet perceptions of the United States as an arrogant imperial power, ruthless enough to be checked only by immense military might. These wars also open possibilities that U.S. troops, like those in the Rapid Deployment Force, might resort to atomic strikes if sufficiently surrounded and besieged.

Nixon considered just such a choice at Khe Sahn in Vietnam; in 1954 atomic-armed bombers flew into Nicaragua to buttress our overthrow of a Guatemalan government which had offended United Fruit; the United States has made nuclear threats over Korea, Cuba, and Lebanon: our warheads have most often been brandished during Third World interventions. Even in situations in which use of atomic forces is unlikely, intervention fans war fevers at home: again making every nation an expendable domino in the endless East-West conflict; inviting Americans to rally behind the brave boys on the line; debasing our language with terms like Dinks and Slopes, body counts, pacification teams, and interchangeable terrorist enemies; feeding further cycles of revenge and retribution. By pushing us to cede moral judgments to the military experts and by making commonplace profound violations of rights and dignity, these wars proclaim our right to destroy whatever humble human refuges exist in order to save them.

The arms race feeds on what E.P. Thompson terms "consequences of consequences" in other ways as well. When it strip mines our common capital, we lose resources that could be used to research and purchase technologies, both present and pending, that can move us towards sustainable ways of living. Unable to "afford," for instance, even the most basic conservation measures, or to develop renewable and flexible sources of heat, light, and power, Americans use one third more energy per capita than citizens of West Germany and twice that of those of Sweden—both nations whose standards of living have now surpassed our own. Our brittle and externally dependent energy system is, as a consequence, profoundly vulnerable to sabotage and accidental breakdown: a vulnerability for which we compensate by proclaiming (as Jimmy Carter did in his final State of the Union address) an implicit right to begin a nuclear war over Middle Eastern oil. We might compare our nation to a family barricading their house against alien barbarians by doggedly transferring foundation stones from the pilings below.

On both sides of the East-West divide, the arms race makes cultures less stable, and, therefore, more likely to embark on reckless confrontations. Imperial arrogance is not new in human history: our democratic predecessors, the Athenians, were only too willing, during their war with Sparta, to destroy the island of Melos when its inhabitants attempted to maintain neutrality. Yet because we now face consequences far more terminal than the sacking and salting of defeated cities, we cannot ignore our actions' broadest consequences.

Cultural polarization can be assuaged by the encounters of ordinary citizens. Two of Millicent's fellow Seattle actors visited the Soviet Union as part of a Russian-language version of "Peace Child," as did a "Peace Chorus," which sang phonetically transcribed songs in the churches and schools of Leningrad, Moscow, and Tashkent. Soviet-American meetings of doctors, scientists, and other professionals have become commonplace. A one-hour discussion between two American and two Russian physicians was broadcast, uncut and uninterrupted, on Soviet national television, and was succeeded by a parallel binational panel in which Carl Sagan and other noted scientists addressed the implications of the "nuclear winter." Satellite "space bridges" have allowed thousands of individuals from the countries of the two implacable enemies to witness reciprocal cultural presentations and even hold joint forums. Further proposals suggest massive visitor exchanges to bring the presently adversary cultures closer through direct human bonds, and to enable individuals to consciously choose, through a presence in the targeted lands, to deter the use of their own governments' weapons.

At times this citizen diplomacy directly challenges Cold War hegemony. When Petra Kelly of the West German Green Party met with East German leader Erich Honecker, she wore a t-shirt with the prohibited "Swords into Plowshares" symbol of that nation's dissident peace movement. In December 1981, 100 German writers, led by Gunter Grass and other leading literary figures, held a peace symposium in East Berlin, out of which came a book that has sold consistently on both sides of the East-West divide. The small group of Moscow scientists, doctors, artists, and academics who formed the Group to Establish Trust Between the U.S.S.R. and the United States were attacked precisely because of their organization's links with Western activists and their general rejection of Cold War ideology. The platform of European Nuclear Disarmament, a body helping coordinate peace efforts from Britain and West Germany, to Holland and Greece—and working as well with independent groups in the Warsaw Pact countries—proposes "detente from below," explaining, "We must commence to act as if a united, neutral and pacific Europe already exists. We must learn to be loyal, not to 'East' or 'West,' but to each other."

The benchmark of our time is severed connection: While American life continues on, unaffected and innocent, the U.S. Congress can support a massive and largely unreported El Salvadoran air war, fund contras to massacre Nicaraguan teachers, health workers, and peasants; and prop up murderous regimes like those in Guatemala, Turkey and Chile. And as the warheads build, day by day, our ordinary worlds continue to appear as solid as ever. To challenge the distant cataclysms requires breaking entrenched cycles of betrayal and despair.

At its strongest, the necessary understanding connects remote actions of state with our intimate lives. After novelist Ken Kesey's son died when the ramshackle bus carrying the Oregon wrestling team skidded off an icy mountain road, Kesey wrote to Oregon Senator Mark Hatfield. He explained how his first response had been to turn the other cheek, accept the tragedy as fate, and absolve individuals or institutions of any blame.

"But what," he continued, "if the other cheek is somebody else's kid? In some other slapdash rig? On some other ill-fated underfunded trip next wrestling season? Or next debate season? Or next volleyball season? Moreover, what if this young blood has been spilled not merely to congregate people and their feelings, but also to illuminate a thing going wrong?"

Kesey considered blaming the university wrestling coach "for driving a borrowed rig over a treacherous pass without snow studs, or seatbelts, or even doors that closed properly"; or the state of Oregon for not better funding the program; or the National Collegiate Athletic Association, for "fostering a situation where more energy is devoted to monitoring the ethic of the few 'stars' in the sports firmament than to the actual welfare of the untold thousands of unknown athletes traveling to their minor events all across the nation." He mentioned other accidents on trips of other schools, then asked:

> But what can they do? . . . It's hard enough to pass a school budget in Oregon without asking for fancy protection. Just not enough money in the communities. Nobody wants to increase property taxes, not even for safer playgrounds, let alone for safer activity buses. . . .

Then, the other night, as I watched the national news, it came to me. We were lobbing those 16-inch shells into the hills of Lebanon. The Pentagon spokesman said he wasn't certain exactly which faction we were hitting, but he reassured us that we were certainly hitting *somebody*. Then he was asked what each of those shells cost. The price was something enormous. I can't remember. But the spokesman countered by saying that the price for national defense is always high, yet it must be paid.

And I began to get mad, Senator. I had finally found where the blame must b~ laid; that the money we are spending for national defense is not defending us from the villains real and near, the awful villians of ignorance, and cancer, and heart disease and highway death. How many school buses could be outfitted with seatbelts with the money spent for one of those 16-inch shells?

Kesey concluded by saying he might have to join "those old long-haired peaceniks on the railroad tracks when the next White Train full of nuclear warheads rolls across our land." He thought it maybe "the job God has dealt this hand around."

© ryph gar cia 1986

# 7.   Village Politics

## The Secular and the Sacred

Given that the loss of Kesey's son leads him back to the necessity of acting in the world, how does belief in the connecting force he calls God come to bear in the present time? What distinguishes a Jeff Dietrich or Dan Delaney from a James Watt or Jerry Falwell? What is the difference between blockading an Air Force base as an act of religious witness, or waiting for Armageddon and the rapture of the saved? Between the faith of Kim Wahl and that of a local fellow Catholic who wrote, admonishing her, "Be content with resisting the evil within yourself."

Discussing the functions served by religious faith in individuals' lives, sociologist Thomas O'Dea speaks of consolation: "emotional support in the face of uncertainty, disappointment, and failure," a balm for the afflicted and wounded, a sense that all is occurring as part of God's plan. Religion also offers security, "established points of reference amid the conflicts and ambiguities of human opinion," and identity—through a set of beliefs about human nature and destiny—which one can either draw on for self-definition and strength, or project outward to distinguish the chosen faithful from the barbarians outside the gates. As when religion sanctifies established society's norms and values, these purposes are essentially conservative: circumscribing the power and right of individuals to act in ways not defined by the hallowed textual words, and furthering the acceptance of violence and injustice as a seemingly regrettable, but ultimately necessary part of God's plan.

Oppositely arrayed are religion's prophetic strains: the paths of Moses, Isaiah, and Jeremiah; of Jesus driving the trinket-sellers from the temple and breaking Sabbath laws to feed the poor; of Bill Cusak's Christ, who would not shoot the Russian to save his life; of Martin Luther, announcing "Here I stand. I can do no other." Much as a call to serve higher truths can breed purely inward piety, it can also furnish standards against which to measure our lives, as in Bonhoeffer's path of discipleship, or Charley Meconis's statement that "Christianity is risky business, not just to give you comfort, at least in the short-term way that the society defines, but to put you in a difficult situation."

As Charley pointed out, it is a trap to look solely at the religious resisters and forget the far-vaster constituency of those Bill Cusak termed "the radio preachers": those leading the shock troops of a callous, arrogant culture that is all too ready to push the planet to destruction in God's name. At a Los Angeles demonstration, a red white and blue van pulled up, decorated with a huge picture of a bible and the words, "If no Jesus—Hell." A frightened nine-year-old stepped out clutching his own bible and flag, while a lean man yelled from a bullhorn: "God bless Reagan. God bless bombs. God is a man of war." Jerry Falwell routinely presents only slightly more moderated sentiments directly to our president, who publicly muses on whether we might be entering the Biblical end times. *Sojourners* circulates 60,000 copies, whereas *The Plain Truth*, which explains that the atomic threat will be stopped only "by the returning Jesus Christ," distributes seven-and-a-half million.

It remains to be seen whether Baptists can or will reach Baptists, and whether the religious abolitionists can successfully challenge those willing to fight World War III as a crusade or prophecy. Will the mainstream churches be able to overcome the strain of accommodation which insists that Caesar's world is inevitably corrupt, that one cannot hold nations to standards of individual virtue, and—in a position staked out in the initial Cold War era by Reinhold Niebuhr, then extended, secularized, and stripped of all moral qualms by individuals like Henry Kissinger and Jeane Kirkpatrick—that one can only support a perhaps-flawed American system against the ultimate Soviet evil? Biblical examples aside, Charley questioned how much religious institutions have ever challenged secular authority except where their own prerogatives were threatened.

Yet numerous churches are taking on activist and visionary roles, in part as a legacy of the Civil Rights Movement and Vietnam era resistance, denominational silences during the World War II holocaust, and liberatory currents that have shaken Christianity during the past two decades. Against an all-leveling consumer culture and a Gatling-gun pragmatism, religion can uphold—as Jim Watkins stressed in his talk to Congaree Presbytery—values transcending those of the given social order. And if faith includes even the barest notions of stewardship, when could the exercise of these values be more needed?

Seattle's Raymond Hunthausen, the Catholic archbishop who termed Trident "The Auschwitz of Puget Sound," has called individuals "to love one another as we love ourselves." God "won't force us," Hunthausen says. "If our world is destroyed by nuclear fire it may be that God will be sad—if God can be sad. But he gives us that choice, and I think the choices are clear."

Because religion often addresses notions like a historical end time, it can furnish language to help us explore the implications of ultimate global annihilation, and to teach us that the earth is not ours to do with what we will. By releasing our dreams of mastering all nature and all humanity, we can reject that "nuclear idolatry" by which, to quote Amarillo Bishop Leroy Matthiessen, "whatever God we formally profess, we bow before, we tithe to, we [now] place our trust in quite different gods—gods of metal."

Religious vision can also define a clear framework for hope. As Charley Meconis said, it matters if some higher power exists to redeem the individual actions that often seem incapable of slowing the ongoing juggernauts of history. In the words of novelist David Bradley, we can believe "that somewhere, never mind exactly where, something good and right and fair is happening which someday, never mind exactly when, will make itself apparent; that in some distant constellation a star has flamed to unaccustomed brilliance, and what we must do is wait for the arrival of the light." We can take consolation in the promise that we are not alone, even in a time of fear and uncertainty, and that much as the weapons culture can defeat or destroy individual lives, it cannot destroy the fundamental forces that move the earth. As in the case of the debates within

Congaree Presbytery, or the groups springing up in Catholic parishes as a consequence of the bishops' Pastoral Letter, churches can become venues of human contact, dissenting community, and public life beyond the domains of the office, mill, or shopping mall. Vesting moral questioning with broader legitimacy, theological doctrine can offer historical and biblical bases for a tradition that links closeness to God with the pursuit of justice and views the divine kingdom in everyday acts of love and solidarity. The choice becomes not how history will turn out, but how we will respond to the cries and wounds of our fellow humans, and how we will recognize that, as Elie Wiesel has said, "Any person, by virtue of being a son or a daughter of humanity, is a living sanctuary whom nobody has the right to invade."

At its best, religious vision avoids abdicating moral engagement through cynical relativism, by retaining a voice capable of stating: "This is wrong. This is unjust. We must find a different way to live." But the faith that can give religion its strength, also risks exclusivity: a view of one's perspective as the sole legitimate truth, like that of the fundamentalists who would condemn to hell all not sharing their particular words, symbols, and rituals. Those acting out of theological faith should be wary about legislating particular beliefs as universal visions.

At times religious traditions also seem to prize God's creations— life in its raw biological state—far more than human culture and creation. The mystics are right in warning against seduction by routine comforts and routine existence. But thin gruel also grows tiresome. The path of the martyrs may carry its own double message of disdain for the very ordinary worlds for which we fight. Unless the peace and justice movements offer visions richer, more sensual, and more rooted in fundamental human desires than those presently offered by our culture, it is unlikely that the bulk of American citizens will give up even their manufactured dreams.

Many of deep religious faith clearly acknowledge this. Dan Delaney fights on the side "of good beer." Lutheran Jon Nelson chides the Coast Guard for seizing from the *Plowshares* his prized jar of pickled herring. In the future, explains the Jewish Talmud, "each person will have to give account for having seen wonderful foods— and not having eaten them." And, as Jonathan Schell makes clear, "since a love of life may ultimately be all that we have to pit against our doom, we cannot afford thoughtlessly to tear aside any of its manifestations."

Secular perspectives, although they carry less risk of fundamentalist absolutism or ascetic detachment, have a more slippery task in explaining how courageous moral actions will be redeemed. In the words of Max Weber, "The Christian does rightly and leaves the results with the Lord." Without an equivalent faith and ethic of conviction, individuals can too easily feel isolated and powerless, or withdraw inward to follow the developing cataclysms as if they were weekly baseball standings. When difficult times come—as in the case of Reagan's MX and contra victories, or the overwhelming weight of an often blind and destructive culture—it becomes tempting to retreat to pessimism, despair, and what Bob Willard called the "fortress of comfortable indifference."

Given that secular activists find enough difficulty merely in working to reverse weapons escalation, it may seem an additional burden to have to also invent a broader vision. Yet it is a trap to treat the arms race as a purely technical problem that can be resolved with mere elbow grease and can-do spirit. This approach risks so circumscribing perspective that individuals may end up gaining their immediate demands—as in the 1950s opposition to above-ground nuclear testing—while the arms race continues essentially unchecked. Those who take this approach also ignore not only the underlying currents that produced the present state of affairs, but also the necessary hope that, in trying to save the world, their actions will also make it, if not millennially perfect, at least a bit more hospitable to modest human dreams.

Traditionally the secular left has trusted a historical promise: one positing a general motion in the direction of human freedom. Yet this history is now threatened with instant termination, making all futures quite contingent. However deformed by the iron cordons of the West, existing revolutionary societies have replicated enough of their own barbarism and oppression to give pause to those who would embrace their models as instant salvation. A few nations—from Sweden and Holland, to Yugoslavia and Nicaragua—have made salient innovations in political or economic liberty, but still compromise with certain forms of unaccountable wealth or power. Historical examples also flicker—Spanish anarchism, the 1956 Hungarian workers councils, the fledgling hopes of Polish Solidarity, an American heritage of socialists and populists—to remind us of what may be created with human courage and vision. But they hardly guarantee a benevolent future.

The point is not that each peace organization must create some ultimate political manifesto. But, as is occurring with numerous activists who initially addressed only the nuclear threat's most narrowly defined aspects, questions of global annihilation can at the least be linked with the root politics of ongoing proxy wars, like those in Central America and the Middle East. Secular activists should begin to ask, as do the best of the religious visionaries: what values allow life to bloom in all its diversity and variety; what strengths of character and gifts of everyday existence are most worth prizing and nourishing; what social, economic, political, and cultural arrangements most further human dignity; how can activists achieve these arrangements using means consistent with their ends; and how can ordinary individuals summon the courage to take the risks and make the sacrifices appropriate to our time? The answers may not be the same for all those acting; they certainly will be expressed in different language and through diverse political approaches. But these answers need to offer more than abstract calls for survival or appeals to realpolitik and self-interest. Peace workers can follow the religious example by talking of ideals, moral values, and transcendent visions—by being open advocates of their own most utopian dreams.

Central to articulating these dreams is the notion of connection to other humans and to the natural world. As Lifton has stated, to live fully we need to feel part of something beyond ourselves. In the judgment of Leo Baeck Rabbi Leonard Beerman, American culture has made a mistake in always stressing independence: "Liberation of the individual from the weight of the past. Not being bound by dead ideology. Even, in the Reform tradition of which I'm part, treating Judaism as something to be discovered, not inherited. We bless a child so they may grow up a strong human being and stand on their own. But we don't discuss interdependence."

This interdependence may also be expressed in secular terms. Activists may use a biological model by recognizing that despite distinctions in race, sex, physique, nationality, moral character, or political ideology, humans share a gene pool that is ninety percent the same. Or they may find this connection in the community of individuals who have joined to act on common conscience. E.P. Thompson envisions a new " 'International' of peace movements, nonaligned nations and movements for civil rights and liberation," seeking together "the enlargement of spaces for national autonomy, the peaceful breakup or melding of the [Cold War] blocs and the refusal of every syllable of the vocabulary of nuclear arms." On a more intimate level, individuals can take heart whenever they encounter others who act for a vision of justice, who act, like Erica Bouza, because they feel they must.

Religious and secular perspectives may differ in the relative stress placed on membership in a common human family or on differing interests and roles. "When we first got together," Marv Davidov once recalled, the church-based people said " 'We are all just as guilty as Honeywell management. We are all guilty.' And I said, 'Wait a minute. Let me explain something that I've learned. The management at Honeywell profits from this. They make millions out of murder. They're conscious of their choices. Therefore they're guilty in a different sense from the guilt that you're talking about. You may be guilty to the extent to which you pay your taxes or fail to act when you know. But you're not guilty the same way.' "

He said that the religious people offered, however, an important vision: one of continuance, of doing what was right regardless of cost, of understanding the core commonality shared by all human beings. "They spiritualize us," he said. "And we secularize them."

This convergence and reciprocity offers hope for overcoming the tendency of most political movements to adopt what Weber called an ethic "of ultimate ends," an instrumental pragmatism where, because the goals are noble, one can make whatever manipulations or compromises are necessary to achieve them. The meeting of secular and religious visions counters as well the tendency of many religious activists to believe that pure intentions and a desire for reconciliation will automatically heal all ills. Alternative movements are perhaps strongest when they balance a fundamental insistence on truth with engagement in a direct and public world, and share as well common concepts of grace and rebirth, which may be ascribed either to a divine external presence, or to those mysterious realms of dreams and hopes that lie at the human core. As poet Gary Snyder has written, the sacred "helps take us out of our little selves, into the larger self, to the whole universe."

Rosalie Bertell, a Roman Catholic nun who has used her Ph.D. in mathematics to become a leading expert on radiation and human health, compares our situation with that of the Israelites during their sojourn in the wilderness. The tribes wandered the desert after their exodus from Egypt, and many soon longed for the nourishment and familiar security of their previous bondage. When they were fed by manna from heaven, many resisted and held back. Bertell says we need to know how to take in new nourisment, new manna, from the hopes and community created by our efforts. It is inevitable for us to look backward, near-inevitable for us to mistrust. Like Moses, we might only be able to glimpse the promised land we seek to bring into being. But we have to take the first steps out of Egypt.

## Fractures in the Dream

As we begin these journeys and continue bringing them to fruition, we face not only external obstacles but also those we ourselves internalize. As in the case of Nixon's Vietnam-era atomic threats, the movement's impact on governmental choices may well be hidden. We often find it difficult, therefore, to accept the manna of a chance to act in a time that may matter more than any other, or to accept this chance without recrimination at the slowness with which our efforts make their visible mark in the world. Far too often we slip into doubt and despair.

These feelings stem in part from the sheer difficulty of overcoming our culture's social numbing. Friends or coworkers shrug off our talk of warheads, atomic wastes, or the Salavadoran air war, as if it were only a personal obsession equivalent to bowling, exploring caves, or collecting esoteric spoons. It is easy to become bitter and disenheartened as the continued escalations grind on, or to retreat into an abstracted concern—yes, of course we care—while leaving the world to others presumably less burdened and more noble. Yet those who give up from frustration with the task often rationalize their retreat by citing the movement's internal failings.

These failings center, for many, on moments when the actions of movement participants have refuted their high-sounding ideals. Marv Davidov recalled a Vietnam-era incident in which the Maoist sect, Progressive Labor, demanded podium space at a major demonstration outside Honeywell's shareholders meeting. In return, PL promised not to rush the building doors and to follow the demonstration discipline. But a group led by PL members—and including possible FBI infiltrators—charged the building, hurling beer bottles. A near-riot resulted, in which police covered their badge numbers and maced the ordinary marchers caught in the middle. Coverage of the confrontation threatened to displace focus on Honeywell's cluster bomb production. Years later, when Marv saw some of the former PL members, he told them, "look, you made an agreement with us and you broke it. You're out of the movement and we're still here. Think about it."

Progressive Labor's actions were an extreme case. Yet former Vietnam-era activists still cling to the hurt of wounds from considerably more modest betrayals. Just as Good Samaritan crimes—in which individuals rob or rape those responding to their presumed need—particularly erode fundamental ethics of compassion and concern; just as the Hitler-Stalin pact helped turn a generation of former radicals into Cold War supporters; and as, on a far less global level, Michael Lowe left the Baptist church forever after his congregation tore down the hand-built teen club for a parking lot, so betrayals individuals accept routinely from institutions of power leave far deeper scars when initiated by their comrades. Arrogance or callousness by those supposedly seeking a better world attacks not only the direct relationships involved, but the ideal of change itself.

Beyond going back on their word, the PL members also dangerously romanticized provocation for its own sake, forgetting that to toy with images of insurrection in a time of popular confusion and uncertainty is to invite being cast as part of the threat by those who are more than willing to manipulate common fear. Marv said the movement needs dignity and integrity, which is not to be confused with mealy-mouthed equivocation or polite "moderation" for fear others might take offense—much less with becoming sentimental polyannas. The peace movement can afford neither to dissipate its efforts in brittle rhetoric, millennial projection, or fights over turf—nor to leave a trail of spent activist casualties in its wake.

Current disarmament efforts seem unlikely to debase their vision with talk of "offing the pig" or becoming "outlaws of America." This rhetoric hardly marked the dominant strain in a decade that embodied primarily a tremendous release of hope and an opening up of fundamental social, political, and economic questions. But the seemingly endless, grinding Vietnam War did produce its domestic complement in bitter factionalism and eventual cheerleading for the tortured vision of the Weathermen. Granted, nuclear resisters build on the

Vietnam-era's challenge to indiscriminate and technologically distanced violence; SDS in fact wrote in its founding 1962 Port Huron
Statement, "Our work is guided by the sense that we may be the
last generation in the experiment with living." Yet for all the diversity
of those who ended up opposing that war, their efforts were anchored
primarily in the strengths of youth, passion, and immediacy, what
William Blake called "songs of innocence." And they made the nuclear threat merely one item in a litany of ills—almost preferring,
as historian Paul Boyer suggests, to bury any notion of linkage to
the earlier ban-the-bomb movement, which they viewed as timid,
fastidious, and obsessed with middle-class respectability.

In contrast, those spearheading present peace efforts are older,
more experienced, and far more extensively woven into the fabric
of our culture. Where a significant strain of Vietnam-era resistance
ended up harking back to classic traditions of the Russian Revolution,
the crowds storming the Bastille, and the peasant uprisings that
produced Mao's China, the resisters proceeding now—perhaps because present history seems so evidently tenuous and fragile—seek
a path that both confronts and reconciles.

We see some of this shift in Kesey's letter about the death of his
son. Twenty years ago, he played cultural shaman, and helped define
major strands of the era's common visions. His characters were heroic
individuals standing tall against all comers, cool and indomitable:
the Oregon logger; the Cuckoo's Nest rebel; the acid cowboy, im-
presario of war paint, blinding light shows, and a rainbow bus. Now
Kesey talks of loss and limits, of responsibilities linking him with
the community of other frail humans, of the job being dealt this
hand around.

If the peace movement's model is no longer lone defiance, or classic
insurrections; less a breaking of bars than a questioning as to what
checks on human endeavors may be necessary, then its potential
traps are commensurate with its respectability. In part because the
initial post-Hiroshima atomic weapons opponents acted at a time
when critical social questioning was banished and when the U.S.
government had far greater political legitimacy, they tended to treat
the arms race as a problem demanding either primarily technical
solutions or the panacea of a benign world government. Political,
economic, and social currents that would feed the arms race's relentless progress were primarily ignored, along with any sense that
the United States had been wrong in twice using the weapons on

civilian populations. The bombs were acknowledgedly terrible. The notion that they ushered us into a new world resounded from *Time* and *Life* to *The Saturday Evening Post* and *Ladies Homes Journal*. Yet because discussion of the new future portents floated in detachment from broader contexts, the very fear spurred by citizen outcry almost seeded the ground for promises of peace through eternal weapons buildup. Even the dissident scientists were so bound by their stature that most soon turned their focus on rationally steering an escalation whose inevitability they'd resigned themselves to accept. In part because it so moderated its vision, the initial ban-the-bomb movement's momentum was readily deflected by institutional resistance, Cold War polarization, and the allure of peaceful atomic uses. And nuclear dissent disappeared almost entirely following later modest victories like the Above-Ground Test Ban Treaty.

Present peace efforts may also see themselves far too much as wholly of our society, and, therefore, risk traps as dangerous as those embodied in taking as one's sole model the rebel outsiders. Narrowed visions and respectable approaches can contain, as discussed, their own double messages, conveying a sense that ordinary individuals are powerless to act outside electoral campaigns and letters to their leaders. Or a judgment that things in the world are basically fine, and we need only a bit of constructive tinkering.

Important as moral consistency is, at times its lines are hard to draw. Marv Davidov pushed for being absolutely rigorous, avoiding the easy seductions and resultant blurring of visions that come from jumping towards whatever support is offered. The Vietnam era Honeywell Project turned down, following lengthy discussion, the chance of a sympathetic *Playboy* article, and argued with those in the local movement who sought Honeywell Foundation support for political plays and cultural efforts. "I think we were right to take that position," Marv said. "Dorothy Day tore up a $100,000 check from the Ford Foundation when the Catholic Worker desperately needed it, and then wrote in the *Worker* paper, 'this is everything we need. We can't take money from the Ford Foundation.' The money came in, in fives and tens. If Honeywell drops a bomb contract, let them give money for housing for every bomb contract they drop. Then it may be all right to take some of it, otherwise no."

Others, more comfortable with pragmatic compromise, would disagree, arguing that sympathetic allies can be found in unexpected places, and that the tasks faced are difficult enough without limiting the movement's reach. Besides, since all wealth flows through an interconnected economic system, and most money is in some ways tainted, activists would at least use it for a greater good. These divisions echo Weber's classic choice between the paths of ultimate ends and ultimate means, of moral vision and practical politics. If they could be reconciled, it might only be through acknowledging compromise's costs.

Yet potential traps go beyond being bought and lulled, or the flip side of revolutionary millennialism. More commonly, activists create protective enclaves, where the chosen few, considering themselves the rare jewels of conscience and concern, huddle against the world. Feeding isolation, they begin to doubt their own legitimacy, yet hope the magic leaflet or speech will make everything fall into line. Activism demands a bridging, like that cited by Marty Coleman when she talked of how the Los Angeles Peace Sunday gathering brought together her "sleepy Presbyterians" and the "guys who were writing 'Fuck You' on the walls of Berkeley." The more beleaguered we feel, the easier it is to remain inside the cocoon, produce a few benefits, form a few study groups, or else to style ourselves as a radical flying squad, running frenetically from blockade to blockade, vigil to vigil, assuming our fervor and pain will by itself carry the day. Like *Dr. Strangelove*'s General Jack D. Ripper prizing his "precious bodily fluids," activists caught in the enclave sensibility can become obsessed with abstract purity: nesting within the movement's familiar language and values; fearing contamination from outside interlopers with less-than-perfect political consciousness; ending up, as Win Olive said, "run by what we dread instead of by what we want."

No matter which choices we make, there will be differences and disappointments. Even as we take responsibility for moral choices, we need to avoid endlessly ressurrecting old wounds and condemning either others or ourselves for at times venturing down fruitless paths. Minister Jim Lawson cited the response to one disagreement in the Los Angeles peace community as a model of how to handle the inevitable strains.

In Spring 1981, L.A. activists began discussing a major event to knit together diverse strands of the movement. For four years Alliance for Survival had both raised money and highlighted nuclear issues through concert rallies at the 30,000-seat Hollywood Bowl.

A task force suggested a far larger event to fill the Rose Bowl; secured commitments from Graham Nash and Jackson Browne to participate and bring in Bob Dylan, Stevie Wonder, Joan Baez, and other key musicians; and began actively planning the following January. But Interfaith Center decided that a major march would have more impact and, when the option was rejected, pulled out to focus solely on church education and on the Freeze.

"We refused to battle over this," Lawson said, "but simply went ahead and sent out letters inviting all the Protestant and Catholic heads to participate. When the event happened, we gave Interfaith spokespeople—Harold Willens and Rabbi Leonard Beerman—places on the speaker's podium and the center a share of money we raised."

When I asked if Interfaith's withdrawal left hard feelings, Lawson laughed and said "there's something called the spirit of forgiveness." He'd worked with Interfaith activists before and would again in the future. The issue had to be big enough for diverse approaches, he felt; we could either embrace what he called "the global vision" or hold our grudges, fight over turf, and surrender to the predatory "geopolitics of the Kissingers."

As Rabbi Beerman made clear, humans are now clearly interdependent. The movement had "a difficulty of different egos clashing, different beliefs grinding each other up. But maybe that's inevitable. Like the Talmudic statement, 'The more flesh, the more worms.' " We need forgiveness for ourselves as well as others—release for not being able to solve the crisis in an instant.

Whatever path peace activists take, they must seek to build not only their anger at our present course, but also visions and ways of proceeding that will avoid pushing people to soar for six months in bright intense involvement, then burn out, cynical and dispirited. Even with the best intentions and most compassionate approaches, we can readily enough blind ourselves with facts and figures, convinced that our mere knowledge of the world's evil will change things. We can collapse as well into a judgment that no matter how many facts are amassed and passionate voices raised, the majority of Americans will remain stolidly unmoved. After attending enough meetings and passing out enough leaflets, acting until our voices break and our shoulders ache, we may wonder why we should carry the burden; we may even envision ourselves looking on, righteously cursing, when at last the bombs are ready to fall.

But this stance places us outside of history, outside of life; it denies our connection with those other humans who the warheads equally hold hostage. It denies as well a respect due to our actions' potential strength. In China after the revolution, peasants developed a ritual, "bitter sharing," in which they confessed not sins, but hurts and sorrows, seeking to forge a common bond. At present, we also are bound by both fears and hopes, bound not to a narrow clan or nation, but to all those jeopardized on the planet. Just as the situation of the powerful blurs their vision and compassion, so living under the sword-threat of ultimate weapons offers us all a glimpse of the vantage point of the dispossessed. It allows us to recognize that isolated survival may no longer be possible.

This recognition is fed by our understanding of the bonds that link us to others. When this understanding is absent or squeezed into narrow confines, we find it harder to question and act. We end up with a majority of Americans who fear nuclear war, yet are reassured by a few pacific phrases, a few negotiations, the notion that because no one wants a global holocaust, it is certain not to happen. As Daniel Ellsberg points out, polls show overwhelming U.S. public support for a bilateral freeze and opposition to the use of atomic weapons even if the Soviets invade Europe or Japan. Yet the vast majority also believe that we should let the other side think we'll hit them with everything we have. Acceptance of this bluff leads directly to embracing the presumed big-stick leverage provided by continuing to stockpile additional warheads, and even leads to rationalizing first-strike weapons.

## The Politics of Place

Challenging not only the horror of nuclear war, but also the arms race's inner logic requires complex discussion—more than can be conveyed in a one-minute Freeze ad or a ten-minute spot on a talk show. Not that the high-tech roads are irrelevant, but shifting popular sensibility requires a dialogue less transient and more intimate. Discourse on fundamental questions must be reclaimed as the property of more than just experts on a distant stage.

In the absence of direct human discussion, the previously mentioned political void prevails. In recent elections, U.S. urban centers have, by and large, rejected the vision represented by Reaganism.

Rural communities have elected such strong military critics as Iowa's Democratic Senator Tom Harkin and Republican Congressman Jim Leach. But in state after state, the suburbs provide the winning margin for visions of the United States as an armed camp against the world. To some degree, this difference is a function of wealth. Cities remain respositories for the old, the poor, the black, red, yellow, and brown—those our society disdains and discards. Rural areas are beleagured with debt. Suburbs are, as a rule, far more clearly affluent. But the differences may go beyond class, demographics or subculture distinctions. Whether their focus has been media work, demonstrations, or village-by-village outreach, peace efforts have primarily focused on the metropolitan centers. Because they are close-knit, rural communities can foster discussion of contending ideas. But in the suburbs (with some salient exceptions) life is more private, whether in comfort or in poverty. Information funnels through the shopping mall and TV news. Judgments occur behind closed doors. While democratic dialogue can take place in a cafe, bar, garage, dry goods store, or neighborhood grocery, it rarely occurs in a Safeway or Sears, much less a Burger King or Wendy's. Even when one's neighbors take on global issues, the results most often appear downtown, distanced from view.

The politics of retreat evolved during a period when many of those who once challenged America's Vietnam role buried their disconcerting knowledge about our tendencies towards empire, leaving the dominant public discourse to the Cold War's long-term proponents. If we recognize the tendency of Cold War ideology to drown out critical thought with the sheer white noise of distraction and suggestion, the goal of village politics becomes clearer: to find mechanisms to reach, question, teach, inspire, and engage with those in our society's ordinary, nonpolitical spheres—and then use the shared peril to build further community. Activism now flourishes in numerous churches in part because they offer a place for individuals to congregate as equals: a human context that more secular dissidents have found hard to create. Much as social change requires broad, nationwide actions, it inevitably begins more modestly—like the four teachers at Brookline High, who came together around common craft, or the Florence group that met each Thursday in Bill Cusak's office. Because even the most noble political visions cannot of themselves sustain continued engagement through the inevitable wilderness, individuals need the complex resilience that grows out of what William Blake called the "minute particulars" of ordinary life.

Instead of constantly pointing us towards Washington. D.C., human-scaled efforts at their best ask how we might live—within what bounds, with what expectations. If individuals challenge, for instance, Boeing's cruise missile production, they are pushed to explore what might replace it, to examine their regional economy's possibilities for a different course. We need to counterpose the vast interconnected military enterprise with the recapturing of local community, culture, vision—with the diffusion of power and control.

Such village politics may emerge in unexpected contexts: historian William Appleman Williams cites the stolid Utah and Nevada Mormons who rejected President Carter's original MX basing mode because it would squander their water, corrupt their communities with boomtown rowdies, and make them targets for theater nuclear wars. The MX lesson suggests that every place—certainly every place in a nation possessing 30,000 atomic warheads—is, like it or not, already a potential battleground: whether Florence, South Carolina; Framingham, Massachusetts; the central Los Angeles community addressed by James Lawson, the Minneapolis suburbs that produce both judges and lawbreaking grandmothers; or the Washington State waters, home to the Trident submarines. Each community either fosters the prevailing silence, or uses its resources, traditions, and webs of acquaintanceship and culture to begin the path of discussion and contestation necessary to help reverse the global course.

In a recent essay in *CoEvolution Quarterly*, Karl Hess distinguishes between addressing citizens, who must be dealt with in their full human complexity, and voters, who must simply be persuaded to pull the right lever on an appropriate Tuesday or Thursday. As with the ESR teachers, village politics can allow individuals to be judged on more than just charismatic command. As Hess writes, "to carry the message of a cause in a community when you are a generally respected neighbor is far better than when you do it as virtually your sole activity in public." By forcing us to be responsible to our fellow inhabitants, rootedness in place pushes us as well to define the visions of progress, security, and liberty we put forth, and the values on which our social visions are based.

The intimacy of this approach contrasts with anonymous petitioning of distant governmental powers. Where traditional local politics ignores those vaster historical forces that whip-saw ordinary lives and communities, village politics looks outward, asking how we might join in meeting the call of our time. Making human action once again the center of history, it brings critical planetary questions into the domains we already inhabit.

We see this in Ground Zero's white train campaign, as small towns along the tracks make it increasingly difficult to ship finished warheads to their destinations; in the Mormons' fight against the MX; in New Zealand's ban of atomic armed ships from its harbors. Or, village politics can be seen in the numerous challenges that follow the model of what has been termed "civic disobedience"—as when the Cambridge City Council refused to participate in federal Civil Defense evacuation plans and instead allocated money to mail a pamphlet to all voters on the dangers of nuclear war. Or when similar material was distributed or stances of noncooperation taken by agencies governing cities from Boulder, Colorado, and Montclair, New Jersey, to New York, Houston, and Greensboro, North Carolina— and by the states of California, Maryland, Massachusetts, New Mexico, and Washington. Some Nuclear Free Zones not only prohibit local atomic weapons production or deployment, but also ban governmental purchases from corporations significantly involved in the arms race. Others have sought to halt ongoing atomic weapons-related activities, like a Cambridge Nuclear Free Zone initiative that gained over forty percent of the vote despite a half-million dollar opposition campaign funded by a roster of America's top military contractors, including Rockwell, Northrup, Raytheon, Sperry, Honeywell, General Electric, and the Cambridge-based Draper Labs—corporations who pumped in thirty dollars for each vote they received. We see similar local resistance in the various cities that have independently established sister links with communities in the Soviet Union or Nicaragua, or have declared their municipal bounds a sanctuary, following the lead of churches who've made profound political statements through the basic acts of feeding, housing, and transporting those Salvadorans and Guatemalans who our government calls illicit refugees.

As Bebe Verdery made clear, traditional community organizing seeks the winnable issues and modest gains that build citizen heart and spirit. It is difficult to win these victories on the atomic weapons issues. Either activists take the pragmatic road of lobbying against specific systems, which removes politics to the distant stage, or they educate, resist, and do whatever might create the necessary shift of sentiment, institutions, and policy. In either course, more organized communities at times merely shunt the arms race burden to others that are more compliant or fragmented, as when Seattle citizens' groups convinced their city council to balk at a proposed naval base, only to see the facility embraced by a nearby lumber mill town that had recently been hit by massive layoffs. It is also easy to become virtuously parochial, taking pride in reaching a few other citizens and losing sight of everything larger. Or to forget key practical matters, Bill Cusak's "nuts and bolts," as when the Southern California Alliance for Survival and other local groups filled the Rose Bowl by assembling 100,000 people for the June 1982 Peace Sunday rally and concert, but neglected to collect names, pull together computerized lists for further contact, or in any way make it likely that those who gathered would become more than just a transient community that applauded the music and then scattered home to their private lives.

When activists do weave the links that invite others to broader engagement, village politics allows individuals to proceed at different paces in Florence or Augusta than in Madison or Cambridge, in communities where merely raising a voice is close to treason, and in ones where local noncompliance can be pushed to the point of community-wide work halts, tax revolts, boycotts, peace encampments, or other far more directly challenging paths. In all cases, local media can be engaged and pressured through ongoing dialogue and monitoring. Resources and ideas can be shared, as when civil rights workers moved from Montgomery to Birmingham to Selma, or when the Freeze leaped from western Massachusetts to states across the nation. Local fights can become both pivots and models. Because arms race support systems extend to all corners of the earth, resistance in any place can not only force major shifts in official plans and help trigger further challenges, but also rebound back on those political mechanisms that presently keep the warheads being deployed.

## Ecology of Peace

Village politics rests on a notion of the sacred. As members of what Christian tradition calls the kingdom of God, we share a common bond, a common kinship, and are equally part of a greater whole.

We are also sacred in our differences—which make every human being ultimately a mystery to every other. To the minimal self nothing is sacred, for that creates too great a burden; but to those who recognize these broader links, diverse lives are never interchangeable: we have a responsibility to ensure that other humans are not reduced to mere numbers on strategic planners' screens and their places of habitation are not made expendable battlefield theaters.

At its best, the voice of particularity insists that individuals must, in Wendell Berry's words, "identify their own interest with the interest of their neighbors and of the country (the land) itself," as opposed to embracing whatever course is defined by distant corporate or governmental entitites. Aldo Leopold expressed parallel sentiments in his notion of a "land ethic," one that "changes the role of homo sapiens from conqueror of the land community to plain member and citizen of it. . . . A thing is right when it tends to preserve the integrity, stability and beauty of the biotic community. It is wrong when it tends otherwise."

The fights waged by the South Carolina environmental groups offer examples of resistance to the destruction that proceeds even as warheads still rest in their silos. Like the churches at their most engaged, these groups are organizations of community. Their languages of challenge, affirmation, and moral connection develop through a parallel national exchange, as when Sierra Club articles filtered down to chapters in places as remote as Savannah River, or when Seabrook protests helped inspire the early Barnwell demonstrations. Their visions of community can both challenge immediate weapons culture encroachments and provide glimpses of directions necessary to do justice to who we are and the gifts we have been given.

By the early 1980s, a half-dozen years after the founding of the group that became Palmetto Alliance, South Carolina legislators routinely approached Michael Lowe, praising the stands he was taking. The press ran front-page stories, as atomic workers quit over shoddy welding. With Governor Richard Riley questioning atomic transport and waste disposal, a new plutonium production reactor appeared likely to end up in the more sympathetic climates of Idaho's National Engineering Laboratory or Washington's Hanford complex. And, in the end, the Barnwell reprocessing plant was halted indefinitely by a combination of local discontent, national apprehension regarding a plutonium economy, and the government's refusal to bail out its corporate owners by purchasing the $362 million, two-thirds-completed facility.

To inhabitants of nearby communities, the threat of radiation from Savannah River plant existed in a psychological present that seemed far closer than warheads people assumed would never be used. Though disputed by Department of Energy (DOE) scientists, a potential hazard impossible to see, taste, or feel was undeniably seeping into the air and water that nurtured soybeans, tobacco fields, and local families. In the areas nearest the plant, silence accompanied the benign leash of government pay. But where the paychecks came from the farms, textile mills, or other industries, the risk seemed greater. Citizens were angry at what appeared to be just another attempt to hand the South the nation's cast-off refuse.

When the Barnwell plant was begun in 1971, most Americans still believed in the peaceful atom, and its steadily building presence had helped assuage concern about the largely invisible warheads. Since then, South Carolina's environmental challenges have not only stopped Barnwell and curtailed a massive importation of wastes. They also delayed for several years the renovation of a 1950s production reactor intended to fuel the new atomic warheads. This reactor also, incidentally, threatened to destroy 1,000 acres of virgin wetlands, and to pollute a major source of Georgia and South Carolina's water—the Tuscaloosa aquifer. In addition, activists helped bring to public attention increases in local cancer, heart disease, and infant mortality; repeated discharges of radioactive contaminants into the atmosphere; and leaks into the soil of over 600,000 gallons of high-level nuclear wastes.

In responding to developments like these, environmental challenges address direct potential harm, cast doubt on the legitimacy of expert prescriptions, and provide ways to halt particular weapons systems while the slow institutional debates grind on. Focusing on biological hazards involves less ideological debate and provokes less outraged patriotism than directly criticizing the arms race, although it doesn't erase the politics by which the nuclear industrial complex attempts to discredit even its own studies when they produce unsettling findings. The effects of atomic production's by-products foreshadow those of the warheads themselves.

One could consider the radiation's toll a Grand Inquisitor's choice, updated for the nuclear age: a question, again, of declaring that individuals are expendable in the quest for a presumed greater good. Such individuals might be those without money, pushed to take jobs regardless of risk; those who believe the government assurances; those unfortunate enough to live downstream and drink the water, or downwind and breathe the air. The singling out might not even be deliberate.

Yet focusing solely on the biological hazards of weapons production has its limits. National security, unlike the electricity generated by commercial atomic plants, is a good demanded in infinite measure, on which no price can be placed. If activists do not question the "product" as well as its incidental consequences, those supporting the weapons culture can first dismiss the harm, then insist, as an ultimate position, that the choice is simply necessary. If myths fueling endless escalation are never addressed, activists may find themselves fighting for the worthy particulars of local lives and environments, yet being accused of betraying the also-incalculable commodities of liberty and security. Or, as in the case of Savannah River's renovated production reactor, they may force the acknowledgement of critical environmental safety issues, then find they are addressed as mere technical problems. Much as regions can defend themselves unilaterally, some coordinated national efforts are needed: in the words of a Palmetto Alliance lawyer who organized Vietnam-era sailors in Charleston and later took on atomic power and wastes, "We tried seceding once, and they shot back."

Yet, as with any politics rooted in place, challenging the arms race's incidental toll can draw necessary lines. Exponents of a new regionalism, like William Appleman Williams and Wes Jackson of the Land Institute in Salina, Kansas, suggest that certain massive projects inevitably crush local communities. The deployment of a Trident submarine forges a chain of dispossession and victimization from uranium tailings stored adjacent to Navajo villages in New Mexico, a forward base imposed over the local constitution in the Micronesian island of Palau, and microwave links bisecting Wisconsin and Minnesota farms, to the watershed pollution in Carolina's Tuscaloosa. To use an ecological term, these projects strain local carrying capacity, destroying livelihoods, cultures, and surroundings. And when indigenous inhabitants refuse to cooperate, the projects may, again, end up being blocked.

In an essay on the transformation of agricultural husbandry to an extractive industry like strip-mining, Wendell Berry explains: "If it does happen, we are familiar enough with the nature of American salesmanship to know that it will be done in the name of the starving millions, in the name of liberty, justice, democracy and brotherhood, and to free the world from communism. We must, I think, be prepared to see, and to stand by, the truth: that the land should not be destroyed for any reason, not even for any apparently good reason."

In other words, certain relationships should be inviolable. If choices depend on objectifying and destroying them, these choices should not be made. Certainly community needs often supersede those of individuals. But when distant, unchallengable institutions obliterate local lives and culture, or create areas of national sacrifice for the presumed necessity of building highways, airbases, or reactors, something unacceptable occurs. This process is masked, of course, by the way in which resource extraction by centralized institutions separates benefits from costs, creating a situation where, as David Orr writes, "the winners are cooled, coiffured and entertained electrically," while the distant and powerless losers "are stripmined, irradiated, and polluted." And where this distance breeds ignorance and indifference.

The bumper stickers proclaiming "Don't Dump It In Dixie," or the attempts to save Savannah River wetlands, embody the beginning of a refusal to accept this situation. Like Archbishop Hunthausen's notion of the earth's bounty as a gift we have the choice to cherish or destroy, ecological perspectives at their best acknowledge that, in Wendell Berry's words, "We can make ourselves whole only by accepting our partiality, by living within our limits, by being human—not by trying to be Gods." We might even recast Deuteronomy's classic choice "between death and life" as one between a prevailing trust in universal technical fixes and the humbling recognition that true strength exists only in diversity, and that no people has the right to destroy another for the sake of even the most supposedly noble dreams.

Diversity becomes both the vision activists seek to save from the all-leveling reach of the warheads and a basis for the movement itself.

Just as the strongest ecological system is not a monoculture of solid corn or wheat, so no single culture or tradition can sustain the peace work of individuals in every corner of the earth. Agriculturalist Wes Jackson retells the Old Testament Tower of Babel story as a warning against human pride and the dangers of adopting a sole human language. The tower was possible, Jackson said, because power concentrated in a Babylonian empire whose drafted workmen built the endless ramps into the heavens. The tower promised eternal invention with neither check nor limit. When it was stopped by the fracturing of tongues, people had no choice but to return to ordinary lives.

Jackson's lesson was neither to embrace the planet's competing armed camps, nor to condemn all technologies since the Bronze Age. But he suggested the kingdom of peace—sought equally by the Florence marchers, Los Angeles precinct-walkers, Dutch resisters to the Pershings and cruises, and beleagured dissidents in Warsaw, Moscow, and Kiev—can only flourish based on particular cultures and languages, diverse styles and approaches. In challenging the forces seeking to reduce complex human communities to interchangeable pawns in grand global designs, we begin to question accumulations of power that exist beyond accountability or restraint, begin to recognize that true strength emerges not only from our undeniable bond as a common human family, but also from our specific uniqueness.

Antoine de Saint-Exupery described this sense, writing on the death of a slave (a former king) lying on the Saharan sand: "What was painful to me was not his suffering (for I did not believe he was suffering); it was that for the first time it came to me that when a man dies, an unknown world passes away."

Similarly honoring the particularity of individual worlds, Carlos Fuentes has suggested we can define our cultural vision by seeking either: "a uniformity imposed on all by two rival power centers; or . . . a diversity shared and nurtured by all and springing from multiple centers." As when the group of rock-ribbed Florence Baptists listened to the local rabbi's peace sermon, humans change when we exchange belief systems and symbols, use our varied heritages to strengthen a broader bond. Baptists can still work to reach Baptists, Harold Willens's businessmen to address their peers, but this process proceeds best when those involved understand that theirs is only one path towards a common goal.

Acceptance of diversity unites the religious visions of the Trident mystics, the businessmen's pragmatism, Modjesca's wry persistence, and the flip play of Kathy Bryant and Sheila Strobel. It lets individuals choose which part of our interconnected global problems they will make their passionate cause, through efforts that, as Michael Lowe said, whether addressing "atomic weapons or environmental safety or whatever," raise common questions of democratic choice. Decisions on what issues to take on will always stem from particular situations, particular callings: as in Michael's judgment that, although he would walk in peace marches and help stuff occasional envelopes, his skill and experience pushed him to stick primarily with challenging atomic reactors and waste. Yet at their strongest, the diverse visions nurture each other.

## Jesters and the Kings

Variety of approaches can create difficulties as well as strengths. When Levon Hucks, the young Methodist minister from the small South Carolina town, attended a Savannah River Plant rally held a month after the respectable Florence march, he was disappointed. The participants were young, often unkempt and dirty; they seemed like imports, not local natives. Some were even gay or had a punk look. Although Levon liked the speech of a Furman College religion professor, who shared his own interest by approaching the issues from the standpoint of faith, the others had no such concern—just a general humanism, which left Levon feeling far less comfortable.

It is tempting for social activists to attempt to blend seamlessly into our culture, offend no one, pay homage solely to conventional expectations and roles. Yet, as anthropologist Karen Kahn has explored, familiar assumptions have been profoundly challenged in projects like New York's Seneca Falls Peace Camp, where, "as a women's encampment with a large number of self-identified lesbians, we appeared immoral and anti-family; as a support system for women determined to do civil disobedience, we appeared lawless; as women seemingly independent of jobs and families, local residents assumed we were living on welfare and, thus, placing an unnecessary burden on their county." In crossing those cultural boundaries, Kahn said, the campers, "essentially stepped outside of the community's understanding of what it means to be women."

The resulting strains escalated when the peace camp rejected, on a split consensus, flags local residents offered them to fly on Memorial Day and July 4th. Although participating women later made and displayed their own flags, including many of the traditional red white and blue, their rejection branded them as being "outside the boundaries of acceptable social and cultural practice." Even local residents sympathetic towards peace concerns bridled at the seeming lack of decorum and patriotism. The confrontation culminated when several hundred townspeople stood on a bridge, yelling "Commies go home" and blocking a march by the women.

The refusal to fly the initial flags did seem a needless affront to the townspeople's gift (if one admittedly framed as a test of national loyalty), a choice of abstract purity over connection with local residents. The campers were clearly outsiders, and dismissable as such. Yet the Pershings stored at the Seneca Army Depot awaiting European deployment do not threaten only those living adjacent; since all humans are atomic targets, all have a right to address the jeopardy and its triggers. And when the peace women and counterdemonstrators at last began listening to each other, local ministers were spurred to preach on the necessity of questioning the arms race, and even the American Legion met with camp representatives to discuss ways of reducing tensions. The lines often blur between standing firm for deeply felt truths and clinging so tightly to personal style that an outward bridging can not even begin. Yet just as Win Olive and several other blockaders ended up talking with the group who came with their beer keg to support the Trident, so the Seneca encampment may have, in Kahn's words, "opened the way for new interpretations of social reality"; may have broadened the vision of both those who created the camp and the small-town residents on whose world their varied challenges abruptly descended.

We see these new interpretations emerging in a feminist vision that rejects the right of individuals to dominate by physical force; that challenges as well our projection of uncertainties and fears onto those who are presumed dangerous because they are different. The warrior ethic has traditionally stressed emotional armoring, a quality perhaps once necessary for the survival of communities the men have traditionally defended. But along with the virtue of steadfast loyalty, military culture has also fed a contempt toward our fellow humans and toward the land that sustains us. In overcoming primal inhibitions against the act of killing, this culture has particularly demeaned the historically female virtues of nurturance and reciprocity: heralding the soldier, in Robert Lifton's words, as a no-nonsense conqueror "for whom women were either inferior, inscrutable or at best weaker creatures"; even asserting the ultimate retaliation through battlefield rape.

In this context, U.S. Army drill sergeants call their recruits "ladies," "faggots," and "pussys," leading them in slapping first their weapons, then their crotches, repeating, "This is my rifle, this is my gun. One is for killing, the other for fun." President Theodore Roosevelt warned Americans against losing "the manly and adventurous virtues" by turning aside from the revitalizing experience of war. Henry Kissinger spoke of the United States "emasculating itself" should it not provide requested military funds for Angola. American men still enshrine the battlefield as a primal crucible of passage.

Prevailing myths insist that we fight to protect our (presumably white and Christian) women from the barbarian hordes outside. Yet these myths further cast women as prizes to be seized, helping create a continuum between wartime rape and threats omnipresent in a culture where, in the words of Susan Griffin, "the world, even a girl's neighborhood becomes a minefield"—a warning of brutal force constantly hovering. Related dreams of mastery and a related objectification feed the technologies of mass annihilation threatening every corner of the earth, presaging a despoilation potentially terminal.

Even as the soldier's most honorable roles have begun to be limited by weapons that make concepts of courage and heroism often irrelevant, feminist visions may offer other paths towards strength, autonomy, and liberty. Acknowledging difference and variety without retreating into the frozen stances of protector and prize, these visions challenge the right to dehumanize others, even in the name of democracy, security, or love. They challenge as well a prevailing separation of the private sphere, with its promise of nurturance and respite, from the manly public domains, with their ethics of pragmatic mastery. Feminist visions prefer interconnected responsibility to an abstract freedom that denies all limits and ties. As Carol Gilligan stresses, making a world truly fit to inhabit need not involve the surrender of our most cherished wishes and longings. We can act, as Win said, because we bloody well enjoy it.

Although these visions need not be wholly pacifist, they deny any right to turn war into carnal delight, and stress again diverse particularity over the all-leveling prescriptions of distant experts. Diversity is embodied as well in voices of play and invention, lifting citizen activists beyond the mere presence of the warheads, beyond what Denise Levertov terms "the intense familiar imagination of disaster."

Writer Grace Paley recalls talking with a sympathetic policeman at a 1979 Wall Street demonstration. The man mistrusted Long Island's Shoreham nuclear power plant being built near his home, but doubted whether anyone could successfully challenge it.

> Then he said, looking at the Bread and Puppet Theater's stilt dancers, 'Look at that, what's going on here? People running around in the street dancing. They're going every which way. It ain't organized.' We started to tell him how important the dancers were. 'No, no, that's okay' he said. 'The antiwar demonstrations were like this at first, mixed up, but they got themselves together. You'll get yourself together too. In a couple years you'll know how to do it better.'

Yet as Paley implied, maybe the need was not "to do it better," at least not in the sense of replacing the stilt people with sober phalanxes of marchers. Without the imagination that allows us to do more than endlessly hammer the same tired chords, our efforts can soon become grim and sterile. We see the alternative in the brazen humor of Modjesca Simkins calling the august state house legislators a bunch of old hound dogs; Bill Cusak with his Carmen Miranda marching hat; Bob Willard's bumpersticker—"One Nuclear Bomb Can Ruin Your Whole Day"; the cheek of the women who trespassed one Easter Sunday, dressed as giant rabbits, to picnic inside England's Greenham Common cruise missile base; or Bill Ethell dancing to "The Teddy Bear's Picnic" the night before the *Ohio*'s arrival. Such humor helps us to recognize we are all, in Tony Bouza's words, "just slugs on this earth," and returns us from the realms of imperial visions to those of ordinary humans with mud on our feet. It teaches us, at the root, who we are.

The peace movement cannot afford to romanticize the rude jokers whose politics consist solely of farting at the king, but it will also fail if it becomes an effort of only good kids and blue-bloods. Because the politics of the wild edge so lost its moorings in the late 1960s, we have nearly banished it since, offering instead the calm, patient voice, the more-than-worthy attributes of the moral and the sober. Yet we may need as well what William Blake called "the marriage of Heaven and Hell": not just the careful respectability and steadfast compassion, but also hell-bent lust and the mocking, caustic laugh.

In an age of mass annihilation, we need court jesters who laugh at the unthinkable and will not keep silent: individuals willing, in Günter Grass's words, to advise the government whether the king listens or not. Both jesters and poets speak not only to ills now existing, but to what might be possible and to the shadows of all we say and do. They speak, as John Berger said, "to the immediate wound," in a manner difficult for even the most honed and crafted arguments of prose.

We see this where poet Philip Levine writes:

> *When you hide in bed*
> *the revolver under the pillow*
> *smiles and shows its teeth.*

And we see it in a Vietnam poem, "The Teeth Mother Naked At Last," that Robert Bly wrote thirteen years before he would join Erica Bouza and 576 others in being arrested at Honeywell:

Now the Chief Executive enters, the press conference begins: First the President lies about the date the Appalachian Mountains rose. Then he lies about the population of Chicago, then he lies about the weight of the adult eagle, and then about the acreage of the Everglades. . . . And the Attorney General lies about the time the sun sets.

No explanations here, and no apologies: only human voices and what they must say, like the Cambridge first-grader who thought we should simply vote on whether or not to go ahead with a nuclear war, and stop building bombs if the answer was no. As the churches understand, song sustains far more than the chanting of slogans. By revealing what is hidden, difficult, and of unsettling promise, poetry and humor can bend the iron cage of ordinary time. By shifting accustomed litanies, they can both, as Gary Snyder said, break us out of our isolated little selves and fill in the gaps between what can be proved or defined and what we truly need to know.

A Seattle gallery recently combined works by local artists with a traveling display of drawings by atom bomb survivors. One seven-foot-high wooden sculpture was painted in bright Coney Island colors, with cartoon generals saluting as a metal ball rolls through dollar signs, revealing first an escalation of weapons, and finally, a mushroom cloud over a city. People laughed at the comic strip humor, although other works struck starker notes—like a translucent yellow-and-green bowl, entitled "Serene Apathy": bas-relief jets circled the rim, ceramic matches clustered, stubbed out, in the center, and a human figure cowered, striped red and white as if wearing a night-shirt or a winding sheet, mouth open, wholly paralyzed. In back, the gallery viewers were silent as the Hiroshima drawings—special reproductions—recalled the aura of the original event. Unlike the now-familiar black-and-white photos, their colors denoted passion and life; then one looked closer to see a woman's hair rising straight up, blue and iridescent, with bent shapes all around screaming. Stories below described the cries of sisters and mothers, fathers and daughters, calling to be helped by those who are also dying.

The local works addressed these cataclysms from a greater distance, but offered their own unique perspective on our present era and on how we might live if we mastered this threat. Similar efforts have proceeded throughout the United States, as in a national project in which individuals stenciled human outlines on the streets to recall vaporized bomb victims, or the floating of lantern candles like those released each year on a river in Hiroshima, their glowing lights commemorating lives that were lost. On August 6th, 1985, the bomb's fortieth anniversary, a yard-wide, fifteen-mile-long ribbon encircled the Capitol, Pentagon, and Lincoln Memorial. A Denver grandmother thought of the idea, and its 25,000 cloth panels were put together by church groups, Cub Scouts, senior citizens, and steelworkers—citizens of seven nations, depicting what they would miss in the world. In Los Angeles, an Artists for Survival carnival brought 4,000 people of varied races and cultures to toss beanbags at "Kiss the Bombs Goodbye," throw darts to "Pin the Lawsuit on the Reactor," and witness an arcade of artistic dreams.

Whether or not we can invent images this powerful, we can look to them for illumination, sustenance, and a recognition that invention must complement persistence. The tone of the present movement is far from that of Paris in 1968, when wall slogans proclaimed "all power to the imagination" and "it is forbidden to forbid." We now talk less about reinventing the world than about preserving it. Yet in seeking to save our planet's diverse web of life, we need visions that allow us play, creativity, and reach; allow us to turn our culture's relentless push for acquisition and mastery into an ability to address the real work we face as a species; and to soar without emulating Icarus.

## Village Economics

Imagination also allows us to ask basic questions regarding the social and institutional relationships that might allow peace to be possible: to address, for instance, deeply rooted fissures between a predominantly white, middle-class peace movement and those who, as Bill Ethell said, whether in time of war or their ordinary travails, have always ultimately gotten "the chop" from those who own and command.

Recent dissent has not been entirely class bound. Civil rights organizers worked with massively disenfranchised Southern blacks, and drew at least brief support from unions like the United Auto Workers. Resistance by largely working-class Vietnam ground troops and returned veterans combined with a more middle-class domestic peace movement to shift the course of the war. More recent efforts like Bebe's Carolina Action, Shelley's consumer's group in Maine, various feminist projects, and the variety of local activities Harry Boyte termed *The Backyard Revolution*, have asserted the right of ordinary individuals to challenge government and corporate leaders in an array of domains. But like Saul Alinsky's classic community organizing efforts, these projects have often kept their moral and social visions diffuse, and left the the broadest issues of war, peace, and the economic order to individuals with education and status.

In contrast with Bill's Australian unions or Polish Solidarity, the U.S. labor movement has largely accepted a post-World War II compact banishing as "un-American" even the notion that ordinary workers should have a say either in the fruits of their labors or in fundamental economic and political decisions shaping our nation's future. This surrender has been fed by the demise of an earlier, often immigrant-based political radicalism, the development of a permanent military economy, the impact of homogenizing media like television, and reliance on federal agencies like the National Labor Relations Board. But it has hinged primarily on acceptance of a promised stake in what *Time-Life* magnate Henry Luce called "The American Century."

Now, when a generation of the most militant union members has long-since been purged or censored, this compact continues, even as the international order shifts, deficits from wars fought and wars prepared for come home to roost, and real blue-collar wages begin to steadily fall. As International Association of Machinists head William Winpisinger said, comparing our unions with Solidarity, "American labor today lacks principle as a movement"—meaning it has surrendered the far-reaching visions that might allow it to inspire and lead.

But the unions' resistance to peace movement visions arises from more than their internal failings and the greater coercion facing those with minimal say over their day-to-day work. To many blue-collar Americans, the voice of peace activism has often seemed one of insulated comfort. If you work in a mill, a chemical plant, a MacDonalds stand, or any of the other battlefields in our fundamental war against nature, you don't dialogue with the products you produce—you master the suckers and get on with it. Rebellion is less often noble sacrifice and earnest belief than honest loyalty to one's immediate peers, or the bitter humor that lets Alaska fishermen explain, "You don't lose much when the skipper's boat goes down," or Vietnam marines recite choruses of "Tough shit, tough shit, your kid got greased." When activists merely voice Betty Crocker pieties about how war is terrible and we all want peace, they necessarily appear as Pollyannas; and those caught in the economy's harshest grip most often look on in resentful isolation.

To overcome this resentment requires imagination capable of reaching beyond the profound chasms dividing our nation—like educational efforts that brought these issues to students like Amanda Domingo and the Dominic Savio teenagers. But alternative learning alone will not answer how we can continue to live in our communities, earn our livelihoods, and support our families, while emerging from a dependence the arms race has made routine. For this we need not only village politics, but village economics.

We can find the beginnings of this in campaigns like the Philadelphia effort that secured a three-to-one majority in a 1983 Jobs

With Peace referendum, and is now pushing for alternative production uses for the 11,000 employee Philadelphia Navy Yard. A major
local employer since 1801, the yard recently refitted the battleship
*New Jersey* before it sailed to shell the Moslem villages of Lebanon,
and is readying the aircraft carrier *Independence* for future interventions off the coast of Nicaragua, Angola, or wherever we might
choose to exercise our armed dominion. But after 1987 it has no
further contracts. Residents in surrounding communities, therefore,
face an apparent choice between hustling for additional military business or allowing the facility to close. Because demand for commercial
shipbuilding is nonexistent, the Jobs With Peace group has instead
suggested Navy Yard workers could use their knowledge of the
plant's capabilities and their skills to help plan the conversion of the
complex to produce a variety of other products. Proposals include
trolley cars like those now being sold to the Philadelphia transit
authority by a former shipyard of Kawasaki; steel bridges to begin
replacing nearly 10,000 substandard bridges in the state; and floating
generating stations, following the lead of Japanese and Swedish facilities now producing electricity from ocean thermal currents.

As the Philadelphia activists acknowledge, it is easier to win acceptance of alternative-use plans for enterprises clearly threatened
than for those in which the weapons sector down-side is invisible
over the crest of the hill. Receptivity to their message increased
dramatically after a leaked Navy memo detailed planned shipyard
cutbacks; Barry Goldwater included the yard on a list of twenty
targeted for closure, and a key local congressman said he might have
to accept this choice. Daily headlines soon helped campaign organizers approach community leaders in the areas most affected, and
pushed the city to explore how Navy Yard resources might meet
local needs. Although other military facilities had been closed and
then eventually reconverted (including a former naval ordinance plant
in nearby York, Pennsylvania, that now produces motorcycles for
AMF Corporation), in no case had a popular movement spearheaded
this process. Activists chose to begin at a point where the military
culture was vulnerable.

The campaign's focus on day-to-day economics allowed it to reach
beyond accustomed peace constituencies in suggesting that military
spending threatens American livelihoods. At one meeting of Amalgamated Clothing Workers shop stewards, an economist broke down

what at the time was an over $200 billion U.S. military budget. She translated the staggering numbers into costs per month, per day, per hour, and ended with $7,000 a second. Usually the stewards, mostly black women drained from a full day's work, discussed brief business issues, grabbed a quick hoagie sandwich, and headed home to their families. They sat, this time, through three lecturers, bought every piece of literature available, and even stayed for a final optional film.

The same union passed out 80,000 leaflets during the earlier referendum, joined by individuals like a middle-aged Republican ward leader who had eight children and figured that if he could distribute a thousand leaflets for each one, they'd end up with a better chance of living. A major neighborhood paper ran banner headlines for the campaign's every major proposal. The effort reached individuals who had never talked with peace activists in their lives.

The arms race's economic fallout is clearly evident on one level. Michigan's Employment Research Associates calculated, in a 1982 study, that occupational groups comprising ninety-two percent of the labor force are primarily losing from our present path. Although the Machinists union represents more weapons workers than any other in the country, the Pentagon's high technology focus has caused the number of machinists in defense sector jobs to diminish, even as military spending increases. The weapons cornucopia swallows investment capital, lowers consumer spending, forces cutbacks in state and local governments, and syphons national taxes into a narrow strata of golden sector projects. It also skyrockets interest rates, drains skills and resources, and threatens the profitability of enterprises not feeding from the warfare trough. With military spending—even throughout the supposedly pacific 1970s—running, as a percentage of GNP, twice that of Germany and ten times that of Japan, it is little wonder our streets are filled with Volkswagons and Volvos, our living rooms with Yamahas and Sonys.

Much as massive weapons budgets ultimately destroy work opportunities, military contracting remains a rare growth sector in a spurt-and-stagger economy, in which the alternative may be, in Bruce Springsteen's words, working "down at the carwash where all it ever does is rain," becoming just another rider "on a downbound train." As Richard Barnet has pointed out, weapons contracts represent the United States' sole acceptable industrial planning mechanisms in an era when it has become nearly unthinkable to talk of using common resources for a common good. And although a nuclear freeze, for instance, would ultimately create a significant increase in nationwide employment, it would also jeopardize, during its initial institution, the paychecks of between 100,000 and 300,000 workers. Given a choice, these individuals and others dependent on weapons work might well prefer other employment, and in the process release their Cold War rationalizations. But the conflict between global responsibility and paying the monthly rent can only begin to be resolved when we detail how our society might better use the lives and resources currently vested in producing annihilatory weapons.

In another nascent effort, the Charleston United Electrical Workers group has proposed that the nuclear turbine plant scheduled to be shut down by General Electric instead be converted into an environmental and renewable energy center, combining both research and direct production. A Long Beach, California, United Auto Workers local has worked with McDonnell Douglas and various government and community groups to convert an ailing commercial aircraft plant to the production of light rail and rapid transit cars for regional commuter lines. Perhaps the most advanced conversion model is that of Britain's largest military aerospace contractor, the Lucas company, where workers responded to pending defense cutbacks by meeting shop-by-shop to draw up detailed production plans for 150 alternative products, ranging from heat pumps and combined road-rail vehicles to windmills and dialysis machines. Drawing on knowledge of their own skills and their factories, they stressed not only marketability, but also efficient material and energy use, the social utility of potential products, and the development of industrial procedures that would both employ as many individuals as possible and generally democratize the workplace. Although the overall plan was defeated, following a ten-year fight, by resistance from Lucas and the Thatcher government, it forced the retention of thousands of jobs, spurred new prototype products, and provided a model for ongoing efforts by the councils of London and other major British cities, as well as by groups in other nations.

Because weapons employment is cyclical, even its boom times are inevitably precarious. Philadelphia activists cited as a cautionary lesson the 1977 closure of the Frankford arsenal, which eliminated 7,000 jobs and decimated the surrounding neighborhood. Just as environmental fights often subordinated discussions of the warheads' ultimate threat to the immediate toll levied on those downriver or downwind; so conversion efforts often framed themselves primarily in terms of saving local employment. Their challenge to the arms race became a secondary theme, implicit in the organization's name, and elaborated in the discussions that grew as trust built between peace activists and the unionists and community people who previously viewed such dissenters as a disreputable fringe. In part because the Philadelphia effort cut across expected political lines, it was able to draw at least tentative support from the state AFL-CIO, Mayor Wilson Goode, the city's congressional delegation, and even a key shipyard union leader. Activists also convinced the local Private Industry Council to give immediate funding for neighborhood job banks.

Peace conversion faces a fundamental paradox. Production of mass annihilatory weapons, and certainly of destabilizing systems like the Tridents, Pershings, and Star Wars components, can be judged an objective evil—creating what Daniel and Philip Berrigan have termed "property which has no right to exist." But weapons workers are not initiators of the economic system in which they participate. Other work simply may not be available. If they quit their jobs, they risk not only financial hardship but also the shattering of accustomed community. It can be arrogant for those with other livelihoods to command all who work at military facilities to instantly put down their tools and leave.

These contradictions have at times split those activists addressing weapons facilities: some stress that every bomb, shell, or warship fuels the deaths or probable deaths of innocent individuals; others let these consequences momentarily ride, while trying to offer the weapons workers alternative future visions. Philadelphia Jobs With Peace staff person John Goldberg describes a conversation in which a local community leader, a retired career Navy officer, said he'd like to simply close the shipyard the following day, because the warships it rehabilitated destroyed human lives. Goldberg said, no, he would not, because the stakes included the jobs of 10,000 people, and any action should take their welfare into account.

Goldberg's focus on economic choices was in part a pragmatic tack: challenging the arms race for the dollars it takes from rebuilding our cities and educating our children; framing opposition to global intervention by stressing how Americans lose jobs when dictators like Pinochet crush their nation's labor movements and create factories paying twenty cents an hour. And it could still not easily overcome the addictions fed by weapons dependence: the Long Beach, California, conversion efforts largely collapsed after McDonnell Douglas began bidding to build a new C-47 military cargo plane. But Goldberg cared about the unemployed just as he did about halting the weapons march. He valued the campaign's deliberate outreach to new allies and local institutions, with the imagination and vision their perspectives might bring. He was frustrated, in contrast, with those content to stick with the familiar meetings and vigils, speaking continually to the already committed, and with those who said they didn't need a strategy because if they only witnessed to the truth, God would handle the results.

Similarly, George Lakey, a Philadelphia Jobs With Peace cofounder and veteran Quaker activist involved primarily with nonviolent direct action, valued the current outreach both for those it invited into the movement and for the ways it pushed traditional activists. He hoped the campaign could provide an antidote to a situation in which dedicated individuals challenged the military state, but were so isolated they could simply be swept aside. "We're doing our homework," he explained, "so that when it's confrontation time and this small group is out there getting arrested, they will be representing a whole lot of people who aren't there. People will be saying, 'this is happening to us': like what happened in France in 1968, a sense of solidarity and mutual grievance where when the students got hurt, the workers said 'hell, we're doing this too,' and ten million struck and occupied their factories."

As in other village politics efforts, personal bonds allowed the Philadelphia conversion workers to eventually discuss their most complex and far-reaching visions. Concepts were kept simple in the leaflets and at the initial meetings and presentations. But when individuals began to work together, varied experiences and visions came into play. At times this raised difficult issues, as when a key Jobs With Peace activist was riding to a community meeting with a black organizer, an ex-prisoner, who began joking about faggots. The activist said that hurt him directly, because he was gay. After the two talked at length, the man who made the joke said the conversation meant a lot to him. Yet it only grew from shared personal trust.

Honeywell Project also tried, from their earliest Vietnam days, both to reach out to the ordinary weapons facility workers, and to keep a compassion for the bombs' present and pending victims. They objected to groups putting out leaflets saying "Honeywell Kills," because while it was true that Honeywell decision makers contributed to the deaths of thousands, and profited quite handsomely in the process, the company's workers, like drafted soldiers, were merely hostages to a permanent war economy. Later, the project incorporated explicit conversion demands; focused the blockades and vigils on corporate headquarters rather than on production facilities that might imply blame lay with the ordinary men and women on the assembly line; made clear that the effects of a weapons production halt could not be simply tossed onto the backs of Honeywell employees. The project invited those on the inside to join in asking how their lives could be better spent.

Efforts like these are stronger for focusing on turf modest enough to be manageable—as when the Philadelphia campaign worked with local community councils to try to fund a full-time organizer for the neighborhoods most dependent on the yard. But activists must also do more than just buffer the dislocations from dropped contracts or push military facilities from one community to the next. Dick Greenwood, assistant to the Machinists' union president, suggests a national system "for channelling [conversion] resources and coordinating activity," one capable of responding to the global reach of corporations like Boeing, General Dynamics, and Rockwell. The Lucas effort raised its new possibilities more powerfully because it spanned all the facilities of a major British contractor. The Philadelphia example offers ways communities might use available resources to build sustainable local economies: drawing steel for bridges, for instance, from the beleaguered mills of Bethlehem, the Monagahela Valley, and nearby Bucks County; allowing individual villages to do more than simply scramble for the leavings of distant capricious powers.

National legislative efforts addressing military dependency include versions of a bill first introduced in the late 1970s by George McGovern, Republican Senator Charles Mathias, and New York Congressman Ted Weiss, following consultation with various unions.

The bill sought to form a federal body to research potential markets for converted facilities, establish alternative use committees at defense plants around the country, and initiate an Economic Adjustment Trust Fund, paid for by a tax on weapons contractors, that would provide dislocated workers with income, benefits, and retraining and job hunting allowances. A related proposal passed the House in 1979, attached to another bill, but was then rejected by the Senate. Versions currently circulating are slowly building support, including a 1985 endorsement by the AFL-CIO's Industrial Union Department; in addition, the comprehensive Freeze bill now incorporates conversion provisions in its text. Including Philadelphia, Jobs With Peace referendums have carried in over eighty-five cities. Legislators in California, Connecticut, Minnesota, Oregon, and Hawaii are debating whether to establish their own state-funded planning and retraining efforts.

As they reach beyond traditional dissenting constituencies, conversion efforts hit entrenched notions that it is fine for the government to subsidize Rockwell, Boeing, and Honeywell, or for corporations to move plants overseas on three weeks' notice, but bordering on treason to suggest our basic economy might be directed by anyone other than its present owners. Just as Martin Luther King was attacked for not sticking to civil rights issues when he spoke "for the poor in America who are paying the double price of smashed hopes at home and death and corruption in Vietnam," so labor organizers are supposed to talk only about wages, and disarmament activists to address just the mute metal hunks of the warheads. Conversion offers unions a chance to speak not as particular "special interests," isolated by lines of trade and craft, but as forces seeking a general good, affirming values that strengthen the nation as a whole, and for their members to challenge the arms race while continuing to honor familiar daily bonds of friendship and community; for middle-class peace activists to confront a privilege that may buffer them from the daily pressures faced by the majority of Americans; for both to address the web of economic relations that keeps the weapons being produced.

Conversion politics can be taken too pragmatically: replacing individuals' original concern over whether our species will survive, with a paternalistic, "let's talk jobs because that's what *they* understand." And no solution will instantly erase entrenched institutional and psychological resistance. But these experiments can at least invite those under the weapons culture's most direct economic sway to consider how their work might serve a more human future. By examining our nation's root productive base, conversion efforts can explore, concretely and specifically, what should be produced, how we should produce it, and how we might create fulfilling work for all. They can push our society to make these choices the domain not of a remote elite group of owners, managers, or planners, but of those ordinary citizens most intimately affected.

## Justice and the Curse

We Americans like clear results. "If you're so smart, why ain't you rich" not only judges individual progress on the fabled ladder to success or failure. It also questions the moral worth of any opposition movement that does not visibly affect established power. Even after we have rejected the war industry's promise of eternal security, both military and economic; even after we have overcome our numbness towards the threat, we still don't know if our efforts will succeed. Our culture's divisions remain massive and often daunting. The impact of what we do is often hidden. Nothing guarantees which of our campaigns will mesh with popular mood and historical caprices to successfully bring new strength to the movement. Yet proceeding as acknowledgedly fallible humans, we act, as Michael Lowe said, to preserve our inherent dignity; act, in Win's words, because "to be a real person you must do something about it."

To take a related example, few would have expected the profound growth of the American antiapartheid movement that began after Reagan's 1984 reelection. Admittedly, it's easier to challenge violence and injustice 8,000 miles away. Yet U.S. support for the Pretoria regime did not waver until direct human actions—across lines of race and class—spoke to common conscience. Like many of the disarmament efforts, or those of Polish Solidarity, these demanded that each of our social institutions—whether universities, churches, municipal governments, or corporations—ultimately serve a common good. By refusing to detour through the endless rationalizations and pious legalities, individuals raised the blunt, basic truth that we can choose whether or not to cooperate with murder and oppression.

Whether our concern is with South African lives or the atomic peace issue, we come up against the same prevailing current of righteous selfishness. Village politics fulfills its promise only by going beyond parochial complacency. Whether through recognition of a fundamental biological bond, or through religion, artistic imagination, connection with the land, nurturance of diversity, or a striving for work of meaning and dignity, all sustaining visions, as Lifton put it, allow one to, "wildly or gently. . . . psychologically travel outside oneself in order to feel one's participation in the larger human process." These visions converge, or can potentially, through nurturing of community and a parallel sense of responsibility, whereby instead of endlessly "colonizing the future," we seek to become its stewards, heeding the cries of our fellow humans who live, along with us, beneath a common sky.

To stress these visions is not to disdain the pragmatic organizational structures needed to pass a state conversion bill or link Florence, the Leo Baeck peace circle, the educators' caucuses, or affinity groups of blockaders. Nor is pointing out the traps of a sole electoral focus to spurn all engagement with the ballot. It is just to recognize that the movement must be institutionalized enough for coordinated action and long-term staying power, yet open enough to allow those generous and unpredictable impulses that complement the slow and patient march. The vision is still developing that can knit various streams of human activity into efforts capable of offering new definitions of common security and common good: definitions that cannot be dismissed as special interests or as the whiner's catalogue of ills, but stand as alternatives to a Hobbesian world of cutthroat individualism, bureaucratized paternalism, and what Jim Lawson called the "epidemic of meanness."

This search for kingdoms of justice will not bring an immaculate world. As Peter Weiss writes in *Marat/Sade*:

> *Their soup's burnt*
> *they shout for better soup*
> *A woman finds her husband too short*
> *she wants a taller one . . .*
>
> *And so they join the Revolution*
> *thinking the Revolution will give them everything*

*a fish*
*a poem*
*a new pair of shoes*
*a new wife*
*a new husband*
*and the best soup in the world*
*So they storm all the citadels*
*and there they are*
*and everything is just the same*
*no fish biting*
*verses botched*
*shoes pinching*
*a worn and stinking partner in bed*
*and the soup burnt*
*and all that heroism*
*which drove us down to the sewers*
*well we can talk about it to our grandchildren*
*if we have any grandchildren . . .*

Weiss writes not to scorn human courage or necessary revolutions, but merely to caution against false expectations and the bitterness that lingers in their wake. Even in a society of far greater dignity, what Grace Paley calls "the little disturbances of man" will still endure. Yet knowing, as Marv Davidov said, that humans are creatures capable of "the most beautiful or most hideous" activity imaginable, we need not be saints. We need merely to acknowledge that "the war of all against all" now threatens to become terminal, and that if the bomb does nothing else, it pushes us to honor the fundamental interconnection core to classic notions of living generously in the world.

In its fight to preserve common life, the peace movement is deeply traditional; in its need to overthrow the dead weight of a carnivorous past, it asks radically far-reaching questions. In seeing ourselves as part of, not separate from a broader stream of history, and in making it clear that to risk the annihilation of all is the ultimate sundering of human right and dignity, we begin to join ethics of invention and of responsibility; we link true altruism and true self-interest. In the words of psychologist David South, we need to treat our species' profound intelligence as a gift, not "a lethal mutation."

If it is indeed a gift, it is one requiring a community of justice, like that which Marv had sought to build in his thirty-five years of engagement. His sensibility began with private hurt: growing up poor, as his father managed a supermarket liquor department, while being surrounded by the wealth of Grosse Point, Michigan; being invited to a sleigh-ride birthday party by a fourth-grade classmate from one of the giant estates, then coming home crying after the child's grandmother said he couldn't come to the party because he was a dirty Jew—crying "how can I be dirty when I take a bath every night?"

But justice requires feeling the other's wounds as well as one's own. Marv learned further lessons when, drafted into the army the week after the end of Korea, his sergeant ordered a blanket party to beat bloody a man who jumped the boat and skipped the fighting. "I'm Jewish," Marv had told the other men in his barracks. "We have family members who went to the gas chambers because people obeyed every order without thinking. So I don't think we should beat him up. I think we should go down and ask 'Why did you jump the boat?' Maybe he had a good reason for not going to Korea."

Marv ended up getting beaten himself, after the others nearly sent the recruit to the hospital and Marv told them he was ashamed. His Jewish chaplain said he should have known there was anti-Semitism in the service, and that he'd do best to keep quiet, serve his two years, and get out and back to college. Marv survived thinking of Montgomery Clift's rebel lifer in the movie "From Here to Eternity," and by meeting "a few other guys who were like me, who were doing it alone." Later he saw black friends scorned and jailed for no crime but the color of their skin. When he met further kindred spirits and joined the Southern freedom marches, it was not just for the Mississippi sharecroppers, but for his own life—a feeling that he had to take this chance "to carry out my deepest private feelings in public."

Speaking to similar wounds and choices, Alice Walker quotes a bitter prayer collected in the 1920s by Zora Neale Hurston:

> I have been . . . blasphemed and lied against. . . . My home has been disrespected, my children cursed and ill-treated. My dear ones have been backbitten and their virtue questioned. O Man God, I beg that this that I ask for my enemies shall come to pass:

That the South wind shall scorch their bodies and make them wither and shall not be tempered to them. That the North wind shall freeze their blood and numb their muscles and that it shall not be tempered to them. That the West wind shall blow away their life's breath and will not leave their hair grow, and that their fingernails shall fall off and their bones shall crumble. That the East wind shall make their minds grow dark, their sight shall fail and their seed dry up so that they shall not multiply . . . that all about them will be desolation, pestilence and death.

Walker marvels at this curse: "at the precision of its anger, the absoluteness of its bitterness. Its utter hatred of the enemies it condemns." She feels in herself its dream of revenge, that desire to "Let the earth marinate in poisons. Let the bombs cover the ground like rain. For nothing short of total destruction will ever teach them anything."

Yet, echoing Modjesca's sense that "everyone goes when the wagon comes," Walker said that the planet was her home and she intended to stay. "If, by some miracle," she said, "and all our struggle, the earth is spared, only justice to every living thing (and everything is alive) will save humankind. . . . Only justice can stop a curse."

# 8.   Nuclear Lives

## After Auschwitz

In Yad Vashem, Jerusalem's Holocaust Museum, a glass case displays a contract to build a crematorium. It is an ordinary business contract, one written between the German government and a company staffed by men and women who may well not even have known the nature of their product. The corporation creating the device simply served the nation and made a profit. At no point were the choices made by those working on it considered exceptional.

It is in this context that Seattle Archbishop Hunthausen called the Bangor Trident base "The Auschwitz of Puget Sound," that resisters blocking the atomic weapons trains compared them to boxcars taking Jews to the ovens, and that former Nuremberg prosecutor Mary Kauffman defended the blockaders by linking the responsibility to challenge the Nazi "crimes against humanity" with that of American citizens in a nuclear age. In the same spirit, the holocaust survivor wrote thanking Erica Bouza for her actions, saying we cannot again stand by while the three-year-olds line up sweetly in their white-and-blue aprons, patiently waiting for the gas.

An image from the novel *Sophie's Choice* may be useful in comparing our present time with an earlier one that still strains reason and comprehension. Sophie is a Polish Christian taken with her two young children to Auschwitz in a general round-up. In perfect German, she pleads for their lives: telling the SS officer that she is not

a Communist, not a Jew, not like the others. She says her children
look like Aryans, and tells the officer to look at how beautiful they
are.

"You're a believer?" the officer asks. Sophie nods her head, showing him her cross. Then he asks, didn't Christ say "Suffer the little
children to come unto me?" He says she must choose which child
will live and which will die.

Because Sophie's choice is an impossible one, she refuses, pleading
and begging; then, when the man begins to seize both, cries "No,
take the baby. Take my little girl." Her situation embodies a far
point of barbarism and powerlessness. It serves as a model for circumstances in which human responses no longer matter.

The United States is different, of course, in that those who build
the cruise missiles, wait in Minuteman silos, or serve on Trident
submarines believe they are averting a holocaust, not creating one.
But the present threat of global death also parallels in many ways
the horror of Auschwitz. To begin with, both situations strain all
rational understanding. As Lifton points out, they destroy not only
individual lives, but also the contexts that give human life its fundamental meaning. Because the Third Reich so collapses our understandings of history, we tend to view it as a covenant not of
individuals but of demons, resurrect it again and again through movies, spy novels, and "Hitler's secret diaries" vest this ultimate savagery with an aura of the erotic. Similarly, we never fully believe
that the continuity of human existence could be jeopardized by weapons we build, so we trust Divine Providence (or omnipotent engineering) to insure they never will be launched. We forget that another
equally unthinkable cataclysm did occur.

The camps, as Hannah Arendt pointed out in her book *Eichmann
in Jerusalem*, were the product of a particular type of barbarism: an
evil not of mad possession, but of banality. Different from ordinary
murder, or even from the sacking and leveling of a medieval city,
they could exist only in a complex technological society. Bureau-
cratically insulated and geographically distanced from the view of
most German citizens, they required the participation not only of
direct executioners, but of normal individuals who simply went about
their business and ignored them.

This is not to say our society is wholly comparable to Hitler's
Germany, but merely to point out that the consequences of our
actions may be as terrible. For those, like the Filipino peasants,

Chilean unionists, or Central American villagers, who have been tortured or killed in our interim proxy wars, the distinctions may be rather academic. The savagery of the German officer, who took Sophie's children and created a situation in which real choice no longer existed, was made possible to a large part by the actions of ordinary people of perfectly good will—people living in a time whose difficulties they believed would ultimately pass. Some Germans knew what they were doing and defended it, in Goering's words, as steeling themselves for a necessary task. But most did not. Their lives proceeded, at least until the Allied saturation bombings, not so differently from the way they always had.

We see this in Dietrich Bonhoeffer's prison letters, where we find not only a struggle for spirit and connection strong enough to sustain resistance through a time of ultimate evil, but also a mundane account of weddings and births, Bach cantatas and popular novels, of Easter dinners, Punch and Judy puppet shows, and the labors of repainting a family house. German citizens made love, went to the dentist, watered their plants, and agonized over buying the right blouse or pair of shoes. The screams in the night were for the most part safely distant.

In Bonhoeffer's case, he took daily life, even from prison, as a source of strength to combat the surrounding barbarism. Yet even in the death camps, one found a curious normalcy in the world of those specialists who, because they had particular skills, were permitted to live so they could lay the crematoria water pipes, wire the electric fences, and play in the inmate orchestras. As camp survivor Jean François Steiner put it in *Treblinka*, "The Jews themselves had to become responsible for output as well as for discipline." Another survivor of the same camp described the dependence of the privileged working Jews on goods that came with the "transports," the clothes and shoes, pots, linen, and food available after each new group was sent off to be gassed. During one six-week period there was a dry spell, when the only arrivals were a few hundred gypsies, so poor they brought in nothing. The workers returned to eating only the meager camp food, and lost weight and energy day by day. They were near the lowest ebb in their morale when, as the survivor wrote:

> Kurt Franz walked into our barracks, a wide grin in his face. "As of tomorrow," he said, "transports will be rolling in again." And do you know what we did? We shouted, "Hurrah, hurrah." It seems impossible now. Every time I think of it I die a small death; but it's the

truth. That is what we did; that is where we had got to. And sure enough, the next morning they arrived.

As anthropologist Lisa Peattie explains, we use similar normalizing devices: an insulation bred by a complex division of labor; a reward and incentive structure that pushes individuals "to undermine daily, in countless small steps, the basis of common existence"; a prevalence of bureaucratic formalism and technological mystification.

Like the good Germans and like those—among their victims and in other nations—who could not accept that the land of Goethe, Schiller, Beethoven, and Brahms could exterminate an entire people, we mask the most urgent questions by immersing ourselves in the very routines the atomic weapons threaten. We retreat in fear, as did those American leaders who refused to try to halt the death camps—whether through negotiating population releases or bombing the crematoria—because they worried about appearing too supportive of Jewish interests. We seek private refuge, saying there's nothing we can do.

In a talk on the need of sanctuary for Central American refugees, Elie Wiesel recalled thinking about the Swiss who lived a mile away from the border of occupied France:

> I could never understand and I cannot understand now how those people in Switzerland, who were free, could remain free and eat in the morning and at lunch and at dinner, while looking at the other side, to occupied France. . . . If ever time was a metaphysical domain, that was it: when good and evil were separated by a man-made frontier. Any frontier is man-made, and yet, on one side people died while on the other they went on living as though the others didn't die.

As Wiesel said, following *The Day After* broadcast, "we are all Jews now." It is because of human choices that the unthinkable occurred and can again. Now as then, our actions will decide the outcome.

Sophie encounters another choice preceding the one in the death camp: resistance workers ask her to translate some German documents, and she refuses. She has her children, she explains, responsibilities that she cannot evade; she fears the Gestapo will find out. Her response is reasonable, certainly comprehensible. Her fate would almost certainly not have been altered had she chosen differently when choice still existed; like the present bombs, the camps offered exemption for neither noble intention nor moral rightness. Yet it was a similar, more general abdication that ultimately doomed her children.

If the gravity of the atomic threat in any way parallels that of this previous horror, we are faced—both as individuals and as a society—with some difficult implications. We are also faced with making decisions that, while troubling even to think about, may well lead to a world that is both more humane and more secure. Those like the Trident Nein, who poured their blood down the hatches of the *USS Florida* and changed its name to *USS Auschwitz*, are saying we must either challenge the potential disaster or succumb to it. And that we cannot pass off to others the fundamental responsibilities of our time.

Unlike forty-five years ago, SS troops will not seize us merely for speaking or simply for being. If we are white and middle class, if our children do not ingest stray radioactive particles or carcinogenic chemicals, and if we work, pay our taxes, and do not disrupt the endless military buildups, the state will leave us in benign neglect for as long as the warheads remain in their silos. Yet America's combination of affluence and formal liberty may lull us into a profound complacency. "It is clear," writes Wendell Berry, "that official policies . . . have come to be routinely justified in this country on the grounds that they will uphold freedom, dignity, and equality of opportunity. There is no official depredation that one can think of that has not been initially so justified. The skids are greased with unctions of democracy."

## Intimate History

With the threat of atomic weapons both deferred and invisible, the prime support of their present evil is neither volitional nor willed. The warheads seemingly get built on their own, insulated through bureaucratic distancing, and removed from general sight. Because there may well be no second chance if the bombs go off, our crisis is in some respects more urgent than those faced in previous eras. Even if we begin to reverse the arms race, building a sustainable peace will be a more than lifetime task.

Our situation presents a seeming paradox. With the deployment of fast and accurate first-strike weapons, and the corresponding shaving of response times, the United States has given Soviet generals six minutes to decide whether or not to launch the presumably retaliatory strikes that will make the world uninhabitable. A century ago, violence and barbarism were widespread; the curse cited by Alice Walker addresses wounds rooted in the earliest human history. Despite this legacy, humans have traditionally assumed our continued tenure on the planet would be lengthy, but this no longer can be taken for granted. Prevailing economic, cultural, political, and certainly technological structures all feed the escalating brinksmanship. Our world can end in less time than it takes to eat our morning toast.

But it doesn't help to live in the panic zone: to replicate our cultural obsession with ever escalating speeds of motion, action, and annihilation—what James Fleming has called the "society of the accelerator." Following the 1968 Chicago demonstrations, Weatherman leader Mark Rudd told Todd Gitlin, contemptuously, "Organizing is just another word for going slow." Before the 1984 election, Helen Caldicott suggested that there was "a mathematical certainty" of nuclear war if Reagan was returned by the voters to office. We often seek, to paraphrase a metaphor of Soren Kierkegaard's, to stop the runaway carriage of our culture by desperately clutching the seat.

Nevertheless, impatience feeds on undeniable urgency: American guns and bombs killed peasants daily in Vietnam, Laos, and Cambodia, and continue to do so in El Salvador, Guatemala, and Nicaragua; first-strike weapons shave further the already-scant nuclear response times. It demeans us when we allow these and other steadily proceeding barbaric actions to continue unchallenged. But the sense that we have no time in which to act often hampers our bringing into being the visions that might bridge across the structures of fear we seek to overcome.

Writing recently in *The Whole Earth Review*, poet Anne Herbert similarly examined the cycle of frenetic motion and rapid burnout endemic to peace and environmental activists. She asked how our choices might differ if we decided we had 100 years to change the world, instead of a foreshortened future constantly threatening imminent collapse. She asked as well whether we could avoid both dulling repetition and endlessly tilling new ground until such overreaching spits us up, once again, as spent casualties.

Herbert concluded by describing her experiences with "organizations, campaigns, whole movements . . . [run with] everybody feeling behind, feeling there isn't enough time, feeling important because every little thing is urgent because it hasn't been well planned." She also noted how those involved at times viewed themselves as near-messiahs, and those they sought to reach not as co-workers potentially creating their own paths of engagement, but merely as "burdens to be lifted or converted." She talked of how Robert Oppenheimer's brother suggested he draw on the awe in which he was held to educate the general public on the dangers of the arms race; how Oppenheimer said, in essence, there wasn't time for that, he had to petition the leaders; and how the statesmen then turned and discredited him for his stands.

Put differently, merely fearing the weapons, or merely knowing we must roll them back, does not tell us how to build a world where peace may be possible. If it has become necessary for individuals to disobey their governments in the process of obeying what international law professor Richard Falk has called "the Nuremberg obligation," this challenge cannot succeed if rooted in Promethean desperation, resentful bitterness, or in the quick fixes that further only dislocation and fear.

In an essay on Peruvian mountain farmers, Wendell Berry describes agricultural traditions so rich and complex even the least-skilled individuals do not erode the fragile land they work. In contrast, American farmers must undertake extraordinary efforts if they seek to rebuild natural support systems, instead of continually depleting them. Extending the comparison, nearly all of us support destructive processes in the routine course of our lives: paying taxes to fund weapons buildups; consuming nonrenewable resources when we drive our cars or heat our homes; buttressing, through routine silence, the images of a world that is comfortably secure. We need not embrace pangs of guilt each time we buy a pair of shoes or a packet of candy— but only conscious efforts to change our culture will counter its reckless, destructive strains.

So we return to choices, personal and global. In Wes Jackson's words, "everything we do—who we shake hands with, who we make deals with, who we make love with—brings us closer to or further away from nuclear war." We have other choices beyond carrying the world as guilt-ridden weight, or adopting sole, prescribed moral codes. But our actions do matter, for all of us. Our future is contingent, without guarantees.

Individual character, like the stream of day-to-day life of which it is part, plays a double-edged role in the present time. As psychologist David South writes, "If enough people would just cultivate their gardens, pay their taxes, vote, learn to meditate (or pray), and love their neighbor, the human race will probably be extinct in thirty years." To the degree that we view ourselves as a nation of good people who mean no one any harm, we blur our role in contributing to an ultimate evil. We can be privately virtuous without ameliorating the atomic crisis in the slightest.

Yet strengths of character can also spur us to gaze beyond our own front doors, to take responsibility for what we can no longer abdicate to others. A retired teacher and cofounder of the student peace group, STOP, explained how Shelley Berman's success as an organizer was rooted less in charismatic eloquence than in the hardly glamorous attributes of ethical soundness and courage to take on difficult tasks: "If he asks you to do something, it isn't just to make himself feel powerful, or create an appearance of motion. You know he will have assessed it, judged it carefully. You can feel proud to contribute, help, and feel that what you do will matter." Florence residents followed Bill Cusak's lead in part simply because they respected him. Coupled with broader concerns, perhaps the classic moral virtues of courage, compassion, and integrity matter more now than ever—like the sense that allowed Ruth Nelson to tell the Coast Guard sailor, "No, no, young man. Not in my America, you wouldn't do that."

Just as the movement flourishes best through a diversity of cultural styles and political approaches, no absolute rules dictate which pieces of the interconnected global crises we each address. Arguments over the relative urgency of challenging the MX missile or the helicopters shooting and napalming Central American peasants miss the point. All such actions are part of our prevailing culture's carnivorous streak. Challenges to any of them can raise common issues of democracy and dignity. In whatever domains we choose to make our prime stand—rolling back the weapons or saving the topsoil, halting the contras, challenging U.S. support of South Africa, or building housing for those who have none—we are stronger for linking their interconnected roots.

Given this, we still face questions of how to act, what constitutes appropriate involvement and risk, when we are rising to the call of our time and when hiding behind those cultural rationalizations that led Jon Nelson to almost prefer the constraints of jail because "on the street it's far easier to cheat." Witnessing the actions of the Berrigans—or the Trident blockaders—we have a sense that if everyone acted as they did, the arms race would promptly end. Yet only a fraction of those involved can bring themselves to take the risks of major prison terms. Most of us still duck out from behind our vigil signs, half-hoping we really won't be noticed. Even the most risky actions can be taken as lessons, not necessarily to be precisely replicated, but for others to confront the seriousness of our situation with all their strengths and gifts.

If we are indeed facing Sophie's choice, must we drop everything except addressing the global crisis—forego having children, building houses, living in the world? Will our actions inevitably progress from attending a march to risking major prison terms by decommissioning missile warheads with hammers and blood? Political movements often echo the classic choice posed to Achilles: whether to live a short and glorious life, falling in battle on the fields of Troy, or a long and humble one, tilling his fields and dying of old age in his bed. Or the judgment of Bertolt Brecht that "We who were to prepare the ground for kindliness—we ourselves could not be kind." Yet even as we challenge what Modjesca called "the chintzy things," the aspects of common culture that blur our vision and stunt our souls, we can still pause to receive those moments of delight and grace fundamental to the birthright we seek to preserve. It was this vision that the *Peacemaker* group honored in savoring their blockade-day breakfast of eggs, oranges, buttered toast, and watermelon. As Marv said, "People have to be able to climb mountains, talk with children, make love, read poetry. And do the actions they feel they can."

Ground Zero member Jeanne Clark, a Dominican nun who participated in the Trident blockade, believed it was "not very probable that children will get into the war rooms or board rooms in the near future and stop the war, but it is possible for us to allow the children in our lives to come close, to interrupt us as we busily go about the business of adults, the business of doing and taking charge. It is possible for us to allow the children to call us to action, action which will help to create a world fit for children—a world without war." Quoting Christ's precept that "Unless you become as a little child, you shall not enter the kingdom," Clark contrasted childhood vulnerability with the frozen detachment that allows the weapons to be designed and deployed. She said we needed their voices to help lead us home.

Because we face a situation that is both immediately grave and of indefinite duration, we miss the point if we frame our metaphors solely in terms of the Warsaw Ghetto uprising, Spanish Civil War, or the charge up Iwo Jima; we risk both making impossible demands on ourselves and excluding all but those willing to lay aside their entire lives for the urgency of their time. We might, instead, compare the movement's task—in the words of Jim Forest, of the International Fellowship of Reconciliation—to that of the artisans who built the great medieval cathedrals, working generation after generation on an effort whose fruition most would never live to see. In the perspective of the cofounder of Erica's peace group, Woman Against Military Madness, the path of involvement was "more a circle than a line." One leafletted, sat at a table, perhaps got arrested and spent time in jail; although the next step might be another arrest, it might also be something entirely different but contributing equally to the same ultimate vision.

Individuals will always act in diverse ways. The Trident blockaders could be viewed as being at an apex of risk and commitment, and some, indeed, continued focusing on major civil disobedience. Jim Douglass and the other Ground Zero members organized the nationwide campaign against the trains that brought the final atomic warheads to Bangor and other deployment sites. A number of them, along with several blockade support people, were arrested along the tracks—including Jim Douglass and his wife Shelley; Kim Wahl and her husband Bill; the grandmother from Ashland, Oregon; and Jeanne Clark and several other Ground Zero nuns. Ted Phillips went on to protest test launches of MX missiles aimed at the Marshall Islands from California's Vandenberg Air Force base. Jon Nelson blockaded Honeywell twice, while Ruth, now wheelchair-bound, sat in vigil in support. Win Olive climbed the fence at Pine Gap, an Australia-based CIA facility specializing in satellite tracking and communications monitoring.

But the blockaders also took other paths. The Ashland grandmother helped make her city a Nuclear Free Zone, as—in his rural Washington county—did the young lawyer who'd worried about losing his right to practice. Kim Wahl joined others leafletting each Thursday morning at the headquarters of the corporation whose trains carried the warheads. A poet and playwright organized fellow writers to speak with a common voice. Bill Ethell worked full-time with the Australian unions.

Charley Meconis spent the three years following the blockade coordinating his ecumenical religious peace group, writing a novel based on the experiences of a Vietnam B-52 pilot who quit for reasons of conscience, and, together with his wife, raising a newborn daughter. When the little girl was two, he decided to join the others on the Bangor tracks, and was asked by friends whether it was wise to risk another sentence and consequent separation from his family.

This reaction disturbed him, because our society readily honors individuals who make supreme sacrifices in time of war: those killed or injured while presumably defending their country. The Trident sailors were routinely gone for long stretches. Yet modestly disrupting our lives was a far reach for many in the peace movement.

This didn't mean, Charley repeated, seeking martyrdom or renunciation. He valued the time with his daughter, cautioned against individuals risking jail unless they felt it so necessary for their own integrity that they could stand by their choices whatever the consequences. Echoing Shelley Berman's mistrust of the voice which insisted "look how good I am. I'm sacrificing everything to the cause," Charley said we had to give up notions of becoming heroic saviors of the world. And recognize that "You aren't in this alone. You're in this together. While you're being frivolous, laughing, drinking beer, someone else is working. And you hope that they'll know the point when they have to rest, and that you'll be able to carry on."

## Hope in Hard Times

Because we will spend our entire lives facing the nuclear threat and its constellation of interwoven crises, we need to sustain our involve-

ments past the next election, demonstration, or blockade. Participants in historic social movements often quickly drink their fill of
shaking the world, then—in response to entrenched institutional
resistance and their efforts' own shortcomings—hit the Thermidor
of exhausted retreat. Yet, given our power to make the world uninhabitable, we cannot delegate the task of its preservation to only
the hard-core committed. Because passion and involvement will inevitably undergo surges and retrenchments, circumstances require not
only that the peace movement steadily bring in new participants,
but also that it nurture, on an unprecedented level, the involvement
of those presently concerned.

As Charley Meconis said, it does not work merely to briefly light
up the sky like a magnesium flare. At times the next necessary step
may be a regrouping, a deliberate slowing even in the face of the
weapons culture's ever-speeded pace. We also need a grounding in
everyday life so we do not swing constantly, rollercoastered by the
success or failure of each peace movement action. If we become too
brittle, embittered, or dislocated, we will replicate only desperate
fear.

Individuals often begin taking on entrenched institutional power
with the belief that if only they sufficiently describe the problem,
people will see. Then they hit the barriers of vested interest and
accustomed complacency, crawl back burned, hurt, and determined
not to be fooled again. Yet, although social movements are obviously
easier to sustain when their efforts bear tangible fruits, we cannot
allow those presently holding power to become the ultimate arbiters
of our efforts. As during Vietnam, those at the helm of the state can
frequently manipulate immediate political consensus. The deeper
impact of social currents may not always be evident. Without surrendering the need to wisely plan our actions, or denying the value
of interim gains, our situation requires us, therefore, to allow the
repercussions of our efforts to echo however they will; we must
forgive others and forgive ourselves. Regardless of apparent results,
we must continue articulating our most passionate, rigorous, and
ultimately most human visions.

These visions contain an inherent uncertainty. If the wrong combination of technical error, global crises, and human madness occurs,
the species as we know it will end. Yet this possibility is part of the
humbling gift of a situation in which the weapons can either destroy

us or bring us together. Individuals like *The Day After*'s experts proclaim their pragmatic advice as the sole realistic course. We who seek a different path can make no absolute promises regarding the human future; we can only suggest that history will depend on our choices. If we recognize the world as a fragile gift, a place where we are guests, not owners, stewards not lords, these choices often become far clearer. They involve not only routes towards dismantling the bombs, but how to live, once more, in a time when our every action matters.

In order to keep on with our efforts, we need to create cultural and political structures, like those of Wendell Berry's Peruvian farmers, that will not require individuals to be saints if they are to make a difference; structures that will sustain momentum even after the adrenaline rush of first concern fades and recedes. In part, sustenance can come from simply continuing: Jeff Dietrich holding on until the stubborn judge released him; Harold Willens asking Jonas Salk until he publicly endorsed the Freeze; Bill Ethell explaining that throwing yourself on the deck of a Trident doesn't mean much unless you're going to do it—or some equivalent—again and again. As Erica said, at a point when involvement had simply become part of her life, "to me burnout's a kind of meaningless word. So one day you're disgusted and one day you're not. Some weeks you do more and some weeks do less. But if it's something you believe in and will keep on working on indefinitely, you don't necessarily expect quick results."

Beyond this radical patience is a coming to terms with the real dread of our age. In part because of the recent peace movement's breadth of reach, most in our culture have been alerted to the horrors of nuclear war. What we lack is a sense of our power to affect this and parallel threats. We fear shattering others with our anguish. Perhaps, as some have bitterly suggested, the nation that twice elected Ronald Reagan deserves to perish.

But, as Alice Walker writes, "Just as the sun shines on the godly and the ungodly alike, so does nuclear radiation. And with this knowledge it becomes increasingly difficult to embrace the thought of extinction purely for the assumed satisfaction of—from the grave— achieving revenge." Using a biological metaphor to move beyond bitter predictions of cataclysm, psychologist Joanna Macy suggests we view ourselves as neurons in the web that makes a living system, neurons that survive only through interdependent connection. Like the mutual strengthening present in the most intimate love, this image refutes the relentless striving to wall ourselves off—individually or as a nation—in armored sanctuaries, and instead links shared vulnerability with common strength. It calls us to view our difficult time as the gift of a chance to do what matters.

If burnout comes from isolation—the sense that we feel the pain but others do not—then we need to carry with us always the knowledge of what is possible within other humans: that we share a power to act, to take those simple though demanding steps that—by causing further sparks to leap—might prove critical in the fundamental turning now required. Echoing Bill Cusak's notion of a choice between following "the source of life" and following the nonlife, Macy says the bomb can teach us "about the hell we create for ourselves when we cease to learn how to live. . . . [That it] is taking us by the scruff of the neck and pushing our nose right into what we do with our greed and sloth, our stupidity and fear and self-righteousness." She believes it pushes us to live as we were meant to.

Cecil Garland, a Utah rancher who has become a nuclear activist, expressed a similar vision, explaining that

> within humanity there is a light, a gently wistful courage that has been with us from the very beginning. It's like a little whirlwind dancing across the desert's dusty face. No matter how cruel, how vengeful, we claim to be, that light never dies. It is the way of the heart, of compassion, nobility, enlightenment, love. Without it we are nothing.

This light returns us to human choices. Modest ones that can nonetheless lead—echoing Modjesca's biblical phrase about "leaven in the lump . . . yeast in the dough"—to profound ultimate consequences. The four individuals who met in Bill Cusak's Florence office did not foresee the emergence of a sustained alternative community in their previously silent town; Charley Meconis did not know that by refusing to manufacture the prison furniture headed for Bangor he would end up drawing the support of the black Muslim pig farm crew; Shelley Berman and his fellow Brookline High School teachers did not envision beginning a national organization whose ideas would ultimately draw the support of the massive union, the National Education Association.

Similarly, the Vietnam era Honeywell Project could not have imagined that they would, in 1985, win a $70,000 settlement from the FBI and Honeywell for illegally infiltrating their organization, with the goal (acknowledged by the FBI, if denied by Honeywell) of stopping them from embarrassing corporate officials. The project turned Honeywell's damages over to an American Friends Service Committee effort that purchased shovels so Laotian villagers could explode buried cluster bombs. After Daniel Ellsberg released the Pentagon Papers, he told Marv how the courage of eight Minnesota activists jailed for attempting to destroy draft board files had helped him make up his mind to send the classified documents to the *New York Times*. A decade later, Marv asked at a meeting with Honeywell and the police whether there was "anyone in this room who can deny that the path that we have taken, of sustained civil disobedience, has deepened and heightened the debate in our community about the production of weapons." No one argued. No one said anything. Then one city attorney laughed and said, yes, that was true.

Standing as a major theological voice, the Catholic bishops' Pastoral Letter on the nuclear issue was also the fruit of a chain of individual actions. Much as it hedged on certain key aspects, this document continues to spur unprecedented discussion in churches throughout the country. Even *Time* and NBC have sanctified its importance. Yet how did the bishops come to their conclusions?

The nuclear document had varied roots, including the legacy of Pope John XXIII and the Vatican II council, the currents of an initially Latin America-based liberation theology, and, in what many would consider an irony, the church's involvement in the abortion issue. Yet it was particularly the product of a loose group of individuals labeled the "peace bishops"—those who pushed the hardest and worked the longest to create a statement of strength. And they themselves did not spring instantly to full-fledged concern and commitment but, rather, each followed particular journeys.

In the case of Seattle Archbishop Raymond Hunthausen, who strongly influenced his peers by witholding half his federal income taxes, he was anguished but silent through most of Vietnam, and only began to seriously reflect on the nuclear arms race after a number of men and women (including Jim Douglass, Charley Meconis, and Jon Nelson) were jailed for going over the fence at the then-unfinished

Bangor base. Perhaps because they shared a common theological language, Hunthausen was particularly influenced by Douglass, who he visited in jail and with whom he celebrated mass.

So we can trace the bishops' letter back to an individual resister, and then to Douglass's enlistment in the Trident campaign by former Lockheed engineer Robert Aldridge, who helped design the Polaris and Poseidon missiles and then quit his job in Sunnyvale, California, after his teenage daughter asked how he could work on these terrible weapons. The girl's lone action, of course, did not create the bishops' letter. But like a feeder stream to a broader current, it combined with others to shake the church and spur further challenges yet to be felt.

It is tempting to describe America as a callous and apathetic culture whose prevailing visions range from the yuppies to Reagan. But pessimism quickly becomes its own confirmation, a cool, easy stance requiring only the knowing assurance that we are, without a doubt, steadily headed for the brink. And it misses perhaps the most critical element of our present situation. Just as our society produces numbing, alienation, and a fatalistic cynicism, it can also produce commitment, resistance, and courage. Individuals like Modjesca Simkins, Shelley Berman, Kim Wahl, Rachelle and Amanda, or Aldridge's daughter are exceptional only in that they have reached beyond the former bounds of their visions to act for broader, more inclusive, kingdoms.

We sell ourselves short, therefore, when we perceive the future as some fixed destination—cataclysm or magic salvation—toward which we speed on eternally fixed tracks. Certainly we face threats and circumstances not of our choosing. But we do make our history, in a world whose continuance is now contingent on our actions. Just as the choices that ultimately produced the bishops' letter began on the humble level of village politics, we need not delegate hope solely to distant actors.

Three years following the beginning of Bill Cusak's four-person group, peace issues had an ongoing presence in Florence. The Peace Links women folded cranes in a local mall; took their film on children's fears to medical wives, nurses, garden clubs, and whoever would let them show it; led discussions based on their experiences as nurses, teachers, computer programmers, and mothers. The pastor of the First Baptist church spoke about the arms race in his sermons. Even members of the local Rotary Club, where, as Bill said, "It was like I had the plague for six months after we showed that movie," were "no longer as sure that military power alone is the only answer." Although the Rotarians didn't wholly adopt Bill's position, they'd begun to ask him about arms race issues they read of in the paper, to joke teasingly about why he wasn't up tying a ribbon around the Pentagon, to no longer treat his perspective as wholly crazy.

Florence saw retrenchments, of course, particularly after the 1984 election, when the Pee Dee activists threw their all into the state Democratic Party: first joining groups from other communities in gaining Freeze resolutions on precinct, county, and state levels, then being swept away by the Reagan landslide. Because they had neglected their own organization and its nurturing, their heart and spirit temporarily died. The group's specific focus had previously begun to broaden, and when Bill considered civil disobedience actions to follow the path of Gandhi, King, Thomas Merton, and others upon whose counsel he'd been reflecting, he perceived greater local receptiveness for action on South Africa or Central America than on directly opposing atomic weapons. But he'd come to feel these issues were all interconnected: that they held common roots in "a warlike thought process fueled by the fear, this incendiary violent attitude that we'll kill anyone in South America who doesn't say the right words or doesn't trade in the right way. Or in South Africa, where the ingrained apartheid is violating people. The same basic attitude, it just has a different face, that 'I'll kill you if I don't get what I want. And I'll get what I want at any cost.' "

Bill believed humans could not survive with that approach. To change it would require not only thinking about the bombs, but also steadying in "for a longer haul," drawing on "what we would call the Holy Spirit, but they'd name it a different thing in different faiths." To help participants nurture their journeys, he was setting up what he called Contemplative Prayer Groups, based on a model developed by the Washington, D.C. World Peacemakers. By stressing a common search for spiritual roots and meeting informally in private houses, the groups evoked the early Christians, who gathered hidden from the scrutiny of Roman eyes. They resembled as well the Basic Christian Communities that have developed recently in Latin America, helping birth both liberation theology and accompanying popular resistance movements. Because the journey was more than just internal, Bill thought that at some point he and others would have to "tell the truth and take the consequences. . . . Stand in the breach and take whatever comes." Coming to grips with the nuclear threat had already been "like a crowbar" in his own life, "cracking my personality, opening up depths to go beyond that superficial intellectual process of peace."

The effects of Bill's crowbar to the soul have continued in other lives as well. After Marty and Bob Coleman sold their $600,000 house so she could volunteer full time at Interfaith Center, they remained in their local Presbyterian congregation, and now teach to enthusiastic response a class on "Choosing Our Future: Rambo and the Nuclear Age." Kathy and Sheila continue their work with NUFFUM. Although Erica Bouza speaks two nights a week to Shriners, Kiwanis groups and the Junior League, she decided she couldn't just stay in the antiseptic world of giving lectures, and was arrested a third time at Honeywell. This was a last-minute decision, and prompted Tony to look up, startled, and exclaim, "Son of a bitch! There goes my wife over the fence."

The shift of war and peace issues from the concern of a few hardy activists to that of individuals in every domain of our society does not erase the steady escalations, the first-strike systems, or the lives lost daily in Guatemala, Lebanon, Nicaragua, Angola, and Soweto. Nor does it instantly overcome the allure of wasting the world in the name of freedom and democracy. But this shift does mean that ground has been sowed, and the cries of activists no longer echo alone in the night.

Marv Davidov sometimes recalled a story about Bob Zellner, an Alabama organizer whose father was a Klansman and a preacher, and who became Student Nonviolent Coordinating Committee's first white field secretary. When a Klan mob tried to lynch him, Zellner wrapped his arms around the tree, holding on with all his strength. It took so many men to pry him off that a Klan leader at last looked down and said, "Anybody who wants to live this much, we're going to let you." Marv remembered Zellner in particular when thinking about individuals like the Berrigans, Ruth Nelson, and all those who kept on, not letting go, trying to stop the warheads' march.

Few of us would wish to spend our existence resisting the arms race, or resisting our governments. Poet Adrienne Rich asks, "How did we get caught up fighting this forest fire, we who were only looking for a still place in the woods?" Modjesca Simkins regrets all the shows she could have seen, the books she could have read, the things she could have done, if she hadn't had to spend over sixty years just "fighting, fighting, fighting all the time." Yet we work not only to staunch the flames, but also to affirm the fundamental streams of existences that the weapons increasingly threaten.

These streams are realized ultimately in community. They are bolstered by a sense that others past and present have worked for similar visions, and that even our pain and fear may become forces to bring us together. When Bill Cusak's daughter asked whether he thought good or evil would have won out if the movement failed and the bombs fell, he said that, at least for those seeking the path of connection he termed being one with God, good would have prevailed in their lives.

Similarly, Elie Wiesel retells the expulsion from the Garden of Eden in the words of a wise Hasidic rabbi, who explained that when God asked Adam, "Where art thou," God knew where Adam was, but Adam did not. "Do we know where we are?" Wiesel asks, and then explains, "my place is measured by yours. . . . My place under the sun, or in the face of God, or in my own memory is measured by the distance it has from you . . . if I see a person or persons suffer, and the distance between us doesn't shrink . . . my place is not good, not enviable."

Some have recently compared the challenge of finding our present place on the earth to that faced by those involved in the nineteenth century antislavery movement: an effort embodying a similar range of visions, from individuals who wished merely to limit the institution's growth—halt its expansion to the territories—to those with seemingly utopian visions of outright abolition. Just as slavery seemed an eternal part of human existence until popular outcry and historical forces made it universally unacceptable, so warfare in general—the warning brushfires preceding the mushroom clouds—may be something our species must, at long last, seek to relinquish. Again, efforts to address violence's root causes will meet profound opposition, just as legal freedom has not eliminated the forces that created black bondage in the first place. But historic leaps and shifts are possible.

As Marty Coleman said, involvement in the movement was far more than the novelty of finding herself suddenly sitting, listening to Bob Dylan and Stevie Wonder in the Rose Bowl. For all that this might be the very worst of times in its terrible potential, it called forth the best of what she had to give. She also saw others beginning to draw on "those things we've always been taught," using their own traditions both to move through the endless tangling obstacles and to gain those moments of joy and succor that reveal the task's necessity and virtue. Like Shelley Berman, she found "a window" to a different way of seeing. At times she even felt exhilarated—like the old man who told Kathy Bryant, "God damn, I'm just so proud of you young children fighting for this world."

If the bomb carries an ironic gift, it is one pushing us to honor the life that persists even amidst our evident capacity for barbarism. We are called to live up to our hallowed phrases about liberty, equality, and fraternity—about being children to a common God. Our species will no doubt remain mulish, contrary and contradictory—these qualities are part of our strength. But perhaps we can no longer afford to capitulate to private fear and greed, a callous bragging nationalism, and the varied streams of nature and entrenched vindictive power that steadily seed our building peril.

Because an atomic war would destroy the fundamental humanity even of any who survived it, the fates of New Jersey realtors are inextricably linked with Moscow nurses, factory workers, and clerks, linked as well with Berry's Peruvian villagers, who till their garden plots wholly unaware of the bombs. In Bob Willard's words, we can sense "the universality of life from the universality of the threat," receiving an opportunity individuals have possessed in no other time. When Einstein spoke of the unleashed power of the atom changing "everything except our ways of thinking," he addressed a shift to a radically different world than the one into which our grandparents were born. In a sense all bets are off—or, more precisely, all possibilities are open.

This makes the arms race as much an individual as institutional concern: one that touches both how we will stop the bombs and how we will live. If those who've made careers of pushing escalation are unlikely to steer us to a different course, that leaves only ordinary citizens, in all our fallible humanity to take up the task. As Gandhi once said, almost anything we do will be insignificant, but "it is very important that we do it."

We can draw sustenance from specific lives without enshrining those who act on some mighty pedestal, without writing them off as heroes or saints. Yet perhaps present hope can best be found in the knowledge that individuals have changed, and in turn nourished further changes in others: have broken the pall of silence that has hung, largely since its inception, over our right to prepare annihilation for the world. These journeys both matter and are replicable. Those who act carry their own doubts, fears, and histories of denial. Yet if they can continue, others can as well. If at last they find strength in risking and speaking, so can we.

# Related Writings of Interest

Arendt, Hannah. *Eichmann in Jerusalem*. Penguin, 1977.

Auckerman, Dale. *Darkening Valley*. Seabury, 1981.

Bateson, Gregory. *Towards an Ecology of Mind*. Ballantine, 1972.

Bellah, Robert, et al. *Habits of the Heart*. Harper & Row, 1986.

Berry, Wendell. *The Gift of Good Land*. North Point, 1981.

Berry, Wendell. *The Unsettling of America*. Avon, 1977.

Bonhoeffer, Dietrich. *Letters & Papers from Prison*. Macmillan, 1979.

Boyer, Paul. *By the Bomb's Early Light*. Pantheon, 1985.

Boyte, Harry. *Community Is Possible*. Harper & Row, 1984.

Camus, Albert. *The Rebel*. Vintage, 1956.

Camus, Albert. "Neither Victims Nor Executioners." Continuum, 1980.

Douglass, James. *Lightning East to West*. Crossroad, 1983.

Douglass, James. *Resistance and Contemplation*. Dell, 1972.

Dyson, Freeman. *Weapons and Hope*. Harper & Row, 1985.

Fitzgerald, Frances. *America Revised*. Atlantic Monthly Press, 1979.

Friere, Paulo. *Pedagogy of the Oppressed*. Continuum, 1970.

Gaventa, John. *Power and Powerlessness*. University of Illinois Press, 1980.

Gilligan, Carol. *In a Different Voice*. Harvard University Press, 1982.

Gitlin, Todd. *The Whole World's Watching*. University of California Press, 1980.

Gordon, Suzanne, and McFadden, Dave. *Economic Conversion*. Ballinger, 1984.

Gutman, Herbert. *Work, Culture and Society in Industrializing America*. Random House, 1977.

Kennan, George. *The Nuclear Delusion*. Pantheon, 1982.

Kohlberg, Lawrence. *The Philosophy of Moral Development*. Harper & Row, 1981.

Koning, Hans. *America Made Me*. Thunders Mouth Press, 1983.

Lasch, Christopher. *The Minimal Self*. W.W. Norton, 1984.

Lifton, Robert Jay. *The Broken Connection*. Basic Books/Harper & Row, 1983.

Lifton, Robert Jay. *Death in Life*. Basic Books/Harper & Row, 1967.

Lifton, Robert Jay, and Falk, Richard. *Indefensible Weapons*. Basic Books/Harper & Row, 1982.

Macy, Joanna. *Despair and Personal Power in the Nuclear Age*. New Society, 1983.

Paley, Grace. "Cop Stories." In *Reweaving the Web of Life*, edited by Pam McAllister. New Society, 1982.

Powers, Thomas. *Thinking about the Next War*. New American Library, 1983.

Rich, Adrienne. *The Will to Change*. W.W. Norton, 1971.

Schell, Jonathan. *The Fate of the Earth*. Avon, 1982.

Schell, Jonathan. *The Time of Illusion*. Vintage Books, 1976.

Schell, Jonathan. *The Abolition*. Alfred Knopf, 1984.

Sennett, Richard, and Cobb, Jonathan. *The Hidden Injuries of Class*. Vintage Books, 1983.

Sharp, Gene. *The Politics of Nonviolent Action*. Porter Sargent, 1973.

Sider, Ronald J., and Taylor, Richard K. *Nuclear Holocaust and Christian Hope*. Paulist Press, 1982.

Steiner, Jean François. *Treblinka*. New American Library, 1979.

Thompson, E.P. *Beyond the Cold War*. Pantheon, 1982.

Thompson, E.P. *The Heavy Dancers*. Pantheon, 1985.

Thompson, E.P., and Smith, Dan, eds. *Protest and Survive*. Monthly Review Press, 1981.

Walker, Alice. "Only Justice Can Stop a Curse." In *Reweaving the Web of Life*, edited by Pam McAllister. New Society, 1982.

Wallis, Jim, ed. *Waging Peace*. Harper & Row, 1982.

Wasserman, Harvey, and Solomon, Norman. *Killing Our Own*. Delta, 1982.

Weber, Max. "Politics as a Vocation." In *From Max Weber*, by Hans H. Gerth and C. Wright Mills. Oxford University Press, 1968.

Weschler, Lawrence. *Solidarity*. Simon & Schuster, 1982.

Willens, Harold. *The Trimtab Factor*. William Morrow, 1984.

Wiesel, Elie. Essay on refugees from *Sanctuary*, edited by Gary Maceoin. Harper & Row, 1985.

Williams, William Appleman. *Empire as a Way of Life*. Oxford University Press, 1980.

Williams, William Appleman. *America Confronts a Revolutionary World: 1776–1976*. William Morrow, 1976.

Wittner, Lawrence. *Rebels Against War*. Temple University Press, 1984.

# Index

# Acknowledgments

A LL books are to a degree common projects. Yet in examining how diverse citizens have sought to reclaim a human future, I have particularly drawn on those individuals who gave me the gift of explaining both their initial pathways to concern and the visions they hoped would continue sustaining their efforts. Some of them became major characters in this book. Far more illuminated that broad context within which I could understand particular lives and choices. Without all who shared intimate dreams, *Hope in Hard Times* would not exist.

Given that my writing and research had me crisscrossing the United States for four years straight, it required support beyond that of an often-resistant commercial market. I drew heavily on various individuals who offered their hospitality, emotional sustenance, financial help, and a wealth of other forms of assistance. Thank you Jane Klassen, Norman Solomon, Ada Sanchez, Carol Prentice, Jane Hatfield, Michael and Laura Lowe, Carol and W.H. Ferry, Paul and Ann Sperry, Schroeter and Mary Boulton, Alan and Andrea Rabinowitz, Rodney Loeb, Carol Summer, Erica and Tony Bouza, Wayne Campeau, Gary Morris, Bebe Verdery, Dorothy and Garvice Murphree, Robert Musil, Sybil Suthergreen, Mary Tucker, Terry Eastman, Dick and Mary Carbray, Kirk Jones, Bruce Johnson, John Milian, Leonard Schroeter, Steven Delibert, Rebecca Sive-Tomashefsky, Cora Weiss, John Deklewa, Don and Phyliss Pennell, Ann Bartley, Boehm Foundation, Paul Schell, Laurel Blossom, Paul Ballard, Pat Hastings, Robert and Nancy Stover, Rick Rapport and Valerie Trueblood, Gary Dreiblatt and Nancy Sinkoff, Marion Weber, Bill Traver, Jean Sieroty, Dick Mayo-Smith, Frances Hart, Philip Stern, Bill Patz, Mark Bloome and Sharon Gantz, Magda Loeb and Fred Waingrow, Corrine Dee Kelly, Dave Hall, Susan James, Bill Nagele, Noelle Hite, Josie Reichlin, Bill and Mary Carry, Margaret and Bruce Beck, George Scheer, Rich Pollock, Abby Brown,

Marilyn Smith, Kathy and Don Rouzie, Bill Hess, David Pollack, Peter Heggie, Pete Knutson and Hing Lau Ng, Dianne Kelso, Kitty Tucker, New Society Publishers and the Health and Energy Learning Project. Rupert Garcia added the grace of his illustrations to more than catch the spirit of those whose lives I've sought to convey.

I also benefited from comments made by various individuals on the book and its component sections. Thank you Ed Dobb, Lisa Peattie, Shelley Berman, Sam Day, Jorge Garcia (who is also a first-rate running partner), Robert Manoff, David Orr, Jack and Lise von Mettenheim, Paul Boyer, Charley Meconis, and Rebecca Wells. Thank you as well my Lexington support team of Jaime Welch-Donahue, Bob Bovenschulte, Pam Constantine, Dick Tonachel, Karen Maloney, and Marsha Finley.

Finally, five individuals helped sustain this project from its most difficult moments to its ultimate fruition. Michele Hirsen anchored me in those very everyday worlds that the movement ultimately seeks to preserve. Liz Gjelten, as with my last major work, exercised the finest craft in editing, honing and rearranging my frequently tangled phrases and thoughts, unearthing those critical threads that would have otherwise ended up lost or hidden, and Joan Fiset fine-tuned the end-point narrative. Wayne Grytting, master fisherman and philosophical consultant supreme, vastly strengthened my analytic arguments, pushing me to explore precisely those demanding questions that I might have been most inclined to duck. And finally, Jonathan Dolger, my ever-patient agent, provided unflagging encouragement, advice, and support throughout the book's lengthy journey in the marketplace.

# About the Author

PAUL ROGAT LOEB was born in Berkeley, California in 1952 and grew up in Los Angeles. He attended Stanford University and the New School for Social Research in New York City. In 1974 he became an editor of *Liberation* magazine, a journal that had been raising questions about peace and justice for twenty years, publishing the work of Albert Camus, Bertrand Russell, James Baldwin, Paul Goodman, Lewis Mumford, and Martin Luther King, Jr., among others. In 1976, Mr. Loeb left *Liberation* and has since appeared in a wide range of publications, including the *Washington Post*, *Village Voice*, *Mother Earth News*, *New Age*, the *Los Angeles Herald-Examiner*, *Nuclear Times*, the *Los Angeles Times*, and the *International Herald-Tribune*. He has also appeared on numerous radio and TV programs, including National Public Radio, Cable Network News, C-Span Public Affairs Network, Studs Terkel's Almanac, the Michael Jackson show on ABC talk radio, and the national NBC-TV show "1986".

In 1982 Mr. Loeb's first book, *Nuclear Culture: Living and Working at the World's Largest Atomic Complex*, was published to national acclaim. In the last few years, Mr. Loeb has lectured and led workshops on material from both *Nuclear Culture* and *Hope in Hard Times* at over one hundred colleges and universities, including Harvard University, Massachusetts Institute of Technology, Columbia University, Catholic University of America, University of South Carolina, Michigan State University, University of Chicago, Reed College, and Texas Tech University. Comments on his presentations include:

"With compassion and respect, Paul Loeb illustrates that the nuclear dilemma is a profoundly personal one, which reaches into each of our daily lives."

Waging Peace Group, Harvard University

"Paul's speech came across beautifully. He found himself pummelled with questions and spent almost an hour talking to students after the class. This was genuinely an A-plus event."

Sociology Professor, University of Missouri

"You tackle the overwhelming dilemma faced by all of us [and] consequently go right to the heart of the moral enigmas of the nuclear age, without being moralistic. . . . You ended up reaching more students than Helen Caldicott."

Sociology Professor, University of Texas

"Not even General Westmoreland, following the end of the Vietnam War, drew such a large crowd. . . . Few speakers have the gift for lifting us from the pessimism and cynicism which surround serious global issues. We owe a debt of gratitude."

Biology Professor, North Arkansas Community College

Mr. Loeb is currently lecturing throughout the United States and is available for speaking engagements and workshops. For further information, contact him through the Nuclear Culture Project, 2225 First Ave. #203, Seattle, WA 98121, (206) 441-1479.

Mark Sullo